Maya® 8 Character Modeling

Gary Oliverio

Wordware Publishing, Inc.

Library of Congress Cataloging-in-Publication Data

Oliverio, Gary.
  Maya 8 Character Modeling / by Gary Oliverio;
  p. cm.
  Includes index.
  ISBN-13: 978-1-59822-020-9
  ISBN-10: 1-59822-020-9 (pbk., companion cd)
  1. Computer animation.   2. Maya (Computer file).   3. Three-dimensional
  display systems.   I. Title.
  TR897.7.O44 2006
  006.6'96--dc22   2006029338

© 2007, Wordware Publishing, Inc.

All Rights Reserved

1100 Summit Avenue, Suite 102
Plano, Texas 75074

Printed in the United States of America

ISBN-13: 978-1-59822-020-9
ISBN-10: 1-59822-020-9

10 9 8 7 6 5 4 3 2 1
0610

All inquiries for volume purchases of this book should be addressed to Wordware
Publishing, Inc., at the above address. Telephone inquiries may be made by calling:

(972) 423-0090

This book is dedicated to my wife, Robin, and our five children. Special thanks to Mike Hovland for the scripting help as well.

Contents

Contents

Introduction

In sitting down to write this book, I really wanted to clearly define an approach that was accessible enough for a beginner to grasp. I have seen many tutorials that are so puzzling that in effect they deter anyone from 3D modeling. The problem most people have is distinguishing the good from the not so good, which can be difficult for the novice who is just getting his feet wet.

I didn't want this to be a tedious string of tutorials that you can't digress from or easily put your own touch on. At each step along the way, I hope to keep it nice and simple. I think this way you can use this book merely as a guide to get you started on your own model instead of just copying what you see in the pages to follow. If, however, you want to do just that, by all means go right ahead! I have included on the companion CD all the files necessary to create the character and a Maya file to accompany each chapter.

In my years of teaching I have found that it is generally difficult for new 3D artists to work out the bugs. If you are willing to see it through, I can guarantee you will get it! I tell students to get in there and break things. Mess up as much as you need to in order to learn from your mistakes. Do it over and over again until you understand what you did wrong. The process of scrapping a model and starting over from scratch will strengthen your skills.

This approach will not go unrewarded. What I hear often from students is the "I don't get it" mantra. I tell them that the Eureka moment will come. It usually does — like a brick upside the head! One day they wake up and they just get it! What I am trying to say is don't get discouraged if it doesn't come easy. If you are determined to learn, then learn you will.

I think the best advice I could give someone who wants a career as an artist is to be *passionate*. No amount of instruction from the best teacher in the world will help you if you are not passionate. Hey, if the Karate Kid wasn't passionate about his training, then a room full of Mr. Miyagis wouldn't make a bit of difference. No passion = no sequel! Seriously though, passion will see you through your darkest hours. It will make up for your lack of skills until you have given yourself enough time to hone them.

Remember that this is art. It should be fun. If it is not something you enjoy enough to put the time and effort into, then you should consider other options. Sitting down at the computer should be as much fun as going out with your friends. If you have the passion, it will be fun.

Chapter 1

What Am I Getting Myself Into?

Who Is This Book For?

This book is written for anyone interested in character modeling. A good understanding of basic polygon modeling and knowledge of the Maya interface are pretty much required to get the most out of this book. Although geared toward the Maya user and with specific

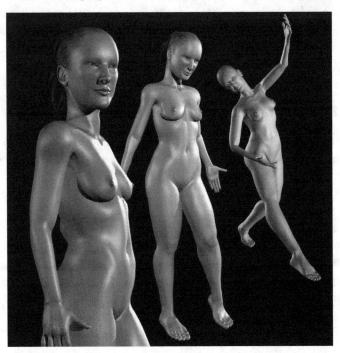

Figure 1-1

references to the Maya tool set, I believe that it can be easily translated to use with the software of your choice. Most of the actual lessons can be performed with any modeling package.

If you stick with me, you will learn how to model, texture, and rig a character. We will look at different approaches where they pertain to game modeling as opposed to higher-resolution modeling. We will also look at different skeletal rigs including the basic skeleton and more advanced control-based rigs. We will not, however, be covering the animation process. Animation is an art in itself. There is way too much to cover and I'm not quite ready to tackle that book. One at a time, if that's okay with you.

There are a multitude of approaches to modeling a character. I've spent a number of years researching this topic and have come up with a pretty concise formula for character modeling based on a number of different techniques. The method I show throughout this book is easy enough for the novice to grasp and will offer some insightful tips for the intermediate to advanced artist.

If your passion is to be a character modeler, then a comprehensive understanding of human anatomy is a requirement. Do you have to know the name of every muscle and bone in the human body? The answer is no, but you should understand where they are and what they do. Having this knowledge will make the character modeling process that much easier.

Looking Forward

Creating characters for games and film is a quite rewarding profession. As a character modeler you will play an integral role in a long process involving texture artists, character riggers, animators, concept artists, etc. In some cases, a character modeler might be required to perform some or all of the aforementioned roles. It really depends on a number of factors. Larger game companies as well as the film industry tend to have people who specialize in specific areas and only perform tasks in their designated field of expertise. Smaller houses, however, might have a larger workload spread out over a smaller group of artists, allowing you to get your hands dirty in a number of disciplines.

Figure 1-2

Either way, character modeling is an exciting career that is always changing for the better. With ever-advancing technology, modelers are being called upon to create more and more believable characters. I can honestly say that this keeps it interesting! With the trend toward creating ultra-realistic characters, it really becomes absolutely necessary for a character modeler to understand the human body and the way it moves. This is something that should not be overlooked, and I can't stress that point enough.

We also see a decline in the need to create models with low polygon counts. This practice applied particularly in the game industry. With advancements in game engines, computers, and consoles, low-poly is becoming a thing of the past. Now more than ever, artists have to be meticulous in creating higher polygon characters.

The increasingly popular use of normal mapping technology has given rise to some amazing advancements in character modeling. Details such as wrinkles, veins, and even pores are being added directly into the geometry. A keenly trained eye is all the more necessary to capture the subtle details of the human form.

The Art of Programming

As scary as it sounds to most artists, it is becoming increasingly necessary to have some understanding of programming; in this case, Maya's Mel scripting. Even a very basic comprehension of Mel scripting will aid you tremendously. Scripting will allow you, for instance, to create your own dialog window that contains your most commonly used commands, or perhaps condense a number of separate commands into a single button.

The skills and job scope of the technical artist have grown rapidly over the past few years, and they form that bridge that spans the gap between technology (programming) and art. Oftentimes, artists and programmers don't quite speak the same language. It is the job of a technical artist to be the interpreter. A tech artist is also responsible for creating scripts that modify the standard Maya workflow to simplify the production pipeline.

Knowing how to script also gives you an advantage when it comes to getting a job. Prospective employers will consider your technical skills a valuable asset alongside your artistic abilities. Anything you can do to give yourself that edge will be rewarded.

To Draw or Not to Draw, That Is the Question...

Many students have asked the question, "Do I have to be able to draw before I can become a good modeler?" I would have to say no, but let me put that into perspective. I have come across a number of people who are excellent modelers but can't draw a stick figure. I think we need to understand that computer graphics is a medium just like painting. Being proficient with watercolors doesn't necessarily make you a sculptor.

Conversely, having the ability to draw the human form gives you a head start on understanding muscle and bone systems and basic human proportions. Simply put, the idea here is to do everything you can to improve your skills. I firmly believe that my drawing skills have made me a more insightful 3D artist. In turn, I can also say that due in large part to 3D modeling, my ability to draw has improved as well.

Figure 1-3

Research and Reference

I can't say enough about the value of reference and research. I have a library of reference books dedicated to human anatomy alone. Books about drawing are also a large part of my collection. Oftentimes it's easier to make out details in a drawing as opposed to a photo.

Here is a list of the more essential books in my library:

Human Anatomy for Artists: The Elements of Form, by Eliot
    Goldfinger, Oxford University Press, 1991.

This book is a great photographic reference of the body in various forms.

The Artist's Complete Guide to Facial Expression, by Gary Faigin, Watson-Guptill Publications, 1990.

This book is essential! Although this book is geared toward the 2D artist, it breaks down the complexity of human facial expressions. Great reference in setting up your character for facial animation.

Anatomy for the Artist: A Comprehensive Guide to Drawing the Human Body, by Daniel Carter, Parragon Publishing, 2005.

This book approaches anatomy from an artistic point of view.

Drawing Human Anatomy, by Giovanni Civardi, Sterling Publishing, 1995.

Drawing the Female Nude, by Giovanni Civardi, Sterling Publishing, 1995.

I really love Giovanni's style — very clean. Great reference.

Stop Staring: Facial Modeling and Animation Done Right, by Jason Osipa, Sybex, Inc., 2003.

This book is gold when it comes to character animation. A must-have if you want to be an animator.

Because I make my living as a character modeler, I have countless reference images of clothing, armor, anatomy, you name it! Anything I find that might be useful either now or in the future goes into this collection. It is also quite useful to collect images of models that were created by other people. Many times you will find pictures of a work in progress, which can give you insight into how the model was structured and the technique used in its creation. Websites such as cgtalk.com, cgfocus.com, and cgchannel.com have forums loaded with these types of images.

Many of the photos used in the book come from www.3D.sk. This is an amazing site with high-resolution images relating to many subjects, including male and female anatomy, armor, animals, and more. These images are excellent as modeling guides or as textures for your models.

I use the term research in the broadest sense possible. There is no limit to the amount of study and preparation you can do on your road to greatness. Just opening this book is a step in that direction.

Chapter 2

Words of Wisdom

Being a grizzled modeling vet (or grumpy old man, as some would call me) in my 30s comes with endless hours sitting at the computer honing my skills. This is an ongoing process and I always feel I have more to learn. I take a lot of pride in what I have accomplished to this point in my career, but I do so humbly. There are many who are much more talented than myself and I strive to be on par with them. I don't claim to have the de facto answers to everything you need to know about modeling. I am merely offering my perspective based on my experience and research. I think you will find that my approach falls into line with what is considered industry standard.

Now that we have that out of the way, I want to present some of my philosophical ramblings. These are some of the things I've learned over the past 10-plus years in the industry, all condensed into the next few pages.

The Secret Formula

I believe in and rely on formula. I always begin a model the same way, regardless of what type of character I am creating. There are many advantages to modeling by formula, and the more you make a practice of this method, the easier it becomes. This also decreases the amount of time spent on the "blocking out" process in character modeling.

A character model should be built the same way you would draw it. When you draw, you sketch out a basic mass for the character before you begin fleshing it out. Generalizing the initial shape of your model allows you to easily adjust its proportions to, for example, give your character a more heroic physique. Once you have your base model adjusted, you can then start adding in details.

The beauty of this approach is reusability. Having a strong base model allows you to eliminate a good amount of preproduction work. Say you need a female character and a guy with a beer gut and moose antlers. By starting with a base model and massaging the geometry, you can tackle both of these characters without starting from scratch.

As you build your models it will also become apparent that body parts can be reused again and again across a multitude of characters. As an example, you create a standard hand geometry for one character, then with some minor tweaking, it can become the hand of your next character. I personally maintain a library of parts that I have created and Frankenstein them in when needed. This is not to say that you should never experiment with new and more concise ways to model. As technology advances, you will need to keep up with it!

Save, Save, Save, Save, Save!

And one more time — SAVE! Saving will keep you from the anguish and gut-wrenching feeling that goes along with losing hours of work. Save often. Every minor change you make deserves a save. Saving is one of the most important things you can do. It is so important it is being repeated here over and over! So here is my public service announcement, and I'm saying it in my most sincere introspective voice: Save — it's the right thing to do.

Keep It Clean

Before we get cracking on an actual character model, I would like to discuss a few modeling basics that I will refer to throughout the book. First off, I want to stress the concept of working *clean*. What I mean by this is keeping your scene free of all extraneous nodes. Maya is notorious for keeping around nodes that are no longer useful to your scene. This increases your file size dramatically. A quick way to remove these "dead nodes" is to use the mhClearDead-Nodes.mel script available on the companion CD.

Another aspect of working clean is to *name everything*! This is a good practice to get into. Immediately name your mesh with something other than pCube1. As you create materials, give them appropriate names. This could save you, not to mention anyone else who happens to touch your file, time later in the creation process.

Transferring assets is a common practice in a production pipeline. Oftentimes you will need to hand off your model to either an animator or a texture artist, and the last thing you need is to have them coming back to you to decipher your scene. Don't be lazy when it comes to naming nodes and you won't be haunted by cryptic names later.

Here is the big one — *polygon accountability*. What I mean by this is that all the polygons on your model should serve a purpose. Simply put, only areas with detail should have a higher concentration of polygons. This is especially true for game modeling, where every polygon counts. Although poly counts are a little more forgiving in film work, it is still important not to waste them needlessly.

Working with Quads

My approach to modeling, like that of many others, is to work only with quads! A *quad* is a polygon that is made up of four points that generally but not always assume a rectangular shape (see Figure 2-1). There is much debate as to the validity of quad-only modeling. Also, working with quads is a bit more difficult than working with triangles, and maintaining a mesh that contains only quads can be quite tricky for the novice. However, I firmly believe that using this method makes you a better modeler.

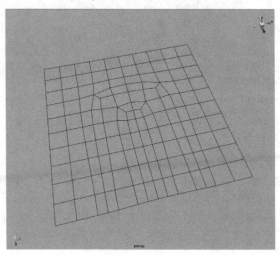

Figure 2-1

I have always taught my students to prepare for the worst and then step back accordingly. In this case, if you can model with quads, modeling with triangles will be that much easier.

There are other factors to support the quad approach. Your geometry will flow better and tessellate cleaner. Deformation during animation will be noticeably smoother, especially around joints. Finally, a great deal of work in high-detailed modeling (see Figure 2-2) is now done by exporting your model to ZBrush (pixologic.com and zbrushcentral.com) or Mudbox (mudbox3d.com). Both of these programs contain advanced tools that allow you to sculpt a model using more than a million polygons! These models are in turn used to create the normal maps that give the illusion of a higher polygon model. ZBrush and Mudbox like to work with quads, so this is something you as a modeler need to address.

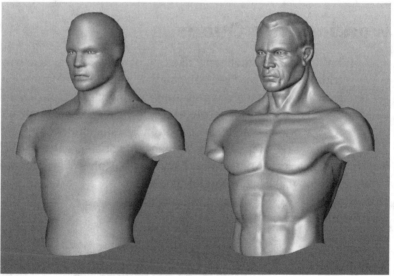

Figure 2-2: Sculpting with Mudbox.

Image used with permission of Mike Hovland

Another thing to mention here is that many game engines deal exclusively with triangles. What this means is that upon exporting an asset from Maya, your model will be broken down into its triangulated form. Oftentimes when creating lower-resolution assets, a modeler will resort to building with tris to accommodate a reduced poly count. Knowing this, however, I would still begin the modeling process using quads and then convert to tris at the end of the building phase to prepare for export.

Suffice it to say, in this book we will use quads for our modeling. If you would like to research the topic of quad modeling vs. tris, there is plenty of information available on the Internet.

Edge Loops

Edge loops. Come on, say it with me — edge loops! Don't know what an edge loop is? By the end of this book you will be dreaming about them, my friend!

An *edge loop* is a continuous edge that loops around the muscle contours of the character's body. You will find that if your geometry follows the muscle structure, your model will animate considerably better. This is especially evident in facial animation. Without edge loops following the muscle groupings in the face, there will be noticeable problems when you animate.

Modeling Reference Guides

Using front and side view image planes or a skeleton on which to base your modeling is usually the best approach; your body proportions are then clearly defined. An *image plane* is the projection of an image in a particular viewport. If you are unfamiliar with the use of image planes, the process is covered in Chapter 4: "Beginning the Modeling Process." When using image planes it is important to have high-quality reference images. Whether they are drawings or actual photos is determined by what type of model you are creating. Be forewarned, however, that photos always contain perspective, whereas drawings can be completely orthogonal. *Orthogonal* refers to flat projection planes such as a front, top, or side view. Such views contain absolutely no perspective. If you are using photos as your reference guides, be prepared to adjust for perspective during the modeling process.

In using image planes it is also important that your front and side views line up at the major features of the body. If you were to overlap these views in a photo editing program, the features should align as closely as possible.

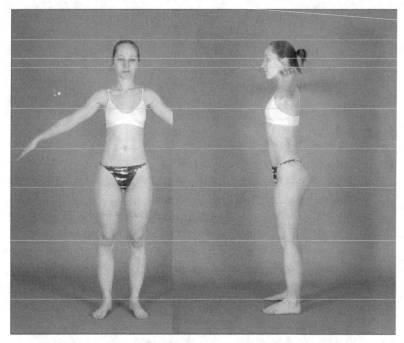

Figure 2-3: Align your reference images so that the body features are aligned.

Before We Get Started...

Let's take a look at the basic human form. I think it goes without saying that men and women have some major differences. Women have softer contours and less defined muscle groups. Women also have wider hips and more narrow shoulders than men. One particular area that seems to give people a lot of trouble is the face. While modeling any head can prove to be difficult, I will say that the softer features of the female face are sometimes harder to convey than those of a male.

One more important thing to mention here, especially if you are relatively new to the modeling process, is to get used to modeling in perspective view. This can be challenging to the beginner but is well worth the effort. Working predominantly in perspective mode allows you to see your object as it will appear when rendered. This is very important to character modeling where your figure will potentially be seen from multiple angles. This can be a simple process if you use the X, Y, Z handles on your manipulator and avoid

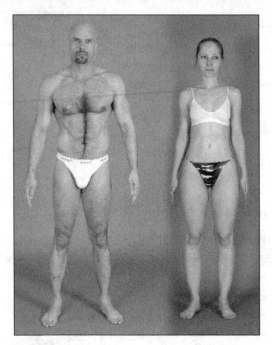

Figure 2-4

grabbing the center box that moves your selection on multiple axes simultaneously. This will guarantee that your selection will move precisely where you want it.

Important Note about This Book

This book contains references to Maya 8 commands as well as Maya 7. Each part of the command will be separated by a vertical bar (|). Whenever the command includes opening the dialog box, a ☐ will follow the command. The Maya 8 command will come first, and the Maya 7 command will follow inside square brackets. Here are a couple of examples:

Edit Mesh | Extrude ☐ [v7: Edit Polygons | Extrude Face ☐]

This example tells you that opening the dialog box is necessary.

Edit Polygons	Polygon UVs	Subdiv
Subdivide		☐
Split Polygon Tool		☐
Duplicate Edge Loop Tool		☐
Split Edge Ring Tool		☐
Extrude Face		☐
Extrude Edge		☐
Extrude Vertex		☐
Chamfer Vertex		☐
Bevel		☐
Cut Faces Tool		☐
Poke Faces		☐
Wedge Faces		☐
Merge Vertices		☐
Merge Multiple Edges		☐
Merge Edge Tool		☐
Merge To Center		
Split Vertex		

Figure 2-5

13

Skeleton | Remove Joint

This one doesn't require you to open the dialog box, and the Maya 7 command is the same as Maya 8.

Whenever it is necessary to go to the additional rollout dialog in a command, it will appear as follows:

Display | Hide ▶ Hide Selection (Ctrl+h)   Figure 2-6

Here, a command is accompanied by its hotkey.

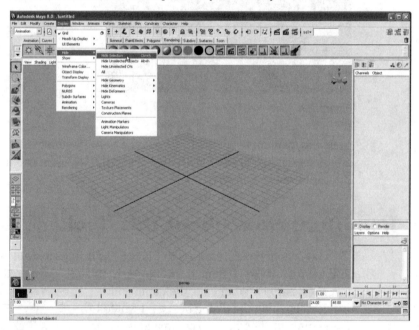

Figure 2-7

I hope that covers it. Let's get crackin'.

Chapter 3

A Modeling Primer

Subdivisions

Refer to Chapter_3 on the companion CD.

In Chapter 2 I mentioned my preference for modeling completely with quadrangles, so let's review a little here. Modeling completely with quads has many benefits that may not be apparent at first. Let's go through a few modeling exercises to get your mouse hand all loosened up, and I'll show you what I mean.

First off, we are going to be building a human, so at some point we will be adding additional geometry to help give the model's surface a smooth quality. This is done in Maya by applying the Mesh | Smooth [v7: Polygons | Smooth] command with our object selected. We'll refer to this as a *smooth node*. Sure, this is obvious to some of you, but hey, this is for the newbies, so go with the flow. What the hell, you might learn something new.

Some of you might prefer to use Proxy | Subdiv Proxy [v7: Polygons | Smooth Proxy]. If you are not familiar with a subdivided proxy, it refers to the process of having your original control mesh represented as a transparent object encasing the higher polygon or subdivided geometry. As you manipulate the control mesh, the underlying high-res mesh will deform as well. I prefer to use the Mesh | Smooth [v7: Polygons | Smooth] command (smooth node) because when working on the control mesh I prefer to see it shaded and not in an X-ray or transparent state.

So that being said, when we apply a smooth node to our object, it will divide each face into four subdivisions. This is why it is also referred to as *subdivisional surface modeling*. Along with dividing each face into four new faces, it also tightens up the mesh. Take a look at Figure 3-1 to see what I mean.

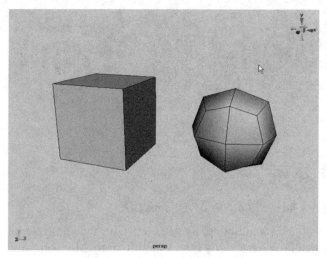

Figure 3-1

You will notice in Figure 3-2 that when you subdivide a cube (Mesh | Smooth [v7: Polygons | Smooth]) you get a somewhat rounded object. If you were to subdivide it again, then each of the faces that

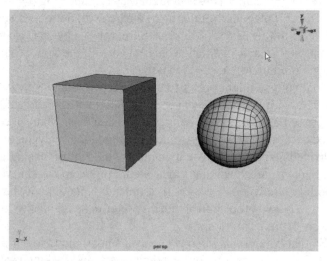

Figure 3-2

were divided into four will now be divided into four again, and so on and so on. With each iteration of subdivisions, you will get a much smoother mesh.

Sooooo, think about the last example. Look at the mesh you end up with and remember from whence it came — the lowly cube. This should tell us something very important: We don't need a whole boatload of polygons to create an organic model.

The base mesh or control mesh doesn't always have to be pretty; that is the job of its cousin, the subdivided mesh. The *control mesh* is simply that; it controls the subdivided surface at the modeling stage as well as during animation. We *always* save the control mesh. It can be a separate entity from the subdivided mesh (subdivided proxy), or it can be in itself subdivided, as long as you can get back to its initial form by removing layers of subdivisions.

One of the most important things about character modeling is to understand how to create a proper control mesh. The subdivisions have a way of taking care of themselves, almost to a fault. You may be thinking, "Subdividing any model always seems to make it appear smooth, right?" The answer, my friend, is a resounding NO. If you take a close look at the actual mesh surface it will probably look something like Figure 3-3. You will see that where there was a triangle, Maya turns it into a quad. The problem is that it doesn't flow the way the geometry was intended to flow and it appears as a somewhat awkward shape.

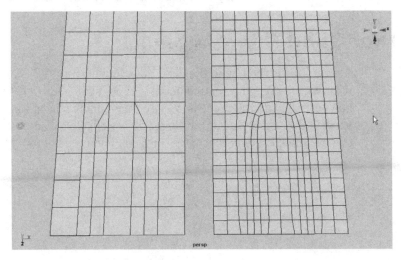

Figure 3-3

Now let's compare Figure 3-3 to Figure 3-4. Notice the difference in the flow of the geometry? I hope you're still with me when you say, "Hey that second example looks ten times better!"

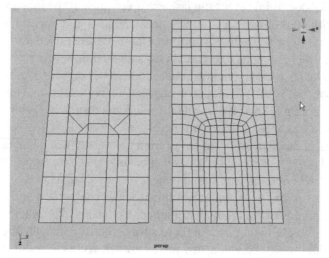

Figure 3-4

The reason it looks better is because the control mesh is made entirely of quads. So you say to yourself, "How do I go about making a model using all quads, oh Knowledgeable One?" Well, there is a secret. Actually it really isn't a secret, and it really is pretty easy.

That Quad Thing Again...

Alright, this is the key to the quad modeling universe! Basically, what we are doing is creating detail without adding unnecessary geometry and, in the process, we are maintaining quads. Let me show you an example here. In Figure 3-5 we have a plane with basic subdivisions. Pretend this is the surface of your geometry.

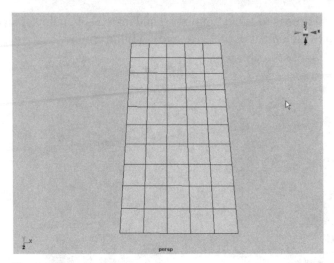

Figure 3-5

Let's say you want to add details to an area, like a big gash or wrinkles. The problem is how do you do so without adding a ton of geometry? Let ol' Uncle Gary show you how.

Many times when creating an edge loop you need to find a place to end it. Oftentimes, people have the tendency to just run it into an existing vertex, leaving one of those nasty triangles.

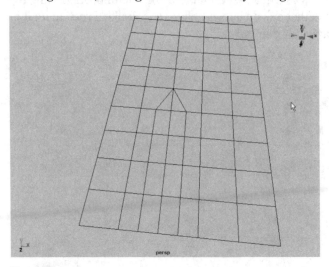

Figure 3-6

The answer is to avoid temptation and instead of ending at a vertex, go to the midpoint of the edge and continue around.

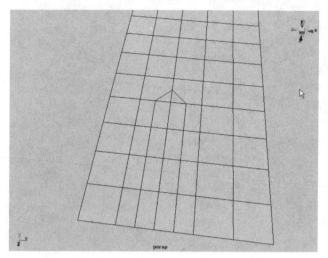

Figure 3-7

Now draw an edge from the midpoint of the angled edge to the near-est vertex. Repeat this process wherever you need to. Even though the shape may still resemble a triangle, it contains the same number of points as a quad (see Figure 3-8). The important thing to note here is that a quad doesn't have to look like a rectangle; it just needs to have four points.

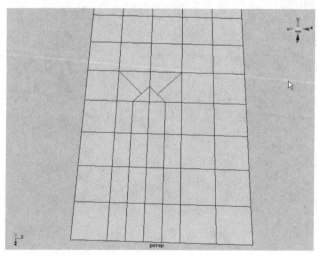

Figure 3-8

This can be repeated an infinite number of times, adding a great amount of detail and, most importantly, you're working entirely with quads.

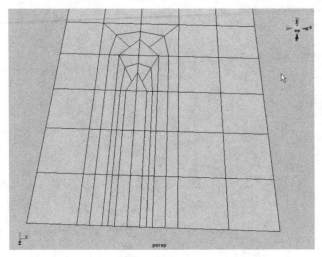

Figure 3-9

Another method of building with quads is to start out in a similar fashion to the first example by drawing your edge to the midpoint and continuing along your path.

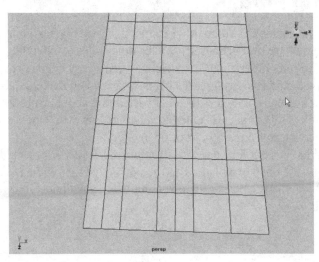

Figure 3-10

However, this time instead of drawing a line from the vertex to the angled edge's midpoint, simply collapse the angled edge.

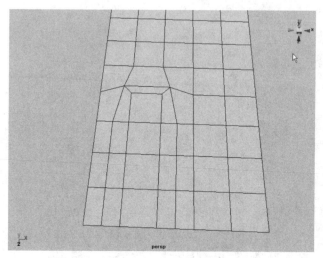

Figure 3-11

Pretty cool, huh? That is all it takes. Now you should be able to build anything with quads, no problemo!

Extruding Pitfalls

Let's take a look at some other issues that may pop up while you are modeling. In this book we will be doing a lot of extruding. One thing to remember about extrusions is that every edge surrounding your selected faces will produce a new face when extruded. Now this is fine and dandy for the most part, and it should work exactly like you would expect. Problems can arise, however, when you extrude a face from a border or open edge.

What is a border edge? An example of a *border edge* would be the outside edge of a plane. But the open edge that you have to be watchful of is the border edge you get when you divide your model in half.

It is a common practice to "mirror" a model when working on something symmetrical such as a character's body or a fighter plane. When you mirror the model you can create an instance of the original that allows you to operate on one side and see the same results on the other. The problem arises when you extrude a face that has an interior open edge, as shown in Figure 3-12.

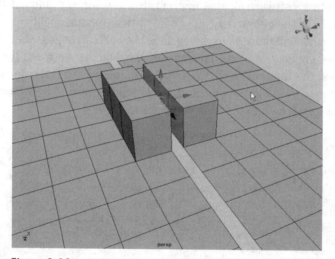

Figure 3-12

When you have a mirrored object you usually don't see the faces that are created inside of your geometry. The problem is that having a face inside the geometry that shares an edge with the outer surface or shell can create unwanted results when smoothed. This is a no-no.

The simple fix is to delete that interior face as soon as you see it. This is just one of those little things to be conscious of while you are modeling.

Can't Get a Hard Edge!

One other issue that seems to pop up quite often is adding sharp detail to a smoothed model, such as adding the hard edge of a belt that looks like it is a separate piece of geometry when it is actually part of the original mesh. The smoothing algorithms in Maya (or any other software for that matter) always want to round out the surface of the geometry, thus giving it that organic quality.

Maya will draw a curved surface between all edges when the smooth node is applied. The smaller the distance between two edges, the tighter the curve. Therefore, the way to make an edge look hard is to tighten up the control mesh by adding new edge loops very close to the loop you want to harden.

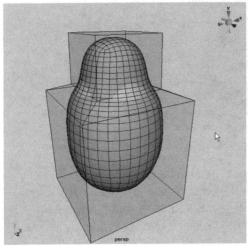
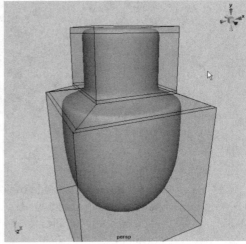

Figure 3-13

Figure 3-14: Add edge loops close to the loop you want hardened.

Normals

When we refer to soft edges we are not talking about smoothing. Depending on your settings, an object such as a sphere may appear to have a hard edge surrounding each face, giving it that "disco ball" appearance. This is referred to as *faceted*.

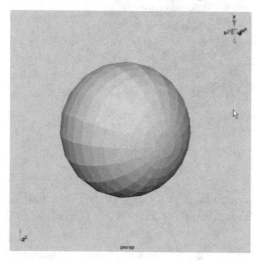

Figure 3-15

In order to get rid of those hard edges, we need to soften them. We do so by adjusting normals; in this case, Normals | Soften Edge [v7: Polygons | Normals]. Normals play a very important role in the 3D realm but are often ignored, especially by the novice user. A *normal* is an indicator of sorts of the direction a face or vertex is pointing in relation to the view. For the most part, when an object is created the normal will point straight out from the face in a perpendicular fashion.

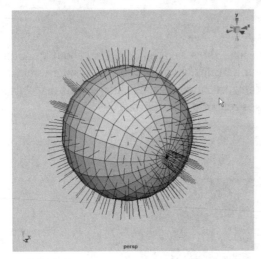

Figure 3-16

Vertex normals are a bit harder to comprehend. They may look as if they are pointing in random directions on the faceted sphere.

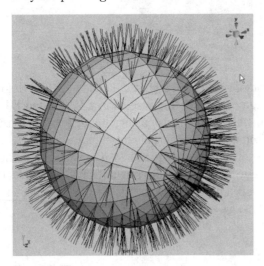

Figure 3-17

In reality, they are pointing to angles that will allow the edges to appear hard. Notice that there are four normals projecting from each vertex. These represent the corner vertices of each face. In this example, four separate faces all share the same corner vertex, and each vertex has its own normal.

What you are doing when you make the edges soft is moving the vertex normals so that they are all pointing in the same direction. This adjustment of a normal coupled with the normals around it give the surface a smoother appearance.

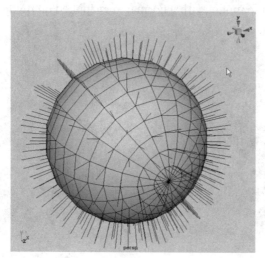

Figure 3-18

Softening the normals, unlike the smooth node, does not add geometry to your object, so you will still have the appearance of hard edges around the outside of your object. You will notice no difference between hard or soft normals when you apply a smooth node to your geometry. Hard edges can, however, be added once you have applied the smooth node. This is not recommended. I always try to add the detail of my character at the base level, not after it has been smoothed.

Normals are often used in game modeling that requires a low polygon count. In this case, maintaining an organic character is done by softening edges. One other place that normals play a role is in matching up the seams of two separate pieces of geometry, such as a hand and an arm. When the vertex from one object shares the exact x, y, z, coordinates as a vertex from another object, they are said to be *co-incidental vertices*. Therefore, normals for each vertex must be identical where two objects meet to create an invisible seam when the object is drawn in the game engine.

27

Finally, and most importantly, normals are key to normal mapping. Go figure. In the simplest terms, *normal maps* are created from calculating each normal in conjunction with the direction of light (vector), thus producing a color indicating how that particular normal is to be represented when rendered. Wow, that's a mouthful! Figure 3-19 shows an example of a low-poly character model on the right and the same model with a normal map applied on the left.

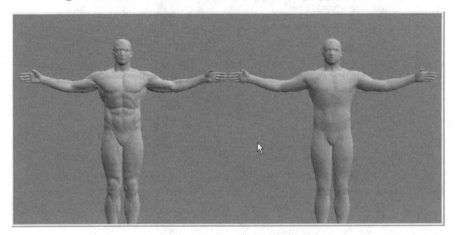

Figure 3-19

UV Layout

Let's take some time here to talk about texture mapping. In almost all cases you're probably going to texture your object. There are numerous ways to go about this process.

The old school way is to get in there and unwrap that thing and then try to adjust your UVs so that there is no noticeable stretching. This approach is fortunately becoming obsolete.

Basically, UVs represent the position of the vertices of your model in 2D space. You will notice that once a UV map has been applied to an object, all of the vertices of your object will be represented as UVs. UVs and vertices are not the same thing. This just seems like the easiest way to explain them. Adjusting UVs in the UV Editor does not move the vertices of your geometry. It merely matches the UVs up to pixels on your texture map.

The ideal UV map exactly matches the face size, edge length, and vertex positions as they appear in 3D space. Any variation will cause stretching and pinching of the texture when applied to the model. Before you get too worried, know that it is not always possible to create perfect UVs. There are, however, new methods to make the process considerably easier.

One of the most common ways to make sure you have minimal stretching of your texture is to use a *marking map*. This is a texture normally comprised of squares that may contain numbers or letters. In many cases, a checkerboard map would work just as well.

Figure 3-20: A marking map.

One of the relatively newer methods is called *pelt mapping*. This process, which was originated in 3ds Max 8, gives the user the option of simply selecting edges that are used as seams. The model is then unfolded in a pelt-like fashion using the seams as a guide (see Figure 3-21). From this point you can make adjustments to ensure that your texture is evenly spaced. Using this pelt method makes it rather simple to eliminate all that stretching that we used to have to fight to get rid of. One of the few downsides to pelting is that it is somewhat difficult to determine what you are looking at when you bring your UV exported image into a photo editing program to paint. This, however, can be minimized by proper placement of your edge seams.

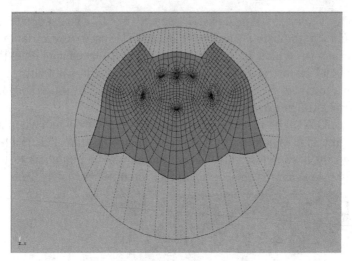

Figure 3-21: A pelt map.

One other new method is a ZBrush plug-in called ZAppLink. This allows the user to export, for lack of a better term, a screen grab of the object. It then ports it immediately into Photoshop where it can be edited at will. When you are through editing that particular view, you simply save it. Back in ZBrush, you merely accept the changes and voilà! The texture now has these particular changes. This can be done with the model at any angle, therefore eliminating stretching of any sort.

The really amazing thing about ZAppLink is that technically you don't have to lay out any UVs; you could let ZBrush do all the work. When you do, a cube map or UVW map is created. What this means is that the texture will be comprised of little squares. So if you were to use the ZAppLink method to completely texture your model, this would not be an issue. In fact, it works great if you intend to use the texture for one unique model only.

Where this cube map creates problems in when you need to produce multiple versions of a texture. A good example of this would be team jerseys for a football game.

The reason cube maps can be problematic is in the fact that if you look at the texture that is created, you have absolutely no idea which end is up. As a standalone map it is indecipherable — just a bunch of squares with no rhyme or reason.

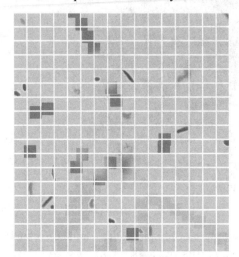

Figure 3-22: A cube map created with ZAppLink.

Even if you use ZAppLink to create your textures, it is always good to create your own UV layout for your model. This gives you total control of the assets you are working with and, believe me, total control is a very good thing. (With total control comes great responsibility, including the pain of laying out proper UVs, which is one of the necessary evils that will pay off big-time in the long run.)

So with that in mind, let's talk about some of the more commonly used texture layouts. As I said earlier, pelt mapping is the current one-stop shop for UV layouts, but I think it is still necessary to talk about some of the more commonly used texture layouts. First and foremost we have *planar mapping*. Think of this like a movie projector shining an image on the screen. This works great for surfaces that are mostly flat or have only a slight curve. You'll notice from Figure 3-23 that the more the geometry curves away from the projected plane, the more it stretches the image map.

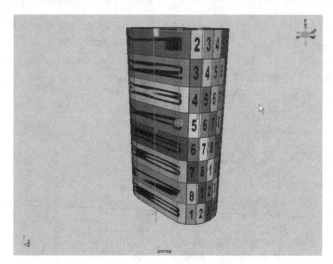

Figure 3-23: Planar mapping

Cylindrical mapping will wrap the object like a label on a soup can. This is good for mapping arms and legs.

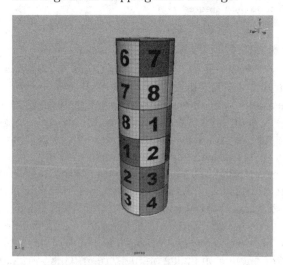

Figure 3-24: Cylindrical mapping.

Spherical mapping is great for mapping a globe. Let's see, it's also really good for mapping... a globe. I think you get the picture. Notice, however, that you will get some pinching where the map meets at the poles.

Figure 3-25: Spherical mapping.

Automatic mapping projects numerous planar maps from four all the way up to 12 different angles. Each face is assigned to each projection based on its angle. It's hard to say that this is ideal for many situations. The problem is that it really can make a mess of your UVs, leaving it up to you to determine where each of the stray faces it doesn't know what to do with belong. There are some good uses for it, however. In some cases it can divide things up pretty well, leaving you with a more manageable cleanup.

Figure 3-26: Automatic mapping.

The Sculpt Geometry Tool

The Sculpt Geometry tool is going to play a major role in our modeling approach in this book. At certain intervals we will use this tool to aid in the modeling process. I use this tool a great deal in order to achieve the smooth organic form of the human body.

As you learn to control the sculpting tool you will become very proficient in fleshing out your character in a short amount of time. This is, however, probably one of the hardest tools to utilize to your advantage, especially in the beginning stages. Like any tool, whether it be a pencil, a paintbrush, or a mouse for that matter, the Sculpt Geometry tool takes a little getting used to.

Let's take a look at the Sculpt Geometry tool. Select Mesh | Sculpt Geometry Tool ▢ [v7: Edit Polygons | Sculpt Geometry Tool ▢]. The Sculpt Geometry Tool window should pop up (see Figure 3-27). The most important things to know about the settings are:

▶ When using the Smooth operation, set Max Displacement rather low — somewhere around 0.005.

▶ When using the Push or Pull operations, the Max Displacement setting should be set to a higher value, such as 0.2 to 0.4.

▶ Using Auto Smooth in conjunction with the Push or Pull operation is recommended. Your Smooth Strength should be set to 2 when using a smaller Max Displacement, and then set higher when you increase the Max Displacement.

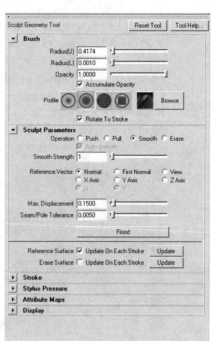

Figure 3-27

There are two approaches that I normally use. One is to work on the object as is, and the other is to apply a smooth node and then use the Sculpt Geometry tool. The trick to the latter approach is to apply a smooth node on the object, then delete the smooth node. This process can be simplified if you utilize the goModTools.mel script. (See the section in this chapter called "Go Tools" for information about this script.) If you use a script you can set up the buttons you use most often into one toolbox. The goModTools.mel script does just this, and is described in detail a little later in this chapter.

What this approach does is allow you to sculpt on a higher-resolution model. The more geometry, the smoother the sculpt. Once you are satisfied with the results, you then step back to your lower-resolution control mesh. The mesh will retain about 80 percent of the tweaking, which makes it a lot less tedious to manually move vertices here and there to form the model. Once you nail down this approach you are going to see vast improvements in your finished model.

The key to using the Sculpt Geometry tool effectively is to use what I call the "touch and click" method. What I mean by this is that as soon as you touch the model, click and release the left mouse button. This is the way to control the effect of the operation. You will find this most useful when using the Sculpt Geometry Tool | Smooth operation. When using the Sculpt Geometry Tool | Pull operation, don't be afraid of moving the geometry out too far. You can easily go back in with the Smooth to make the adjustments.

This process, in conjunction with moving verts on the base mesh, is a rather unique approach, but at the same time is becoming more the norm with the addition of ZBrush to your modeling arsenal.

Let's take a few minutes to experiment with this approach.

1. In a new scene create a sphere with the default settings. Now let's mess with our sphere. If you are totally unfamiliar with the Sculpt Geometry tool, try out its buttons and play around with the tool, changing the settings as you go. Alright, time's up! If your sphere got totally messed up during your noodling, simply delete it and create a new one.

2. Take a look at Figure 3-28. In this case we want to apply one level of Smooth to our sphere. However, we will still want to

be able to step back to our original control mesh. In order to do that, we need to make sure that we have our Construction History on. When the smooth node is applied it actually creates a polySmoothFace node. If you look in the Channel Box, it should show up under the Inputs list. Using the Sculpt Geometry tool, try to recreate Mr. Blobby on your own.

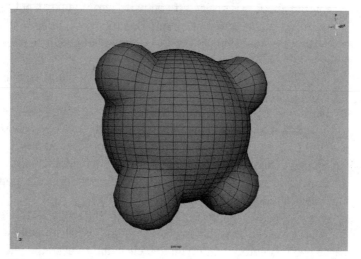

Figure 3-28

3. Now once you are satisfied with the effects of the Sculpt, select the **polySmoothFace** node in the Inputs list. This in turn will highlight the selection in your Outliner. Click on the **polySmoothFace** node in the Outliner and then delete it. This should return you to your original sphere with the modifications you made with the Sculpt Geometry tool. Once again, the Go Tools (goModTools.mel) interface (which we'll discuss in just a bit) will handle this process much more efficiently.

You may notice that the areas that were pulled away from the original sphere didn't look quite as smooth as you would like when the smooth node was applied. This is because as we pulled the geometry out, we ended up with polygons stretching to cover the distance (see Figure 3-29). So, in order to clean this up we will add some additional faces to these areas.

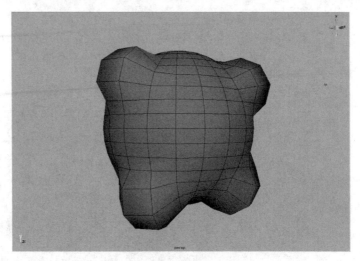

Figure 3-29

4.   Select **Edit Mesh | Insert Edge Loop Tool** ☐ [v7: Edit
     Polygons | Split Edge Ring Tool ☐] and add a couple of edge
     loops to the protruding areas of your control mesh. If you like,
     you can also adjust the vertices. Once you are satisfied, add
     the smooth node again.

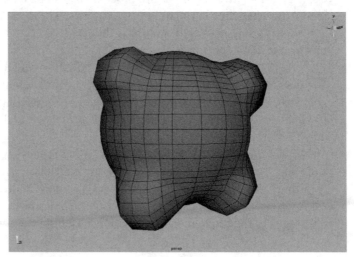

Figure 3-30

5. You will notice that those areas are now considerably smoother thanks to the addition of a few edge loops on your control mesh. At this point you can use the **Sculpt Geometry** tool once again to flesh out your model.

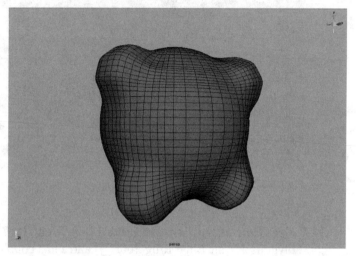

Figure 3-31

So in a nutshell, this is the entire process we will be using as we model our character in the following chapters. The cycle is sculpting, adding geometry, then sculpting, then adjusting your control mesh, and so on and so on.

There is no rule that says this is the definitive way to model. You may feel more comfortable spending your time moving the geometry on a base level to complete the entire modeling process. It will be just as effective as the method I have described above, only slower.

In fact there will be stages in the modeling process where manually adjusting the control mesh will be unavoidable. Either way you go, I think that looking at your mesh with a smooth node applied or using Proxy | Subdiv Proxy [v7: Polygons | Smooth Proxy] during the stages of the modeling progression is essential.

Object and World Coordinates

For some of you this might be obvious, but if you are relatively wet behind the ears, you really need to know the difference between world coordinates and object coordinates.

Take a look in the lower left-hand corner of any viewport. You should see a little XYZ thingamabob. This is actually your world coordinates. It shows you where the XYZ axes are pointing in relation to the camera you are currently looking through.

1. Quickly create a cube. Select it and apply the Move Manipulator by pressing **W**. You should see that the coordinates of the cube are exactly the same as the world coordinates.

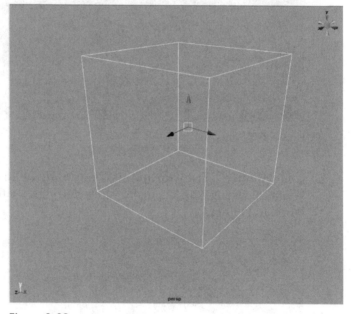

Figure 3-32

2. Now rotate the cube. Press **W** again. Notice that although the cube is rotated, its pivot is still aligned to the world.

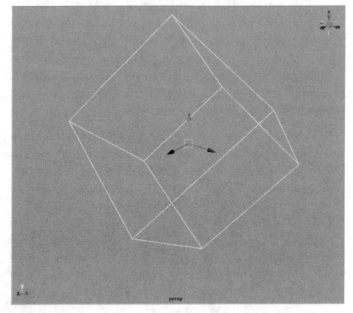

Figure 3-33

3. Go to **Modify | Transformation Tools ▸ Move Tool** ☐. When the dialog pops up, under Move Settings, switch from World to **Object**.

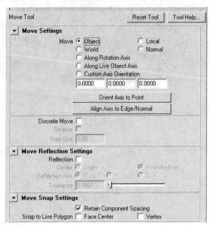

Figure 3-34: Change the Move Settings to Object.

4. If you look at the cube you will notice that now the local axis (pivot) is aligned to the cube and no longer aligned to the world.

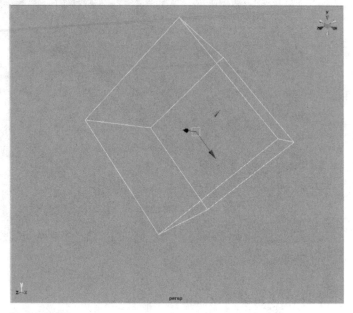

Figure 3-35

There are great advantages to being able to switch back and forth between world and object coordinates. Many times you will want to align an object based on the object coordinates.

5. Make two duplicates of the cube. Scale them so that you have a large, a medium, and a small cube. In perspective view, switch back to world coordinates and try to stack them as shown in Figure 3-36.

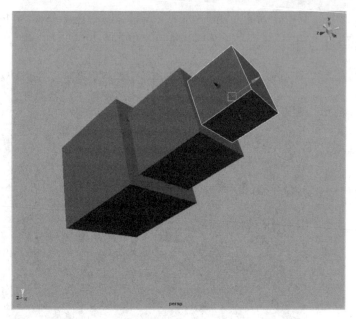

Figure 3-36

Pretty hard to do, huh?

6. Now switch back to object coordinates and stack the cubes. Get the idea?

Go Tools

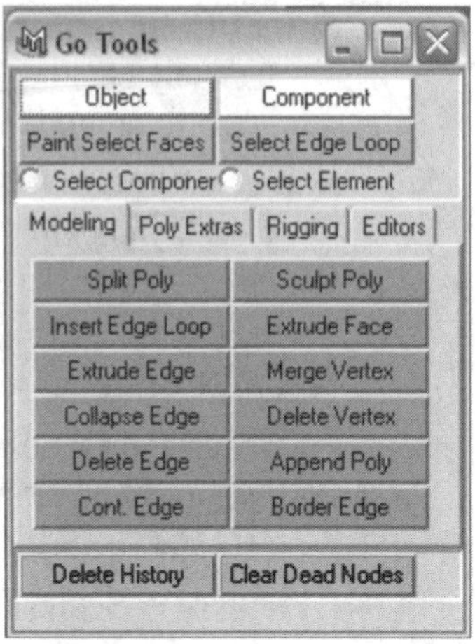

Included on the companion CD are a handful of scripts. The one I would like to talk about a little here is the goModTools.mel script, which creates the custom Go Tools dialog (see Figure 3-37). Oftentimes when modeling you get in a groove and find that some of the smallest things seem to impede your progress. Well, this little script is designed to eliminate a lot of those issues by allowing you to access common commands quickly and easily from one toolbox.

The toolbox itself is split up into various tabs that allow you to quickly move between tasks. I

Figure 3-37

developed this script from my own needs as a modeler. Each time I came across a command I found difficult to access I added it to the script. I hope you find it useful in your modeling.

Here is a list of features included in the Go Tools box:

Object — Switches selection to Object mode.

> Wireframe — Sets selected object to Wireframe mode.

> Shaded — Sets selected object to Shaded mode.

> BFCull ON — Sets backface culling on.

> BFCull OFF — Sets backface culling off.

Component — Switches selection to Component mode.

> Vertex — Escapes tool and sets component selection to Vertex.

> Edge — Escapes tool and sets component selection to Edge.

> Face — Escapes tool and sets component selection to Face.

Paint Select Faces — Sets selection to Paint Faces mode.

> Paint Selected Vertex — Sets selection to Paint Vertex mode.

> Paint Selected Edges — Sets selection to Paint Edge mode.

Select Edge Loop — Performs Maya Select Edge Loop command.

Select Edge Ring — Performs Maya Select Edge Ring command.

Select Component — Sets selection to select vertices, edges, or faces by clicking on or bounding box selecting components (default selection type).

Select Element — Sets selection to select all vertices, edges, or faces by clicking on an individual component. This works like Grow Select but instantly selects the entire contiguous geometry.

Modeling Tab

Split Poly — Accesses the Split Polygon tool.

Sculpt Poly — Accesses the Sculpt Geometry tool.

Fix Sculpt — This button will perform a fix when the Sculpt Geometry tool fails to work. It is meant to work on an object with mirrored geometry.

Insert Edge Loop — Accesses the Insert Edge Loop tool [v7: Split Edge Ring tool].

Extrude Face — Accesses the Extrude Face tool.

Extrude Faces Separately — Extracts each selected face individually.

Extrude Edge — Accesses the Extrude Edge tool.

Merge Vertex — Accesses the Merge Vertices option box.

Collapse Edge — Accesses the Collapse tool.

Delete Vertex — Accesses the Delete Vertex tool.

Delete Edge — Accesses the Delete Edge tool.

Append Poly — Accesses the Append to Polygons tool.

Cont. Edge — Accesses the Edge Loop Utilities | To Edge Loop option.

Border Edge — Selects the border edge of a geometry.

Center Border Edge — Use to straighten the center border edge of a mirrored geometry.

Poly Extras Tab

Smooth — Adds one smooth node to geometry.

Delete Smooth — Removes most recently applied polySmoothFace node.

Instance X — Creates an instanced geometry on the X-axis.

Instance Y — Creates an instanced geometry on the Y-axis.

Instance Z — Creates an instanced geometry on the Z-axis.

Smooth Normals — Performs All Soft on selected geometry.

Subdiv Proxy [v7: Smooth Proxy] — Creates a smooth proxy model for the selected geometry.

Combine — An improvement on Maya's Combine. This will combine the selected geometry and allow you to immediately name the new object. It will also remove the leftover transform nodes that are no longer necessary.

Symmetry Merge — Very useful for stitching together the edges of two halves of a selected geometry.

Center Pivot — Aligns the pivot point to the center of the selected geometry.

Create Layer — Creates a new layer using the new name of the selected geometry. It will also add the geometry into the newly created layer.

Extract Faces — Simplifies the Maya face extraction. As the name indicates, it will separate the selected faces from the geometry.

Duplicate Faces — Creates a duplicate of the selected faces, keeping them as part of the selected geometry.

Rigging Tab

Smooth Bind — Skins a geometry to a joint system.

Weighting Tools — Accesses Maya weighting tools.

Bind Pose — Returns joint system to the pose in which the model was initially skinned.

Mirror Weights — Calls up the Mirror Weights option box.

Delete Bind Pose — This is useful in some cases where you may find it necessary to bind additional geometry in a different pose. It can also resolve scaling issues when the skeleton was scaled after an animation was applied.

Create Joint — Calls up the Joint tool.

IK Handle — Creates an IK link.

Orient Joint Zup — Allows you to adjust the local rotational axis of each joint so that they all point the same direction.

Yup

Xup

Rotation Angle On/Off — Toggles the local rotation angle on or off for all the joints in the scene.

Freeze Transforms — Calls the Freeze Transform tool.

Editors Tab — This tab contains all of the most commonly used editors in one convenient menu.

Delete History — Using this button will only delete history if an object is selected, and therefore will only delete the history on that particular object. This prevents you from accidentally deleting the history on everything in your scene. This could be a big issue, especially if you have weighted geometry.

Clear Dead Nodes — This is an extremely useful script written by Mike Hovland. It will clear out any extraneous nodes that are left in your scene. Maya is notorious for accumulating nodes that are no longer associated with anything currently in the scene. The Clear Dead Nodes script will get rid of these nodes and then save your nice and clean file.

Wrap-Up

So in review, we learned some of the little tricks to creating models that are entirely quad based. We also discussed some of the issues that might crop up while you model and what to do to resolve them.

We also talked a bit about the types of mapping available. We will, of course, go into more detail on this subject in later chapters. We took a quick look at the Sculpt Geometry tools, which we will use extensively throughout this book. In addition, you got a sneak peek at a very useful modeling toolbox.

In next chapter we will start on our character! About time, huh? So from here on out, all the yakking I do will be character centric. Let the yakking begin!

Beginning the Modeling Process

Reference

Refer to Chapter_4 on the companion CD.

We first need to set up our reference. Whether you base your model on a skeleton or images is really up to you. I'll try to facilitate both approaches where it seems necessary. For example, when we model the details of the head, the photo reference will give us more bang for the buck. You can use the reference skeleton and photos provided on the companion CD or use your own.

We will now set up our image planes for our photo reference. If you are already familiar with this practice, you can use the Chapter4_start.mb file on the companion CD and skip ahead to the next section. If this is something new, do yourself a favor and stick with me through the setup process.

1. First, open the **Chapter4_skeleton.mb** file on the companion CD. In your front view on the Panels menu, select **View | Image Plane ▸ Import Image**, then select the appropriate front image. If you are using the images from the CD, select **Lucy_body_front.jpg**. The image will appear in your front viewport. Because Maya has a tendency to randomize the scale of the imported image, look in the Channel Box and set your Height and Width to **30**. You will need to adjust the Center Y so that the feet reside a bit closer to the center grid line.

2. Switch to the side view and do the same, this time selecting
    the side view image (**Lucy_body_side.jpg**) from the CD.
    Make sure you plug in the same height and width settings and
    also any adjustment you have made to the Center Y as you did
    with the front view. You may also find it better to move your
    image planes back behind the gridlines by adjusting your Cen-
    ter Z in the front view and your Center X in the side view. The
    image planes should now line up with the skeleton, as shown
    in Figure 4-1.

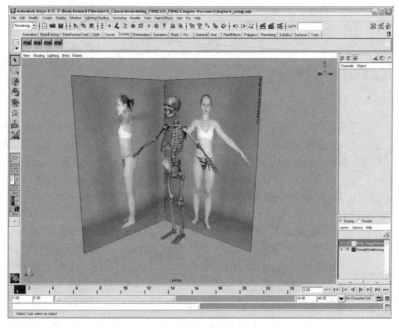

Figure 4-1

You will notice that the images and the skeleton are not a perfect
match. This is not a major concern. Early in the process we will use
the skeleton to merely get the basic human proportions. Later on
when we start adding detail, we will rely more on the reference
images to flesh out the model. The file Chapter4_start.mb on the
companion CD contains this entire scene.

Blocking out the Body

1. Before we start, choose **Edit Mesh | Keep Faces Together**
    [v7: Polygons | Tool Options ▶ Keep Faces Together] and
    make sure there is a check mark next to **Keep Faces
    Together.** This will ensure that your faces will remain
    together when you extrude.

2. We will start the building process with a simple cube. First
    select **Create | Polygon Primitives** and uncheck **Interac-
    tive Creation** on the bottom of the panel. This will default to
    the old Maya standard of creating the geometry at the origin.
    Select **Create | Polygon Primitives ▶ Cube** ☐. When the
    dialog box pops up, set your Subdivisions along the Width to **2**.
    By extruding and cutting in we should achieve our standard
    base model in a short amount of time.

3. Now we want to align the cube with the upper torso. Move the
    cube and resize it as necessary to line up with the rib cage. By
    right-clicking on your cube and selecting **Vertex**, you can then
    line up your vertices so it looks similar to the images in Figure
    4-2. Make sure you are adjusting the vertices in both the front
    and side views.

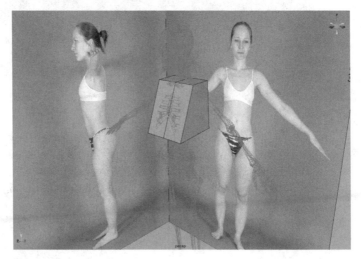

Figure 4-2

Don't be too concerned with the fact that your vertices don't line up with your reference exactly. Remember, we are simply blocking things in right now.

4. Next, we need to extrude the bottom two polygons down to around the top of the hips. With the polygons selected, choose **Edit Mesh | Extrude** [v7: Edit Polygons | Extrude Face]. Once again, use your front and side views to align your vertices as closely as possible to your reference.

5. Extrude the bottom polys down once more to line up roughly between the top of the hips and the base (bottom) of the pelvic bone, as shown in Figure 4-3.

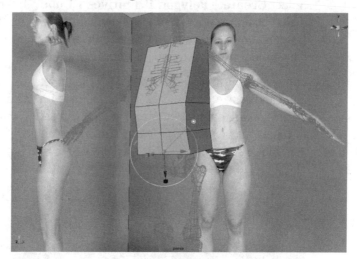

Figure 4-3

6. Extrude the bottom polys one last time so that they line up with the bottom of the pelvic bone. In the front view, scale the polygons horizontally along the X-axis so as to form the crotch region. Now in the side view, scale the polygons along the Z-axis. Go back and adjust your vertices on the model wherever you feel it is necessary. You should now have something similar to Figure 4-4.

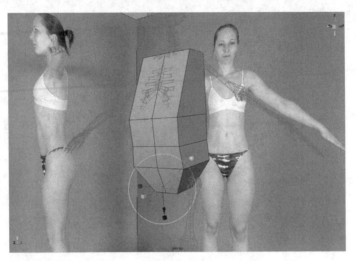

Figure 4-4

7. Next we will use the Insert Edge Loop tool. Select **Edit Mesh | Insert Edge Loop Tool** ☐ [v7: Edit Polygons | Split Edge Ring Tool ☐]. When the dialog box opens, make sure your settings are as follows:

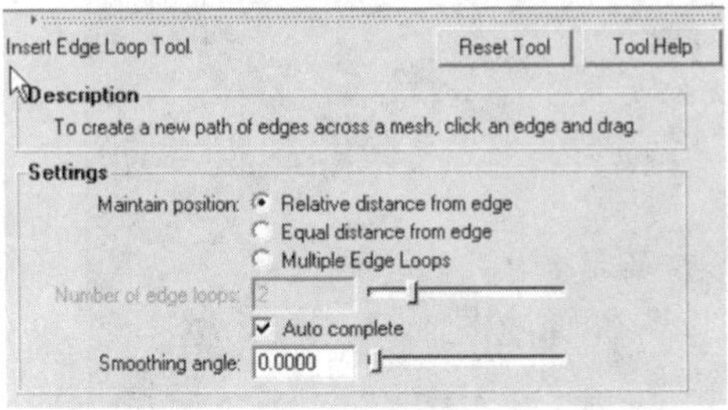

Figure 4-5

8. Use the Insert Edge Loop tool to cut a new edge loop midway down the chest between the shoulders and the bottom of the rib cage. Do the same between the rib cage and the top of the hips. Look at Figure 4-6 to make sure you have it right.

Figure 4-6

9. Select the two faces on the top of the body and use the Extrude tool to scale them in with the X and Z scale cubes on the Extrude manipulator.

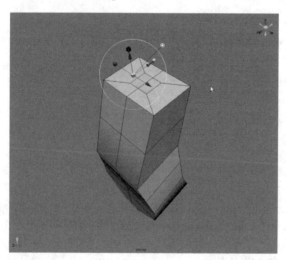

Figure 4-7

10. Now, with the same two faces selected, extrude them up to where the neck meets the base of the skull. Extrude the two faces again to align with the top of the head.

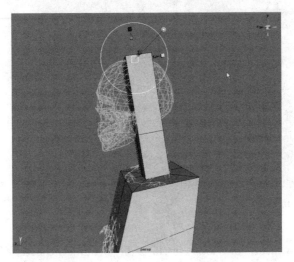

Figure 4-8

11. Select the two faces on the front of the head and extrude them forward to line up with the front of the skull. With the Extrude manipulator still selected, scale the faces down on the Y-axis.

12. Add three edge loops around the neck. Make sure that one is relatively close to the jaw line.

13. Now, select the faces closest to the back on either side of the head and scale them out on the X-axis until they align with each side of the skull, as shown in Figure 4-9.

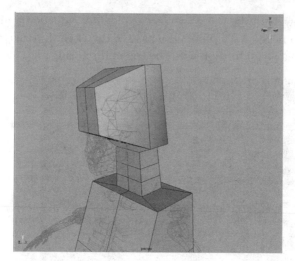

Figure 4-9

14. Add three edge loops horizontally around the head. Create another loop that starts at the top of the head and wraps down under the chin.

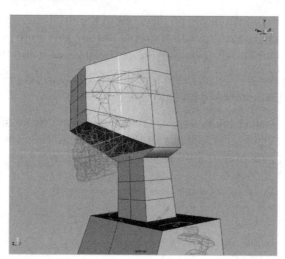

Figure 4-10

15. Still using the Insert Edge Loop tool, create an edge that starts at the top of the head and continues down the side of the body. When you create this loop you should hold down the

mouse button and slide the loop so it is in back of the arm. Finish it out by creating another loop that starts at the top of the head, runs down the side of the head, and continues down around the side of the body. When you create this loop you should hold down the mouse button and slide the loop forward so it is in front of the arm (see Figure 4-11). We'll get back to the head later.

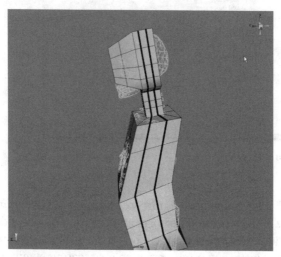

Figure 4-11

16. We should now take the time to do a bit of housecleaning. First off, we need to name our object something other than pCube1. Select the name in either the Outliner or the Channel Box and rename it **baseModel**. Now that we have our model named, we can assign it to its own layer. If your Layer Editor is not currently open on the right side of the screen, turn it on by clicking the **Show Layer Editor** button at the top of the Channel Box. Create a new layer and call it **baseModel_L**. Right-click on the layer and click the **Add Selected Objects** button.

17. **Delete History and save your file!**

18. From here on out we will only concern ourselves with the left side of the body. So let's go ahead and delete half of our model by selecting all of the faces to the left (in a front view) and hitting the **Delete** key. We will now duplicate the remaining half

on the –X-axis by opening **Edit | Duplicate Special** ☐ [v7: Edit | Duplicate ☐]. When the dialog box appears, match your settings to Figure 4-12 by setting the Scale to **–1.0000, 1.0000, 1.0000** and the Geometry Type to **Instance**.

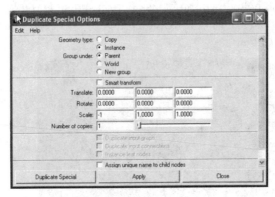

Figure 4-12

You should now have a mirrored version of your original geometry. Whenever you perform an operation on one side of the model, the same action will be mirrored across to the other side. This is a common practice for creating symmetrical models. It makes things quite a bit easier!

19. Name the instanced geometry **baseInstance**. Let's assign the instanced geometry to its own layer. Create a new layer and call it **baseInstance_L**. Assign the geometry to the new layer. For the moment, go ahead and turn off the visibility of baseInstance_L.

    One annoying factor about modeling with mirrored geometry is that sometimes the vertices along the vertical centerline of the model get moved. Sometimes I think they move when I'm not looking. It becomes necessary to stop what you're doing and realign the vertices. You can do this by selecting **Select | Select Border Edge Tool** [v7: Edit | Select Border Edge Tool], and then double-clicking any of the border edges. When you do, all the border edges will become selected. Then you can switch to the **Scale** tool to realign them.

20. An easier way to do this is to use the **Border Edge** button on the Go Tools toolbox. Click the button and then double-click

any border edge. Then right-click the **Border Edge** button to automatically realign the border edge.

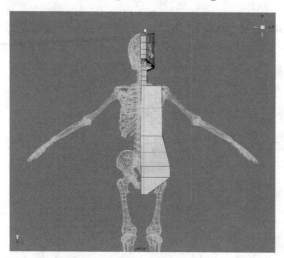

Figure 4-13

21. Using the Insert Edge Loop tool, click any horizontal edge on the front of the torso. You should end up with an edge loop that runs vertically down the middle of the model, from the top of the head down through the crotch.

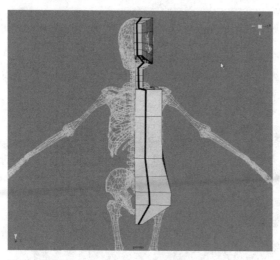

Figure 4-14

22. Select the top edge on the front of the model right around the collarbone and move it down slightly. Now select the top edge on the back on top of the shoulder blades and pull it down as well. On the front of the torso, select the outside edges of your model and move them in toward the center (see Figure 4-15).

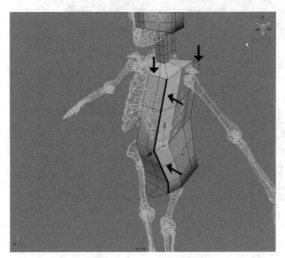

Figure 4-15

23. Select the edge along the outside of the back of the torso and move it forward on the Z-axis.

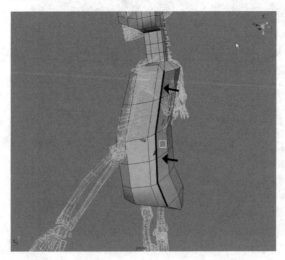

Figure 4-16

24. Now we'll start on the arm. Select the uppermost polygon on the left side of the body (the one closest to the back) and extrude it by choosing **Edit Mesh | Extrude** [v7: Edit Polygons | Extrude Face]. Toggle the manipulator so that it is in world space coords. Do this by clicking the light blue circle that extends outside of the manipulator. Pull the face out a bit on the X-axis by selecting the red handle. Click on any one of the cubes at the end of the manipulator handles. This will allow you to scale the face. Select the cube at the center of the manipulator and scale the face down so it looks similar to Figure 4.17.

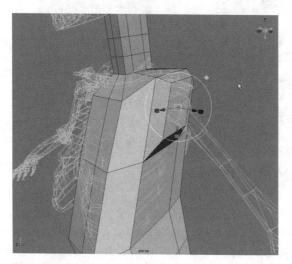

Figure 4-17

25. Extrude the face again, this time down to meet the elbow. You will have to rotate the poly as well to get the correct angle. Make some additional adjustments by scaling the polygon down a bit. Extrude again down to the wrist (keep the manipulator in its default local coords).

26. Now we are going to add a little twist — in the literal sense! Click on the large light blue circle on your manipulator. This will activate the rotational manipulator. Rotate the face along its local Z-axis by grabbing the blue circle. Rotate toward the front of the body so that the face is roughly 90 degrees from its

original position. Doing this accounts for the position of the radius and ulna bones of the forearm.

27. Extrude one final time down to about where the fingers would begin. Be sure to adjust the geometry to match up to your reference.

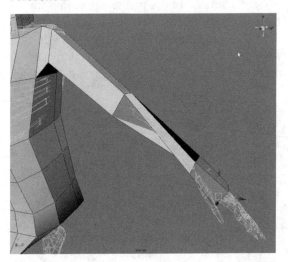

Figure 4-18

If you are finding it difficult to make adjustments on the arm, here is a little trick: Make sure you have both the original and instanced geometry selected and then rotate the two about 35 degrees on the Z-axis or until the left arm is parallel to the ground plane. This way all of the operations on your arm will be aligned to an axis (see Figure 4-19). It is considerably easier to work this way. Just make sure that when you finish tweaking, you type in **0** in the Rotate X panel to bring your geometries back to their original positions.

Figure 4-19

28. Select the three angular faces along the side of the pelvis and extrude down to just above the knee. Again, move, scale, and rotate the polygons around as necessary to match the reference.

29. Extrude again to the center of the knee, and one more time to just below the knee. Finish up by extruding down to the ankle and once more to the bottom of the foot.

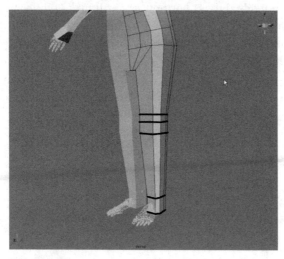

Figure 4-20

30. In Edge mode, select the front edge at the base of the foot and move it up along the Y-axis. If this is not clear, compare the location of the edge in Figure 4-20 to where it is in Figure 4-21 to see what I am referring to. Select the face beneath it and extrude it forward on the Z-axis to right at the point where the toes would start.

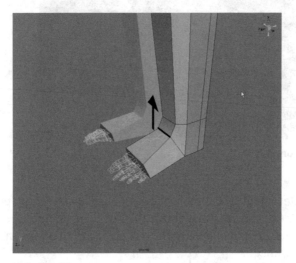

Figure 4-21

31. Later on in the book we will go into more detail about creating the individual toes. For now, we will make one last extrusion to the tip of the toes, giving us the impression that the character is wearing shoes. Let's also add two additional edge loops as shown in Figure 4-22.

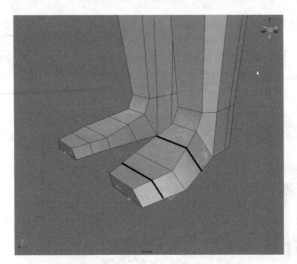

Figure 4-22

32. Before continuing, select the two edges on the inside of the leg, right at the base of the pelvis, and move them in on the X-axis toward the center of the model.

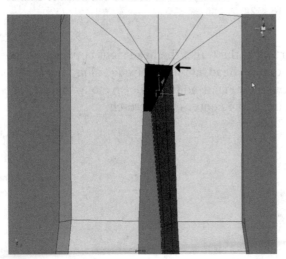

Figure 4-23

33. Starting at the center of your model between the top edge and the one below it on the chest, use the Insert Edge Loop tool to cut a continuous edge along the length of the arm, through the center of the hand, and all the way around the back, ending at the center of your geometry.

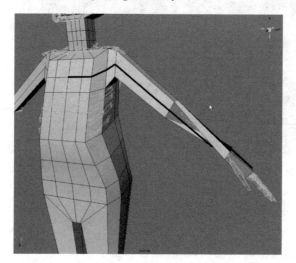

Figure 4-24

34. Starting at the top of the head right between the center and back of the head, cut another edge along the length of the arm, through the hand, and then down along the side of the body, ending in the center of the crotch.

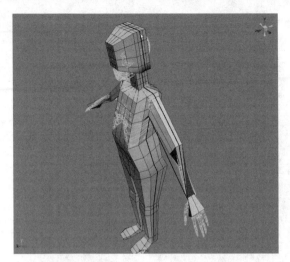

Figure 4-25

35. Now we need to create additional subdivisions on our model by creating more edge loops. With the Insert Edge Loop tool, cut three edge loops around the arm between the elbow and the wrist. Do the same between the shoulder and the elbow.

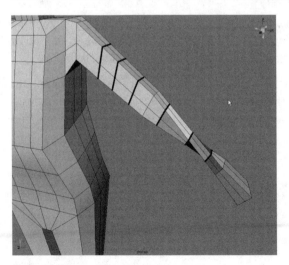

Figure 4-26

36. Place three additional loops between the hip and the knee and another three between the knee and the ankle.

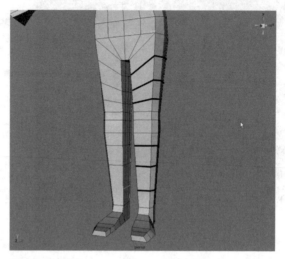

Figure 4-27

37. **Delete History and save your file!**

Now let's shift gears and use the Split Polygon tool. We are going to create a new edge loop between the top of the shoulders and the one below it on the chest.

38. Start by clicking on the centerline of the model, then clicking on the edges across the chest. Now, continue by clicking on each edge over the top of the arm, as shown in Figure 4-28.

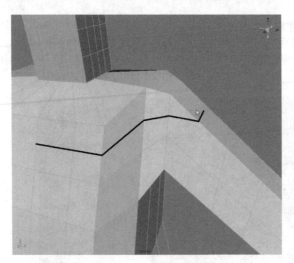

Figure 4-28

39. Now rotate around to the back and continue the cut by clicking on the vertical edge at the base of the arm. Click on the edge to the right and finish up by clicking on the centerline of the figure.

Figure 4-29

40. Again, using the Split Polygon tool, click on the vertex that is right in the middle of the back of the arm where it meets the shoulder area. Click on the back edge of the top of the arm to the left of the previous edge you just created.

Figure 4-30

41. Continue by cutting over the top of the arm and then end on the vertex in the middle of the front of the arm at the base of the shoulder. Press **Enter** to end the command.

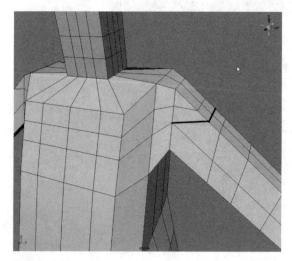

Figure 4-31

42. We'll take care of those nasty triangles in few minutes. Switch to Vertex mode and select the new vertices we created at the top of the arm. Adjust them so that they look similar to Figure 4-32.

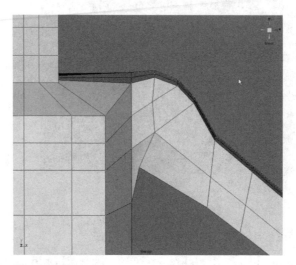

Figure 4-32

43. Before we go any further let's take a moment to soften up some of these hard edges. First, make sure your geometry is selected and select **Normals | Soften Edge** [v7: Edit Polygons | Normals ▸ Soften/Harden ▸ All Soft (180)]. Now you have soft edges, making your model appear a tad smoother.

    Also at this point we could round out the features by averaging some of the vertices.

44. In Vertex mode, select all of the vertices on your model to the right of center, leaving the verts running down the middle of the torso unselected. Go to **Mesh | Average Vertices** ☐ [v7: Polygons | Average Vertices ☐]. When the dialog box opens, set the Iterations to **2** and hit the **Average** button. You should notice that the model has lost a lot of the "boxy" feel and is a bit more rounded out. It also may appear quite a bit thinner, but not to worry. This alleviates a lot of the manual tweaking we would need to do to achieve a similar result.

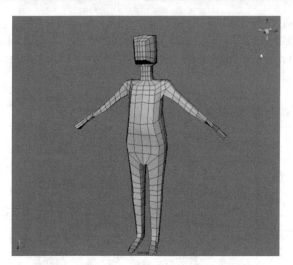

Figure 4-33

45. **Delete History and save your file!**

46. Use the Insert Edge Loop tool to add another loop around the center of the rib cage. Before releasing the mouse button, slide the ring up a bit so it resides closer to the edge directly above it. In Vertex mode, select the vertices as shown in Figure 4-34 and move them down and slightly out as illustrated.

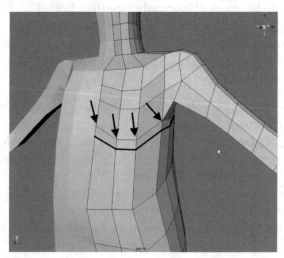

Figure 4-34

47. Now let's take a look at the hand. In Vertex mode, adjust the vertices so the centerline on the hand runs between the middle and ring fingers.

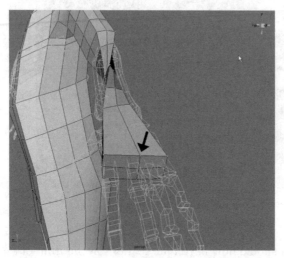

Figure 4-35

48. Using the Insert Edge Loop tool, click on the centerline on the top of the hand. This will create a new loop that runs around the middle of the hand. Now select the new loop to the left of the centerline and click. You should now have a loop that starts at the triangle on the back of the shoulder and continues through the hand and stops at the front triangle near the shoulder, converting both triangles into quads.

49. Now click the same loop to the right of the centerline. This will give you a loop that runs through the back and up across the chest as shown in Figure 4-36.

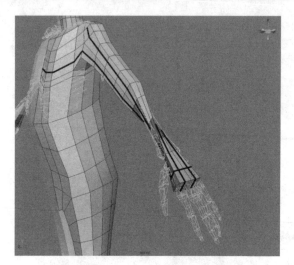

Figure 4-36

You should now have four sections at the front of the hand divided by an edge through the middle.

50. Select the two polygons for the index finger and use **Edit Mesh | Extrude** [v7: Edit Polygons | Extrude Face] to pull them out a bit. Repeat the process for the three remaining fingers and scale the faces so they look like Figure 4-37.

Figure 4-37

51. Select each of the four finger sections and independently extrude them to line up with the tip of each finger on the skeletal reference. Use the Insert Edge Loop tool to create a loop to account for each joint of the fingers. Remember that you can rotate the figure so that the arm is parallel to the ground plane in order to make this process easier. Now adjust the position and scale of each finger to match the skeletal reference. Check out Figure 4-38.

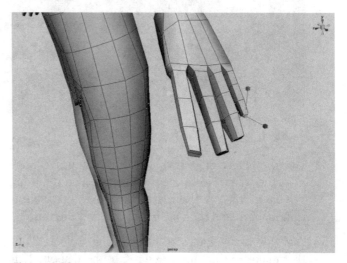

Figure 4-38

52. Create two additional loops between the tip of each finger and the next joint up. Do the same between the rest of the joints on all of the fingers.

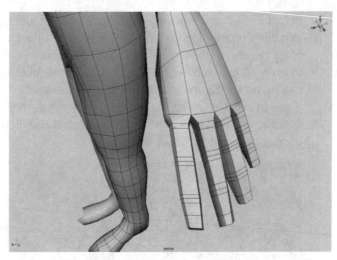

Figure 4-39

53. Use the Insert Edge Loop tool to add another loop on the hand near the wrist. Now grab the two faces on the thumb side of the hand closer to the wrist. Extrude the face out to the first thumb joint, and then again to the tip of the thumb.

54. The thumb involves a bit of tweaking. Select all of the faces that make up the thumb and rotate them about 45 degrees. Create two additional loops between each joint.

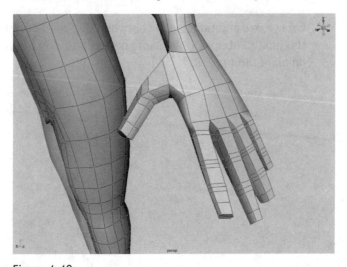

Figure 4-40

55. Let's go back to the body and add a few more edge loops. Add three loops between the bottom of the pelvis and the next edge up. These loops will follow a path down along the front of the leg and around to the back.

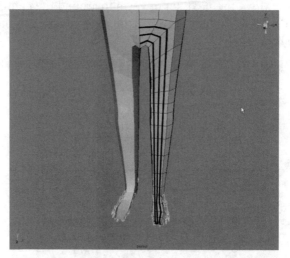

Figure 4-41

56. Let's get back to the head. In the side view, turn on Wireframe mode so that you can see the reference head.

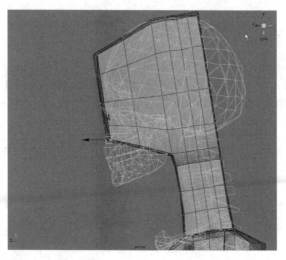

Figure 4-42

57. Select the bottom vertices on the front of the face and move
    them so that they sit at the front of the mouth. The vertices up
    from the ones at the teeth should be moved up to just below
    the nose. The next set up should sit around the middle of the
    nose. Move the next set of verts to around the center of the
    eye socket. The next set up should move down to the crest of
    the brow ridge.

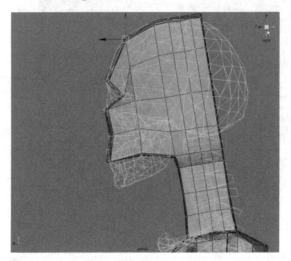

Figure 4-43

58. Compare Figure 4-43 to Figure 4-42 to see how the vertices
    have moved.

59. Continue to move the vertices on the head by following the
    example in Figure 4-44. Compare Figure 4-44 to Figure 4-43
    so that you can see the original position of the vertices as well
    as where they should subsequently be moved.

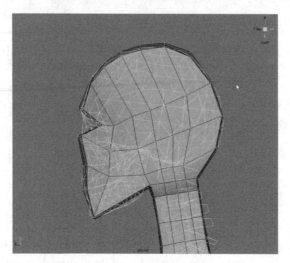

Figure 4-44

60. Select the faces on the side of the head and then switch to a perspective view. Using the Scale tool, scale the faces uniformly by selecting the center yellow cube on the manipulator. It should look similar to Figure 4-45. We'll pick back up on the head in the next chapter, ironically titled "Building the Head."

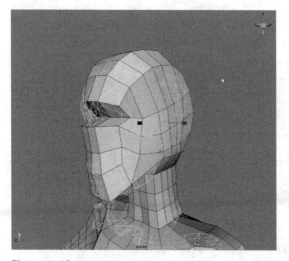

Figure 4-45

61. **Delete History and save your file!**

62. Beyond averaging vertices we could also do a little manual adjustment. Select **Mesh | Sculpt Geometry Tool** ☐ [v7: Edit Polygons | Sculpt Geometry Tool ☐]. When the dialog pops up, select the **Smooth** radio button under Sculpt Parameters and set Max Displacement to **0.005**. Drag the Sculpt manipulator over the geometry. You will see the edges start to become more "rounded." Use the manipulator as a paintbrush to soften and round out the figure.

63. In order to get some of the form in place we could also use the Push and Pull sculpting tools. Be sure to select the **Auto Smooth** check box when using Push and Pull. You may also need to increase the Max Displacement as well. A good Max Displacement setting for Pull and Push would be about **0.2** to **0.4**, with a Smooth Strength of **2** to **4**. (See "The Sculpt Geometry Tool" in Chapter 3 for more information about this tool's use.)

    Don't overdo it. Be sure to not continually hold down the left mouse button. The approach you want to use here is to touch the model and release the mouse button. This gives you the ability to better control how much you are smoothing. You will notice that if you smooth too much, the geometry will tighten up more than you would want. So remember, a little at a time. You should end up with something like Figure 4-46.

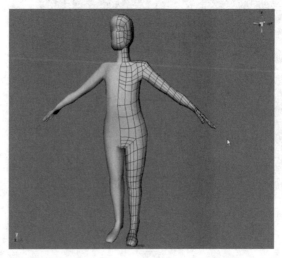

Figure 4-46

Many times throughout the modeling process you may want to apply a smooth node to your model or work with a subdivided proxy to see how things are shaping up. I will often apply a Mesh | Smooth [v7: Polygons | Smooth] and then delete it again and again to see what I need to do on the lower-resolution model.

Here is another neat little trick. During the process of sculpting to obtain more of that organic shape, you can apply a Smooth and continue to sculpt on the higher-resolution model. Then by deleting the polySmoothFace, you will still retain a lot of the sculpt that you performed on the higher-resolution model on the original geometry.

Unfortunately, when you reapply the Smooth you won't get the exact sculpting results, but believe me, it really does make things go a lot easier. One other little hitch is that Maya sometimes gets a bit screwy when you use the Sculpt Geometry tool. You may notice as you are using it that you can't see any changes to the model. The fix is to duplicate the model and then delete the original. The Go Tools toolbox allows you to fix this by right-clicking on the Sculpt Poly button under the Modeling tab.

At this point you may notice that the center of your model may have been altered while you were using the Sculpt Geometry tool. Use the Border Edge command to select the border and then scale the centerline on the X-axis as explained previously. Adjusting the centerline is something you will probably end up doing a lot when using the Sculpt Geometry tool. Using the Border Edge button in the Go Tools toolbox will make the process of straightening your border edge painless.

Important Note

Before we call it quits on the blocking process, let's take a few minutes to make sure our model is lining up with the photo reference. Up until now we have been using the skeleton as reference. Remember way back when I told you that the images don't exactly match the skeleton? Well, from here on out we are going to use the photo reference almost exclusively, so the idea would be to make sure things are lining up properly now while we are dealing with a manageable amount of geometry.

Wrap-Up

Okay, so let's review here. So far we have created a simple model using our good friends the quads. The concept here was to quickly get to a point where we have a solid base figure to work with. Notice I use the word "quickly" here. Once you get the hang of it, you should arrive at this point in no more than 20 minutes. Obviously this takes some practice, but once you have the formula down it will be a breeze. Check out the BaseModel.avi file on the companion CD. In it, I go through the process in real time.

Some additional things you should have learned from this chapter are:

▸ Use the Scale tool whenever you can to adjust geometry. It is a lot easier and quicker than moving vertices, edges, and faces manually.

▸ Rotate your model when necessary to align the section you are working on to the ground plane. This will allow you to take advantage of working perpendicular and parallel to your X-, Y-, and Z-axes.

▸ Use layers to keep your scene organized.

▸ Work exclusively with quads and get an understanding of how to turn triangles into quadrangles.

▸ Use the Sculpt Geometry tool to give your model a more organic form.

▸ Simple lines of scripting code can make repetitive tasks easier.

Chapter 5

Building the Head

Applying What We've Learned

Refer to Chapter_5 on the companion CD.

So here we go. I'll tell you right now that the head is probably one of the most difficult things to model. But you're not gonna let that stop you, right? Oh no, you are a trouper, my friend, and you're going to keep going no matter what! The way we are going to approach the head is the same way we blocked out the body. We are going to use a formula.

If you haven't caught on yet, everything you've learned so far in this book has been a standard formula that you can use over and over, no matter what kind of character you are creating. Once you do it a couple of times you will know it like the back of your proverbial hand! This formula will get stuck in your brain and you will always know where to begin with each character you build.

This is also true of the head, although there are a few more steps. Your head will take shape and I think you will be pleased with the results and how fast you get there. So buckle up and let's get going.

At this stage of the process we will constantly refer to a smoothed proxy of our model to see our progress. You can use the command Proxy | Subdiv Proxy [v7: Polygons | Smooth Proxy] to create a smoothed version of your geometry with a lattice representing your original geometry above it. You can also try applying a smooth node to your original geometry.

The latter option will have you adding the smooth node to check your progress and then removing it to get back your original geometry. This process is simplified by using the Go Tools toolbox described in Chapter 3.

Call me old school, but I tend to rely on this method of adding and removing. I like to be able to quickly switch between my original and the smoothed model. Either way you decide to go is fine. The resulting model will end up turning out the same regardless of how you approach it.

We will also be using image planes more specific to the head. Open Chapter5_start.mb. This contains the image planes already set up for you. The images are contained in the Chapter5 sourceimages folder on the companion CD.

During the course of this chapter I will here and there mention the need to refer to the smoothed model. Ideally, you should be looking at it constantly to make sure things are looking hunky-dory.

Heads Up

Let's get the ball rolling by starting off in the side view. You may notice that our points don't match up to the photo reference quite the same way they did with the skeleton. Like I said before, this is expected because the skeleton doesn't match up exactly to the photos. The idea was, of course, to get a strong base to work from and you have accomplished that. You did read the last chapter, right? Now initially we will deal more with getting all the features in the right place. In other words, don't get too caught up in the likeness right now. We'll worry about that later in the modeling process.

1. Take a couple of minutes to arrange the verts to line up a bit closer to the head in the reference image.

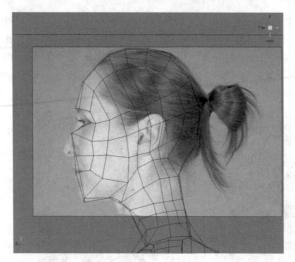

Figure 5-1

2. In a perspective view, select the six faces on the front of the face as indicated in Figure 5-2.

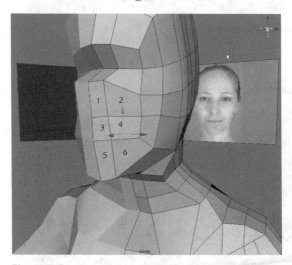

Figure 5-2

3. We now need to extrude these faces in a similar fashion to the neck in the last chapter. We need to open **Edit Mesh | Extrude** ☐ [v7: Edit Polygons | Extrude Face ☐]. When the

dialog opens, set the Offset under Settings to **2** (slider should be all the way to the right) and hit the **Apply** button. (The dialog box may appear slightly different in Maya 7.) You will see the selected faces shrink down, inset from their original positions.

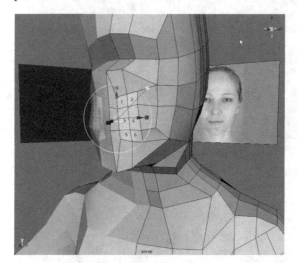

Figure 5-3

4. Next, we'll want to delete the three polygons that were created in the middle of the face when we made our extrusion.

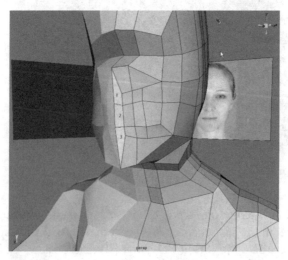

Figure 5-4

5. Select the original six faces that were part of the extrusion and slide them on the X-axis toward the center of the head so that you have a straight line down middle. If it doesn't line up perfectly on the centerline, select the vertices that make up the centerline edge and scale them on the X-axis until they form a straight line, as shown in Figure 5-5.

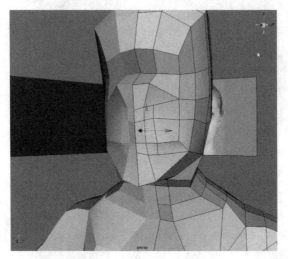

Figure 5-5

6. Make sure you have the extruded faces selected. Then, using the Scale tool, scale the faces on the Y-axis until you get something similar to Figure 5-6.

Figure 5-6

7. With the six faces still selected, switch to a side view. Scale them and move them forward so they line up with the lips.

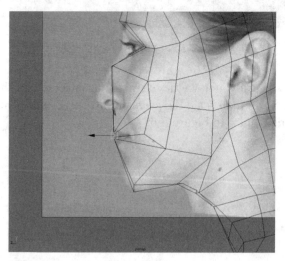

Figure 5-7

8. In a front view, select the two faces in the center of the mouth and delete them.

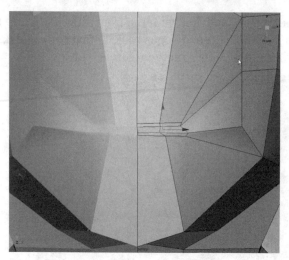

Figure 5-8

9. Now let's go ahead and line up all the vertices we created from the extrusion to the lips of our reference image. Because we don't as yet have enough points, we are looking for the basic form of the lips here. The interior open edges that surround the faces you just deleted should be more or less flattened on the Y-axis so that the top and bottom edges meet.

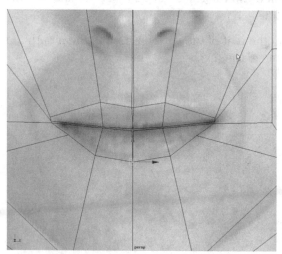

Figure 5-9

87

10. When you're satisfied with the front view, switch to the side and pull the flattened edges back so that they line up with the corner of the mouth on the reference image.

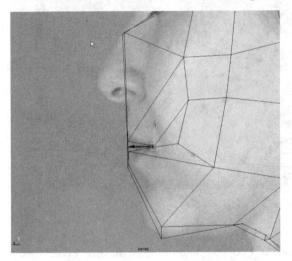

Figure 5-10

One of the more important things to note here is the vertices that make up the corner of the mouth. It is crucial to get the geometry in the right place so that the lips will look natural in the finished model.

11. Align the rest of the vertices around the mouth to form the outline of the lips.

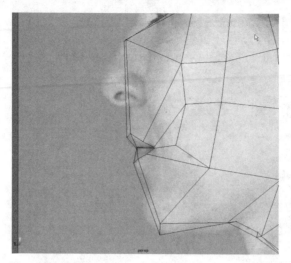

Figure 5-11

12. Next, we will need to add some additional edge loops. First, with the Insert Edge Loop tool, add a concentric loop around the mouth area. Hold down the left mouse button and adjust the new loop so that it is very close to the outline of the lips.

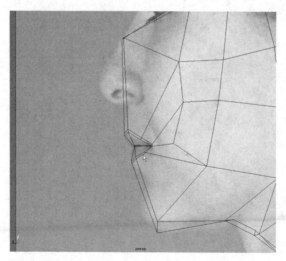

Figure 5-12

13. Add an additional loop, then, in a front and side view, move the vertices so that they resemble Figures 5-13a and 5-13b. Notice that the loop outlines the exterior of the lip shape.

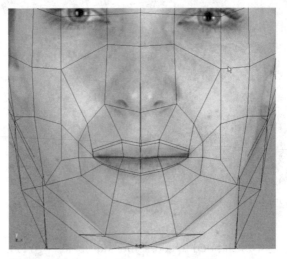

Figure 5-13a

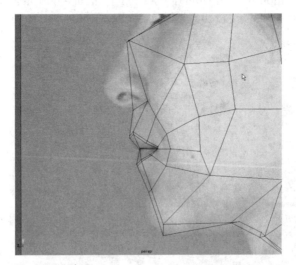

Figure 5-13b

14. Create two additional edge loops — one between the center of the head and the next row over to the right, and another that should be roughly down through the center of the eye. These two loops will continue down around the torso of the model and will be used later to help define the body.

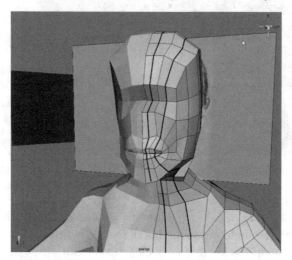

Figure 5-14

15. Now we can adjust the previous edge loops that defined the outline of the lips. Select the vertices on the upper lip and move them down a bit on the Y-axis and then back on the Z-axis. Do the same for the row of vertices on the bottom lip as well. In order to get a good grasp on the position of these vertices, rotate around the head in perspective view to make sure they look correct.

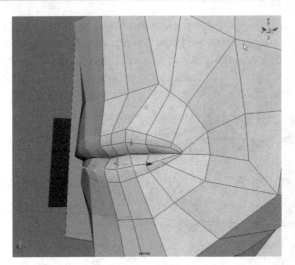

Figure 5-15

16. Add an additional edge loop in a similar fashion to the earlier one, then hold down the middle mouse button and adjust the new loop so that it is very close to the outline of the lips. This will help define the slight edge that is visible around the edge of the lips.

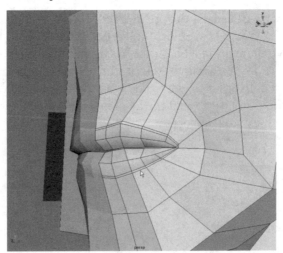

Figure 5-16

17. Select the six faces around the eye and extrude them. If your Extrude tool's offset is still set to 2, the polygons should be inset from their original position.

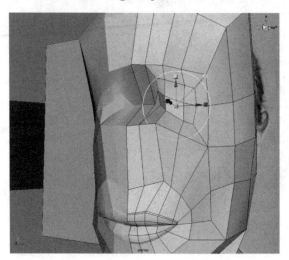

Figure 5-17

18. In front and side views, adjust the verts from the extruded faces to match up with the interior part of the eyelid. When you have finished, select the six interior faces and delete them.

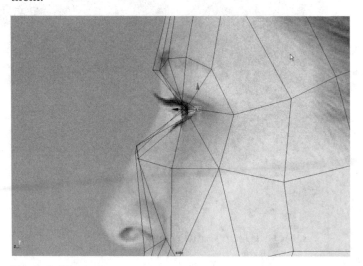

Figure 5-18a

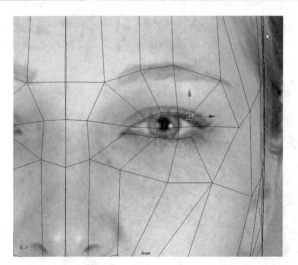

Figure 5-18b

19. Now select the vertex in the center of the head between the eyes and pull it forward until it lines up with the bridge of the nose.

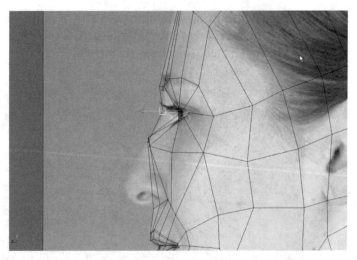

Figure 5-19

20. **Delete History and save!**

The next thing we need to do is start to form the head a bit.

21. First, in the side view, select the vertices on the lower part of the jaw close to the neck. Move them down until they line up with the reference.

22. We also want to move some of the verts along the side of the head to round out the shape a bit. This is known as "tweaking." It is not written in stone exactly how much to move each vertex. We are just trying to get comfortable with the flow of the geometry. In order to visualize this flow we need to be in perspective view.

23. We need to rotate around the head and see if things are going well. Where you need to round things out, select the vertices and move them by dragging on a particular axis handle. This will ensure that they are going exactly where you want them. At this stage we are really just eliminating some of the areas that appear to be flat, mainly around the chin and the side of the head.

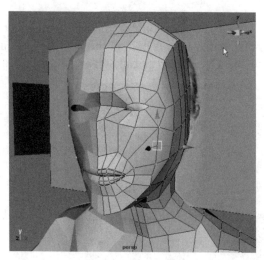

Figure 5-20

24. Now we need to spend a bit of time working on the neck. Use the Sculpt Geometry tool with the Sculpt Parameters set to **Smooth** to "massage" the neck area so that the polygons are a

bit more evenly spaced. You can do this manually by moving the vertices as well.

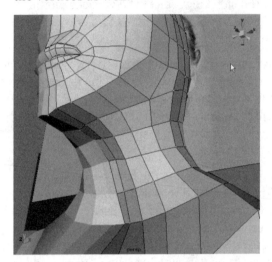

Figure 5-21

25. Now we want to go ahead and adjust the geometry to account for the muscle that begins behind the jaw and ends at the center of the clavicle, known as the sternocleidomastoid.

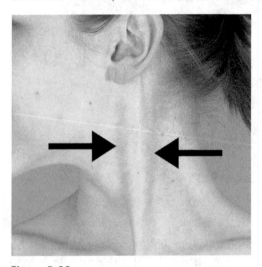

Figure 5-22

26. Rotate the view so that you can see underneath the chin. Starting at the center of the model, select the vertex right where the neck meets the jaw and also the vertex directly beneath it, and move them slightly forward on the Z-axis. Do the same with the next two vertices to the right, and then again with the next set of vertices to the right. Adjust the vertices so that they have a slight arc beginning at the center of the model.

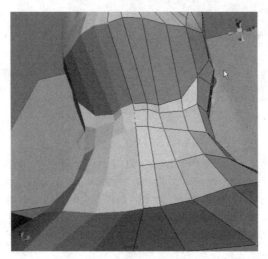

Figure 5-23

27. Selecting the next two vertices to the right, scale them on the Z-axis so that the top vertex is directly above the one below it, then move them back on the Z-axis.

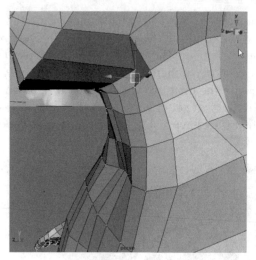

Figure 5-24

28. Select the next vertex over to the right where the neck meets the jawline and move it slightly back on the Z-axis and up on the Y-axis. Skip the vertex directly below and select the next two. Move them forward on the Z-axis.

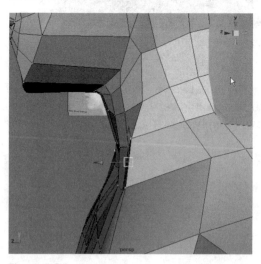

Figure 5-25

29. Adjust the vertices on the front of the neck so that they follow a curve toward the center of the model. That's about it for the neck area for now.

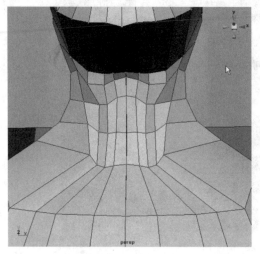

Figure 5-26

30. Next, we will clean up the edge flow near the cheek of our model. Although we have consistent quad-based edge loops, sometimes it is necessary to redirect their flow. Using the Split Polygon tool, start at the end of the edge on the side of the mouth and continue around to the back of the head.

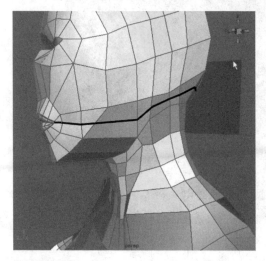

Figure 5-27

31. Now draw an edge that begins at the corner of the triangle on the cheek and continue down around the front of the chin.

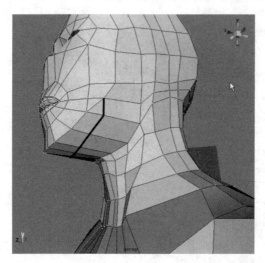

Figure 5-28

32. Select the angled edge on the side of the cheek and delete it. We have now redirected the flow of our edge loops.

33. Let's add another loop that begins just above the eyebrow and circles down the front of the chin.

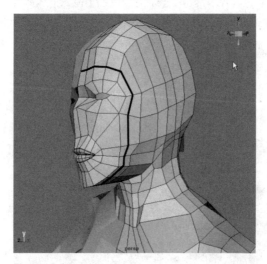

Figure 5-29

34. Use the Split Polygon tool to create an edge loop that begins at the center of the head between the eyes and wraps around the outside of the eye and then back around over the bridge of the nose. I often refer to this as the "Lone Ranger mask."

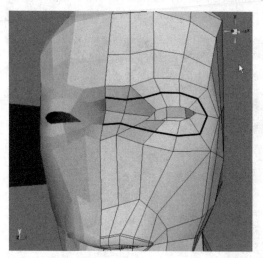

Figure 5-30

35. Go back and collapse the two angled edges near the bridge of the nose.

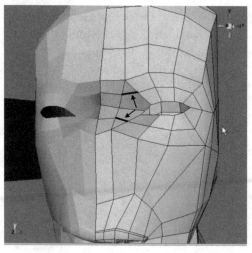

Figure 5-31

36. With the Insert Edge Loop tool, add two concentric circles that begin above the tip of the nose and wrap down around the chin. Make sure that they are close together.

    These will later help us define the nasal labia folds, or "laugh lines," that are most apparent when you smile.

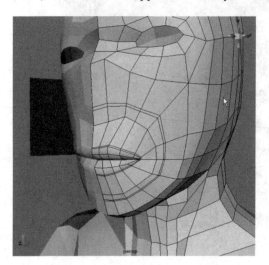

Figure 5-32

37. **Delete History and save!**

38. Take some time and use the Sculpt Geometry tool to soften the edges of the head a bit. Use the Smooth setting and the touch and release method. Avoid the lip area at this point.

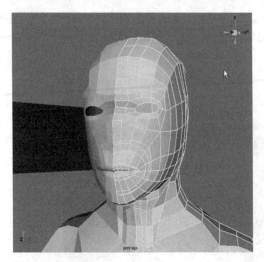

Figure 5-33

39. Use the Split Polygon tool to create an edge loop that begins at the inside part of the eye and then continues around to roughly where the tip of the nose will be.

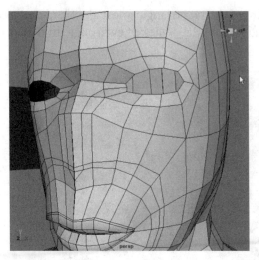

Figure 5-34

40. Inside the loop you created in the previous step, create a loop that starts at the center of the nose and ends at the vertex just to the left of the eye.

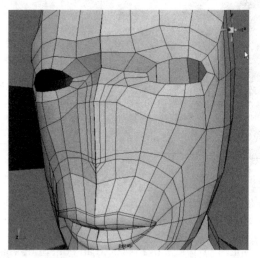

Figure 5-35

41. Take care of the two triangles near the tip of the nose by drawing an edge from the center of each angle to the corresponding vertex.

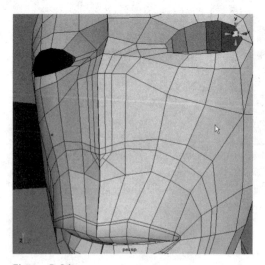

Figure 5-36

42. Let's start to shape the nose a bit. By selecting two vertices at a time — the one at the centerline of the head and the next one to its right — move them to line up with the nose in a side view.

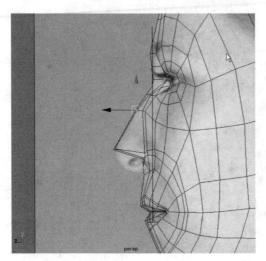

Figure 5-37

43. When you get to the tip of the nose, select the upper two vertices and move them to the tip of the nose in your reference image. Move the two underneath to just below the tip in front of the nostrils.

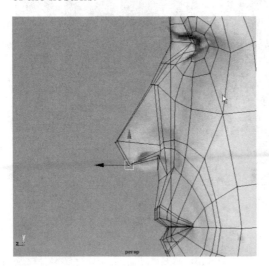

Figure 5-38

105

44. The remaining vertices should be positioned to form the underneath part of the nose.

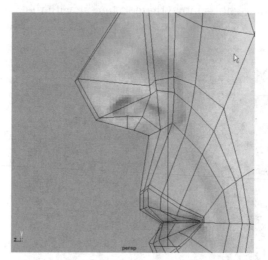

Figure 5-39

45. In a front view, align the vertex to the right to match the outer part of the nostril.

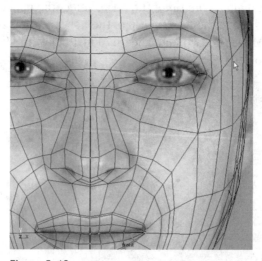

Figure 5-40

46. Using the Insert Edge Loop tool, create a loop that begins at the triangle near the eye and ends up underneath the nose.

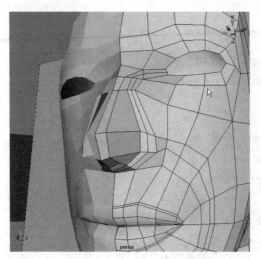

Figure 5-41

47. Still using the Insert Edge Loop tool, create a loop that begins at the inside of the eye and ends up underneath the nose.

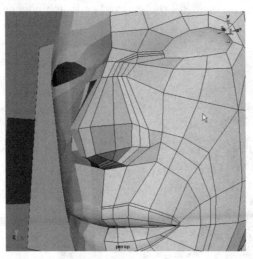

Figure 5-42

48. Create another loop the follows around the "Lone Ranger mask" and another that loops over the bridge of the nose to the chin.

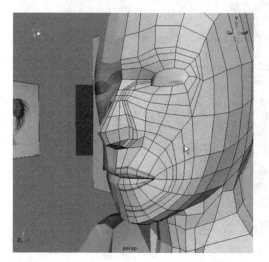

Figure 5-43

49. Still using the Insert Edge Loop tool, create one final loop that begins at the inside of the eye and ends up underneath the nose.

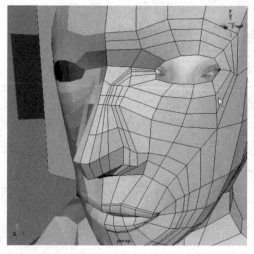

Figure 5-44

Shaping the Nose

We should now have enough geometry to define the shape of the nose.

1. In a perspective view, use the Sculpt Geometry tool to smooth out the bridge of the nose so that it flows smoothly into the cheek of your model. Avoiding the centerline, zoom in close and use a smaller brush size to get the desired results.

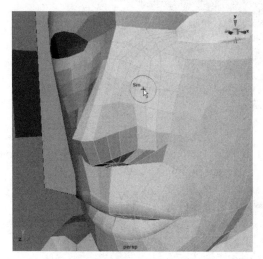

Figure 5-45

2. Since we added additional geometry in a side view, we need to adjust the points so that we match the profile of the nose, making sure to account for the rise of the nostril.

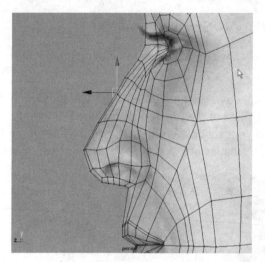

Figure 5-46

3. Now in a front view, line up the outer edge of the nose to that of your reference image.

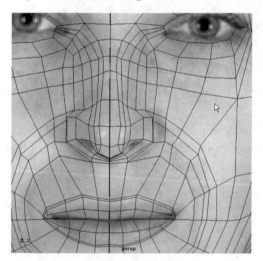

Figure 5-47

The nose can be difficult to define by using only front and side views. It really is necessary to rotate around in a perspective view to be able to get it looking just right. Refer to Figure 5-48.

Notice that there is a slight indent where the nose meets the face. Also, remember the nasal labia fold? We begin to see it taking shape over the crest of the nostril.

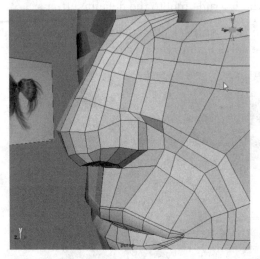

Figure 5-48

4. Rotate the model so that you are looking at the bottom of the nose. Select the six faces and extrude them. Your Extrude tool offset should still be set to 2, so the polygons should be inset from their original position.

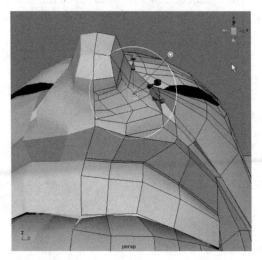

Figure 5-49

5. Before we continue, open the **Edit Mesh | Extrude** ☐ [v7: Edit Polygons | Extrude Face ☐]. We want to go to Edit in the upper left-hand corner and select **Reset Settings**. This will return the Extrude tool to the default settings.

6. With the faces still selected, use the Extrude tool again to push the polys up into the nasal cavity.

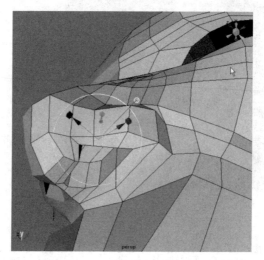

Figure 5-50

7. Add two additional edge loops — one over the bridge of the nose and one over the tip. Both edges will wrap down to the chin.

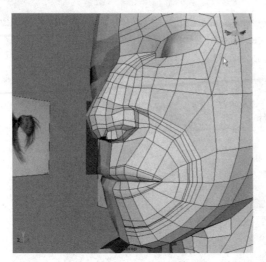

Figure 5-51

8. In a front and side view, adjust the vertices to line up with the nasal cavity. It may also be necessary to adjust the size of the nasal cavity in order to better match the reference. Rotate around and make any additional adjustments. Refer to the smooth version of your model often during this tweaking process.

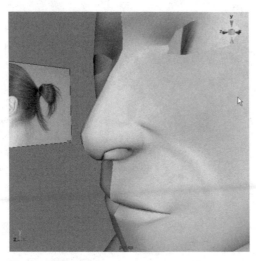

Figure 5-52

9. Let's wrap up this stage of the nose by adding an edge loop inside the nostril, close to the outer edge.

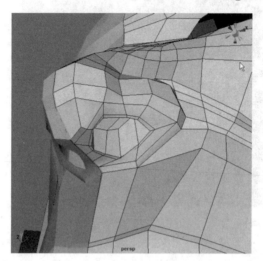

Figure 5-53

10. **Delete History and save!**

The Mouth

Now we need to concentrate our efforts on the mouth and the area surrounding it.

1. Let's start by adding an additional edge loop that circles through the upper and lower lips.

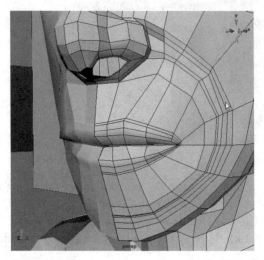

Figure 5-54

2. Rotate to a front view. Let's first make sure that our vertices are properly arranged to represent the outer edge of the lips. In doing so, remember to keep the two edge loops tightly together to define the lip edges.

115

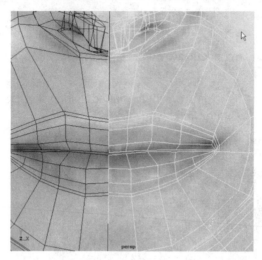

Figure 5-55

3. In order to better shape the bottom lip we need to add an edge loop under the nose and around under the bottom lip. Move some of the edge loops on the chin up on the Y-axis. This will help to define the way the lower lip tends to protrude slightly.

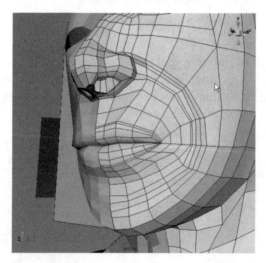

Figure 5-56

4. Add a new edge loop that circles through the top and bottom lip.

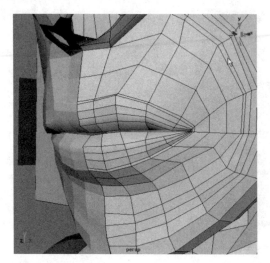

Figure 5-57

5. Moving to interior vertices of the lips, adjust them in the front view so that they are pretty evenly spaced between the outer and interior edges.

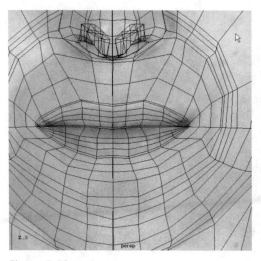

Figure 5-58

6. Rotate to a side view and position the vertices so that they form a nice arc around the lips.

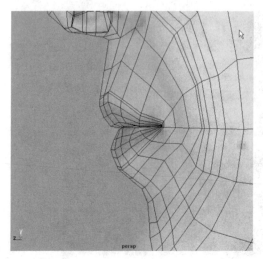

Figure 5-59

7. Now, switch to a perspective view in order to see the way the edge loops are running. Begin to position the middle rows of vertices to give the lips some fullness.

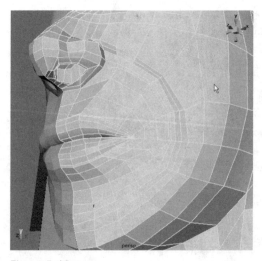

Figure 5-60

If you look at the reference image closely you will notice that the upper lip dips down in the center, then rises slightly, and then dips again. Conversely, the bottom lip dips in the center, then rises slightly. It's also important to note that the upper lip overlaps the lower lip at the corners of the mouth.

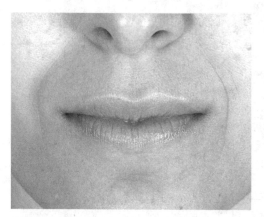

Figure 5-61

8. Let's adjust the points on the lips so that they resemble those of the reference image. Be sure to reference the smoothed version of your geometry to make sure that the lips appear to touch. This might mean that they actually intersect each other in the base model.

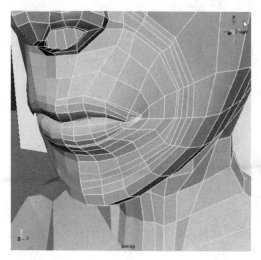

Figure 5-62

9. Beyond shaping the mouth, it is important to have the edge loops follow the flow of the nasal labia fold. In a front view, adjust the points along the edge loops to match the reference image.

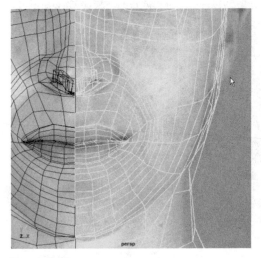

Figure 5-63

10. Rotate to the side view and adjust the points so that they follow the position of the cheek and nasal labia fold.

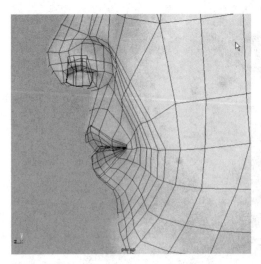

Figure 5-64

11. Rotate into a perspective view and adjust the vertices so that the crease of the fold is represented. Refer to the smoothed model.

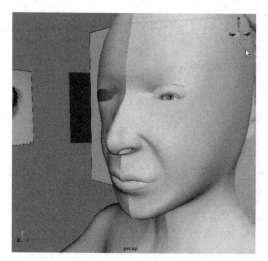

Figure 5-65

12. Let's move down to the chin for a bit o' tweaking. In the side view, move the vertices to follow the shape of the chin on the reference image.

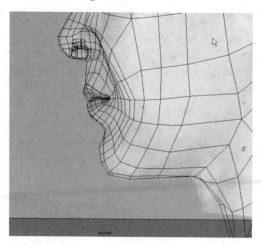

Figure 5-66

13. Be sure to check the front view as well as the perspective view to make sure that the chin and jaw line are matching the reference.

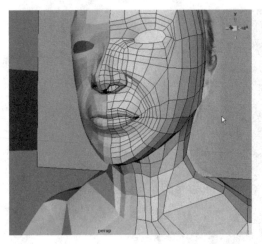

Figure 5-67

14. Take some time to rotate around the model and to view it in its smoothed state to see if there are any glaring issues. Either manually adjust the vertices or use the Sculpt Geometry tool to smooth over any rough edges. Just be careful around the mouth and the nose to avoid any clearly defined edge loops.

15. While you're at it, you can use the Sculpt Geometry tool to soften up the area around the eye so that the edge loops are a little more evenly spaced. This will get us all prepared for moving on to the next step — the eye socket.

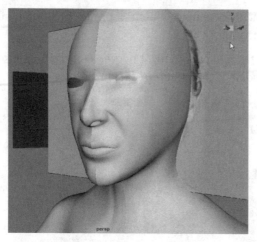

Figure 5-68

16. **Delete History and save!**

The Eye Socket

Back when we started this whole mess, we talked a bit about having to compensate for using photos as our reference. Basically, since any photo you take has perspective, you can't always rely exclusively on the photo when adjusting geometry.

The eyes are one of those features that tend to get distorted in photos, so we need to compensate for this as we move forward. We'll discuss a few tricks to compensate for these issues in Chapter 11. We should also look to some of the reference photos of the head in various poses to help our cause. Please refer to the additional images on the companion CD, in Chapter 5\sourceimages. So let's move on to the eye.

1. In order to get the eyelids and the area surrounding them the proper shape we will create a stand-in eyeball. Choose **Create | NURBS Primitives ▸ Sphere ❒**. When the dialog box opens, set the Radius to **0.30** and the Axis to **Z**, then click **Create**.

123

2. Move the sphere up to match the reference in both the front and side view.

3. Rotate the sphere roughly 4 degrees on the Y-axis so that the center point of the sphere is facing slightly right.

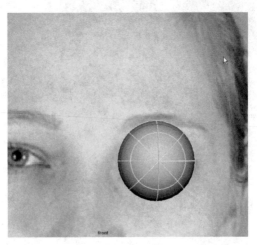

Figure 5-69

The reason we are using a NURBS sphere at this point is so we can take advantage of the Make Live command. When you make a NURBS surface live, all of the vertices we move along the eyelids will snap to the surface of the sphere. This in turn will make it considerably easier to get the eyelids to look correct.

4. So with the NURBS sphere selected, choose **Modify | Make Live**. The sphere's surface is now a live object. This means that the vertices we move should snap to the curved surface of the sphere.

5. Select your geometry again and, starting in a front view, adjust the vertices on the innermost edge loop to match the reference image.

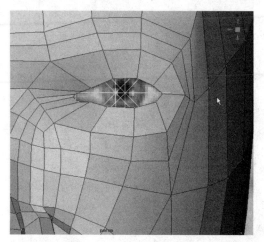

Figure 5-70

6. If you switch to perspective view, you will see that the interior edge loop is following the curve of the sphere.

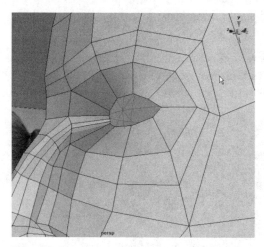

Figure 5-71

125

7. Rotate to a side view and adjust the vertices to match the reference image.

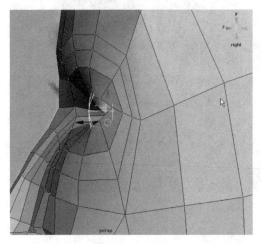

Figure 5-72

8. Select the sphere and turn off Make Live by selecting **Modify | Make Live** again.

9. Add a new edge loop using Insert Edge Loop tool so that it mimics the interior edge of the eyelid. With the edge loop selected, pull it out a bit from the sphere on the Z-axis.

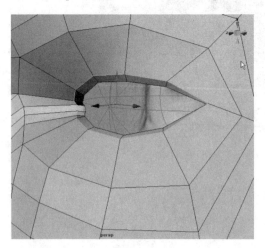

Figure 5-73

10. Create a new edge loop around the eye. Move the vertices to start to define the eyelid itself. Match the points to your reference in both the front and side views.

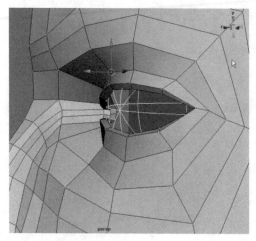

Figure 5-74

11. Add another edge loop. We will move the verts to help define the way that the eyelid sort of tucks itself under the ridge of the eyebrow.

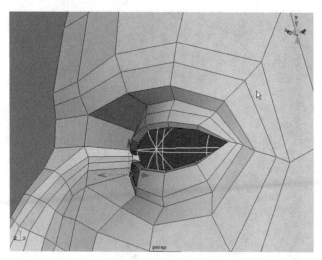

Figure 5-75

12. Create another loop. This one will be used to define the ridge of the overlap of skin over the eye and the pocket that is formed under the eye.

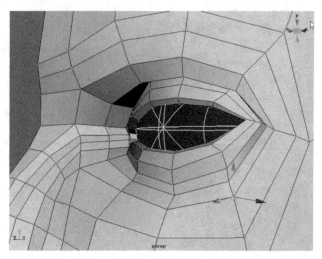

Figure 5-76

13. Create two loops that start at the outside corner of the eye and wrap around to the back of the head.

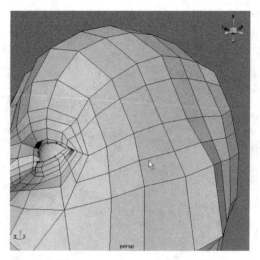

Figure 5-77

14. Add one last loop around the rim of the eyelids.

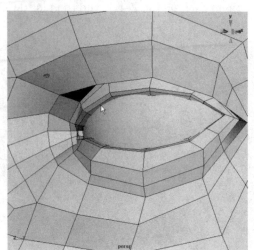

Figure 5-78

Let's go in and do a little bit more tweaking. The inside part of the eye contains a little fleshy area known as the lacimal caruncle.

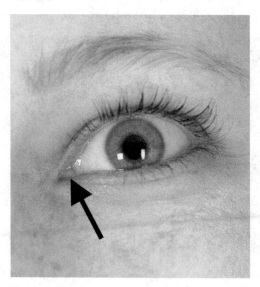

Figure 5-79

15. So let's select the two points on the inside corner of the eye and move them back on the Z-axis and then in toward the nose on the X-axis.

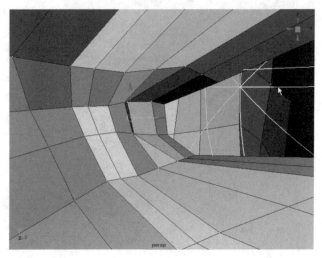

Figure 5-80

16. Select the face on the inner part of the eye and then extrude it out a bit on the Z-axis so that it looks like Figure 5-81.

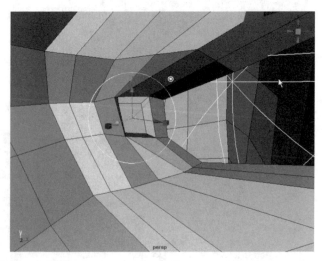

Figure 5-81

17. Select the innermost edge loop and extrude it back into the head on the Z-axis.

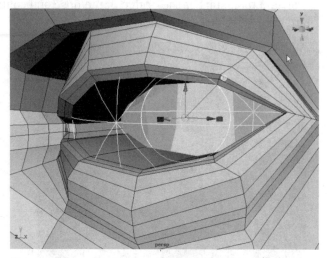

Figure 5-82

18. Take a few minutes to move the vertices on the side of the head near the eye so that the eye socket smoothly transitions into the head.

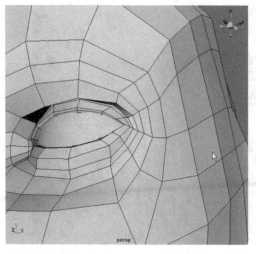

Figure 5-83

19. We'll add two additional edge loops that will give us some additional polys to work with when crafting the ear. Using the Split Polygon tool, start at the bridge of the nose and continue around to the back of the head.

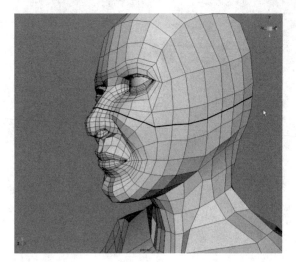

Figure 5-84

20. Collapse the triangle that was left on the cheek.

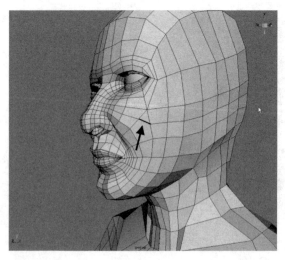

Figure 5-85

Finally, we can add a few additional edge loops to make sure we have enough geometry to capture the likeness and account for animation. These last few loops will also ensure that we have no issues with the geometry not appearing smooth.

21. Using the Insert Edge Loop tool, add three more edge loops that wrap around from the forehead to underneath the chin.

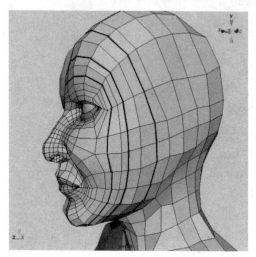

Figure 5-86

22. Add an edge loop that starts at the eye and flows down to the upper lip.

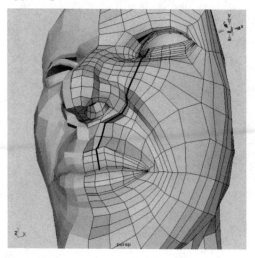

Figure 5-87

133

23. Insert another edge that flows from the inner eye around the tip of the nose.

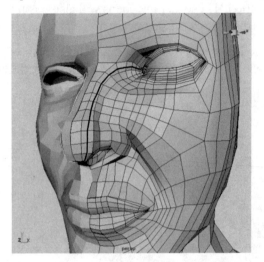

Figure 5-88

24. Create a loop that crosses the tip of the nose and wraps down under the chin.

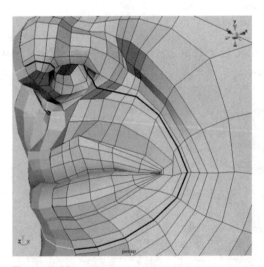

Figure 5-89

25. Create a loop that wraps around the outside of the lips.

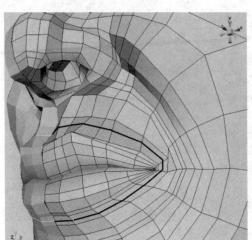

Figure 5-90

26. Add an additional edge loop around the nostril.

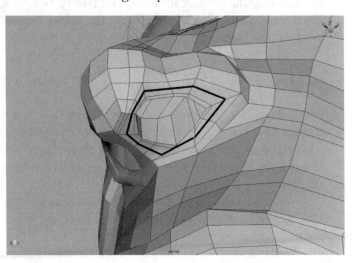

Figure 5-91

27. Finally, we add two edge loops that will give us some additional geometry to create the ear.

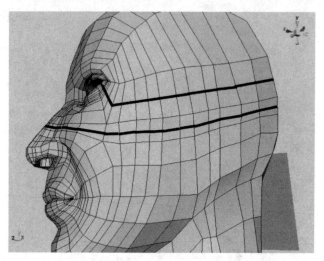

Figure 5-92

This should just about do it for the face, aside from some final adjustments we'll do later on to clean up the rough edges, nail down the likeness, and account for some asymmetry. Don't worry now about your model actually looking like the person you are trying to create at this point.

Wrap-Up

In this chapter we got down and dirty with the character's head. We learned how to use edge loops efficiently to create a head that looks relatively good. At this point, aesthetics plays second fiddle to form as our focus here is to create a clean edge flow that will be easier to animate.

We learned quite a bit about the key elements of the face and how they fit together. You also picked up some big words that you can use to impress your colleagues.

We also learned to utilize the Sculpt Geometry tool as an effective means to model. We will take advantage of this as we move forward. The head is by no means finished. We will be doing some additional tweaking before all is said and done. The next chapter will take us into the dark deep recesses of modeling the ear.

Creating the Ear

Getting to Know the Ear

Refer to Chapter_6 on the companion CD.

The ear. Yes, the ear. They come in all shapes and sizes and carry with them the visual confusion of an Escher drawing.

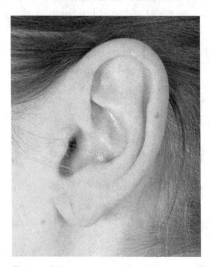

Figure 6-1

I have decided to dedicate an entire chapter to the ear because it tends to be a real showstopper for many modelers. The ears, like the eyes of your character, can easily dispel the illusion of realism if they are not modeled properly.

And, like the eye, the ear suffers from perspective issues as well. If we base the position of the ear solely on the side view reference image, we might end up with an ear that appears too far back on the head. This is because as we look at the side view, the ear is the closest thing to the camera and the features of the face tend to fall away due to perspective. This creates the illusion that the ear is farther back than it actually is. So when we start the ear, we will create it in a different position than it is currently located in the photo.

1. In order to continue to utilize our reference we will temporarily move the side reference image forward on the Z-axis. In the Outliner, select **imagePlane2**. If you can't see it, you need to right-click in the Outliner and uncheck **Show DAG Objects Only**.

2. Double-click on the little icon to the left of imagePlane 2 to bring up the parameters dialog on the right side of the screen (see Figure 6-2). Under Placement Extras, go to where it says Center and change the Z-axis (the third box over) from –0.8 to **–0.5**.

    The ear should now be correctly positioned for us to continue. When we are done with the ear, we can move our image plane back to its original position of –0.8.

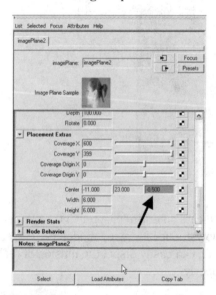

Figure 6-2

Let's Start Building

So with that lofty introduction, let's get back to work.

1. Starting in a side view, create a loop around the ear using the Split Polygon tool.

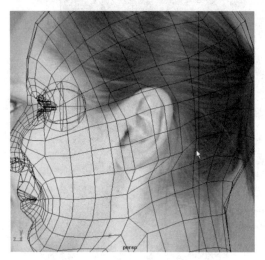

Figure 6-3

2. Go back to the triangles and draw an edge from the center of each to the corresponding vertex.

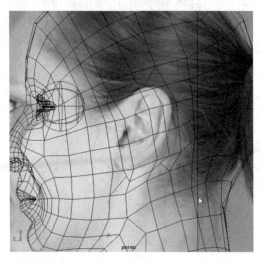

Figure 6-4

We need to move the vertices to accommodate the ear. We just want to get the edges to form a somewhat circular shape to prepare us for the extrusion. Think about the shape of the ear where it meets the side of the head.

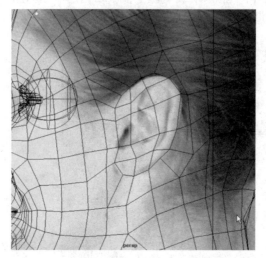

Figure 6-5

3. Select the faces that are inside the ear outline and extrude using **Edit Mesh | Extrude** ☐ [v7: Edit Polygons | Extrude Face ☐]. When the dialog opens, set the Offset under Settings to **1** and hit the **Apply** button. As before, the selected faces will shrink down, inset from their original position.

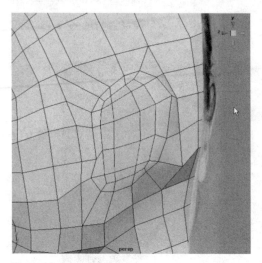

Figure 6-6

4. Before continuing, set the Extrude options back to their default values.

5. Create another edge loop that wraps around the side of the head and goes through the center of the ear.

6. Create another loop that starts at the top of the head and then wraps down under the chin.

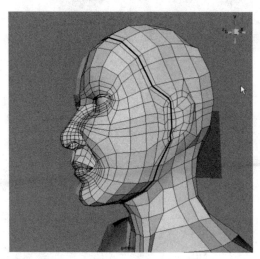

Figure 6-7

7. In a side view, move the verts to align with the ear as shown in Figure 6-8.

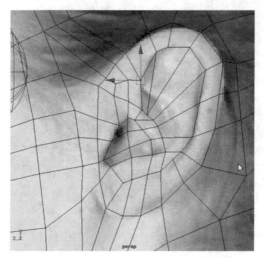

Figure 6-8

8. Create a new edge loop using the Split Polygon tool.

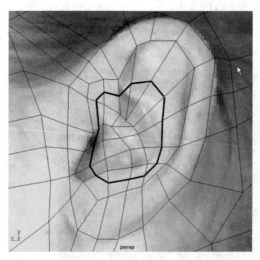

Figure 6-9

9. Kill the triangles by drawing an edge from the center to the corresponding vertex.

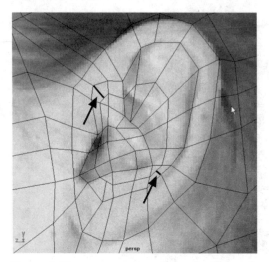

Figure 6-10

10. Position the new vertices as shown in Figure 6-11.

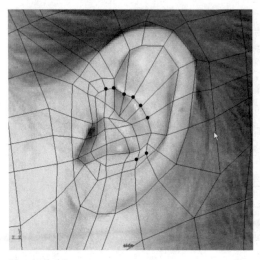

Figure 6-11

11. Select the polygons shown in Figure 6-12 and extrude them out from the head on the X-axis.

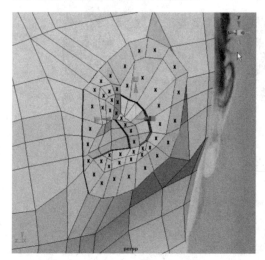

Figure 6-12

12. Now select the polygons and extrude them again.

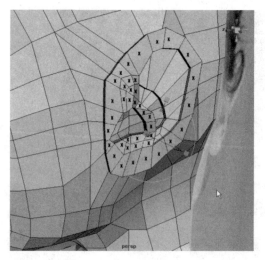

Figure 6-13

13. Select the three polys at the ear canal and extrude them back into the head.

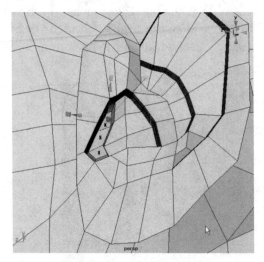

Figure 6-14

14. Select the uppermost polygon of the three you just extruded and extrude it back farther into the head.

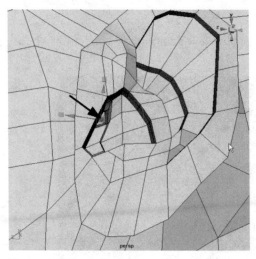

Figure 6-15

15. Select the faces as shown in Figure 6-16. Once again, we need to choose **Edit Mesh | Extrude** ☐ [v7: Edit Polygons | Extrude Face ☐]. When the dialog opens, set the Offset under Settings to **0.02** and hit the **Apply** button. As before, you will see the selected faces shrink down, inset from their original position.

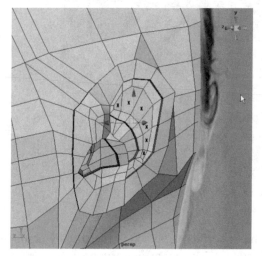

Figure 6-16

16. Back in a side view, position the vertices as shown in Figure 6-17.

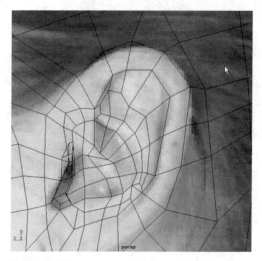

Figure 6-17

17. Use the Insert Edge Loop tool [v7: Split Edge Ring tool] around the faces you just extruded.

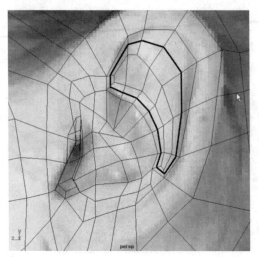

Figure 6-18

18. Use the Split Polygon tool to clean up the five-sided and three-sided polygons.

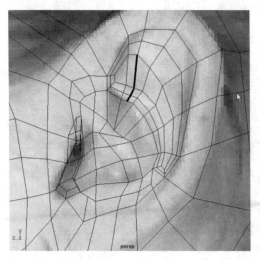

Figure 6-19

19. Select the three faces near the top of the ear and extrude them in on the X-axis a tiny amount.

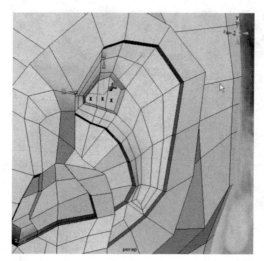

Figure 6-20

20. Select the vertices near the earlobe and pull them down.

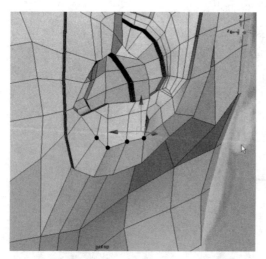

Figure 6-21

21. Create another edge loop around the larger part of the ear using the Insert Edge Loop tool.

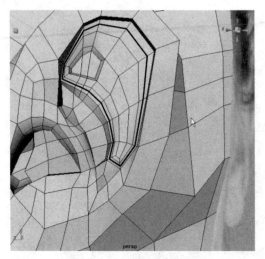

Figure 6-22

22. Select the faces outside the edge loop you just created and extrude them.

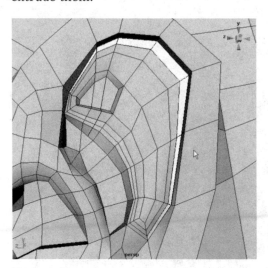

Figure 6-23

23. With the faces selected, tuck them back under the outer ring (helix). Make sure the faces aren't intersecting any other geometry.

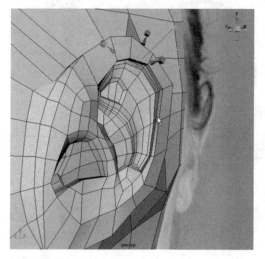

Figure 6-24

24. On the side of the head, create a new edge loop that surrounds the ear.

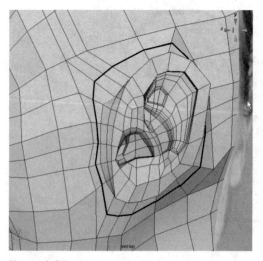

Figure 6-25

25. In a side view, select the vertices that make up the inner part of the ear as shown in Figure 6-26. This would include all of the vertices except for the ones along the outside ring of the ear.

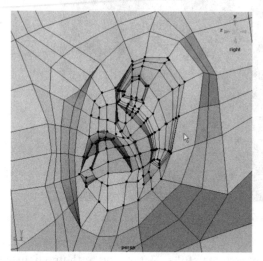

Figure 6-26

26. Rotate to a perspective view. Use the Shift key or Grow Selection to add the first two rows of vertices around the earlobe to your selection, as indicated by the dark lines in Figure 6-27.

Avoid adding verts near the front of the ear. Note that these lines continue around to the back of the earlobe as well.

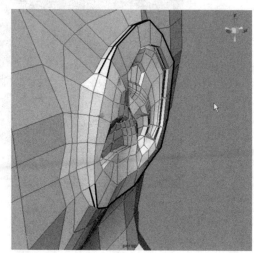

Figure 6-27

151

27. Move the vertices away from the head on the X-axis.

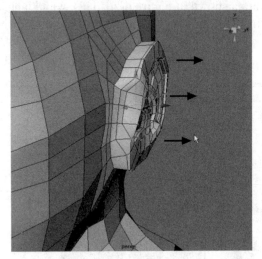

Figure 6-28

28. With the vertices still selected, rotate them slightly so that the front vertices move back in toward the head.

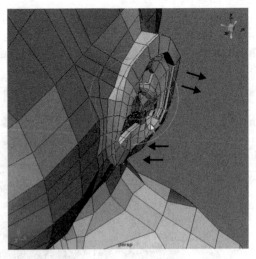

Figure 6-29

29. Rotate so that you can see the back of the ear and add two edge loops using the Insert Edge Loop tool.

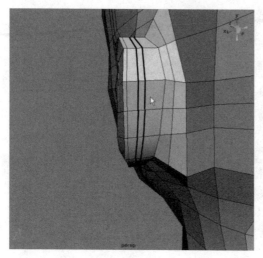

Figure 6-30

30. Work your way around and select the faces closest to the side of the head including those behind the ear, avoiding the ones at the front of the ear.

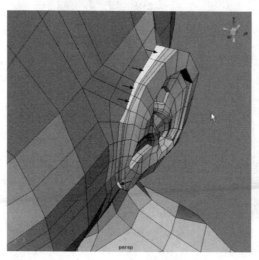

Figure 6-31

31. Scale the faces down on the Z- and Y-axes, and then push them in to line up with the side of the head.

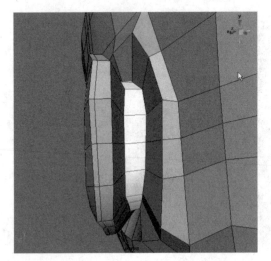

Figure 6-32

32. Add two edge loops around the ear.

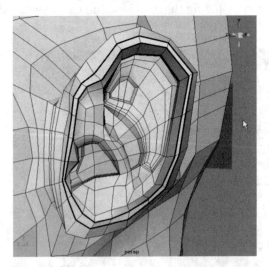

Figure 6-33

33. Pull the vertices of the edge loops out around the outer ring to help define the helix.

    Alright! Now we are nearing the home stretch! What we want to do now is go in with the Sculpt Geometry tool and smooth out some of the areas on the ear.

34. Starting with the front of the ear, smooth out the area where the ear meets the face. Ideally, it should be relatively flat. Check by referring to the smoothed version of your model.

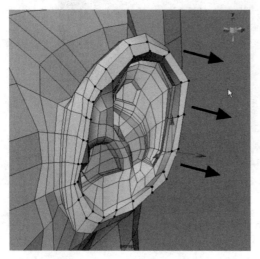

Figure 6-34

35. Add a slight touch here and there with the smooth operation; just enough to rid the ear of any harsh edges and to soften up some of the details. Once again, check by referring to the smoothed version of your model.

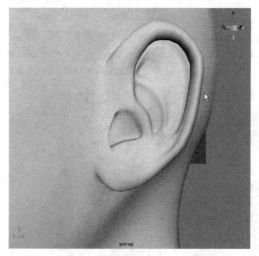

Figure 6-35

36. To wrap things up, use the Sculpt Geometry tool to smooth the head a bit around the ear.

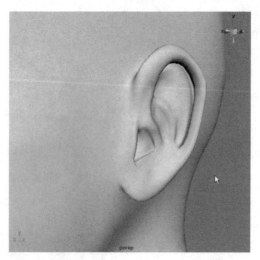

Figure 6-36

Wrap-Up

We have now completed the head for the most part. This was definitely the most challenging aspect of modeling the character.
Besides the fact that you have a finished head, you also have created geometry that can be reused time and time again. The ear is one of those things that you don't want to have to build again if you have one already. It can be altered and adjusted to fit any head you end up creating.

As we move forward there will be some refinements to the head to capture the likeness of our model. These tweaks will be addressed at the end of the modeling process.

In the next chapter we will create an eye that will give our character a little life.

What Beautiful Eyes You Have

The Details

Refer to Chapter_7 on the companion CD.

Earlier, we used a simple sphere as reference to shape the eye socket. Now we are going to create an eye that will give our character a more realistic appearance. The saying goes "The eyes are the window to the soul." Look into anyone's eyes and you get a clear picture of what this statement really means. If the eyes of your model don't look realistic, the rest of the model, no matter how good it looks, will never be quite right.

We will once again begin with a sphere.

1. Choose **Create | Polygon Primitives ▸ Sphere ☐**. When the dialog box opens, set the Radius to **0.3** and the Axis to **Z**.

   At this stage we want to leave the sphere at the origin. This sphere will represent the outer "layer" or cornea, which is the thin transparent membrane that covers the front of the eye.

2. In a side view, select the first two rows of vertices on the left side of the sphere and pull them out slightly to form a bulge in the cornea.

3. Use the Insert Edge Loop tool to add an edge at the base of the corneal bulge, as shown in Figure 7-1.

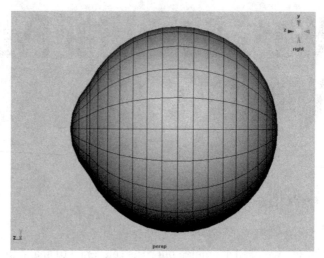

Figure 7-1

4. Create a layer and name it **Cornea_L**. Add the cornea geometry to the layer. Create another sphere and scale it to be slightly smaller than the original sphere.

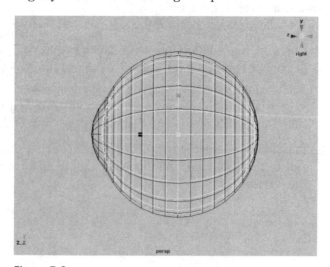

Figure 7-2

5. This sphere will represent the sclera (the white part of the eye) and will also give us the iris (the colored part of the eye). Name the sphere **Eye** and place it on its own layer. To make things easier to work with, turn off the visibility in the cornea layer or turn on templating in the layer so it won't get in the way.

6. Go back to the side view and select the first three rows of vertices on the left. Using the Scale tool, scale them on the X-axis to the right to flatten the front of the sphere.

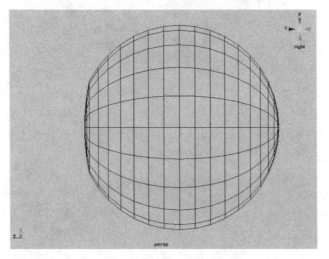

Figure 7-3

7. In a perspective view, select the innermost faces as shown in Figure 7-4 and move them back on the Z-axis.

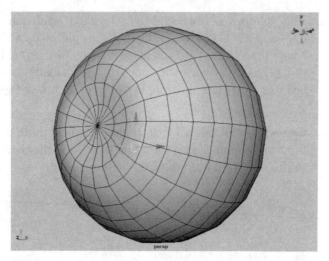

Figure 7-4

8. With the faces still selected, extrude them back into the eye-ball and scale them down.

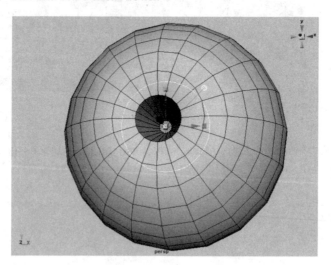

Figure 7-5

9. Add two additional edge loops around the pupil.

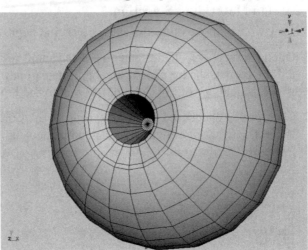

Figure 7-6

That should suffice for the geometry of the eye. What really sells it, though, are the texture and shader settings. At this point we will apply a transparent material to the outer sphere or cornea.

10. Go to **Window | Rendering Editors ▸ Hypershade**. Create a new phong material named **Cornea_mat** with the settings shown in Figure 7-7.

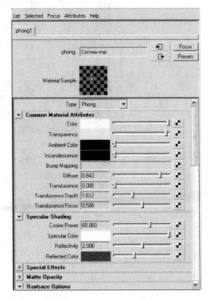

Figure 7-7

11. Select the cornea, right-click on the new material, and choose **Assign Material to Selection**.

    Now we will move on to the sclera, iris, and pupil.

12. Open a new phong shader and give it the same settings as you did the cornea shader except for the Transparency slider, which should be set to black (all the way to the left).

13. Click on the checkered icon to the right of the Color slider. When the Create Render Node dialog box pops up, select **File** from the Textures tab.

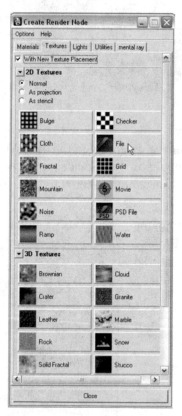

Figure 7-8

14. A new place2dTexture panel will open, as shown in Figure 7-9. When it does, click on the folder icon to the right of Image Name. Browse to the **Chapter 7\sourceimages\ Lucy_eye.jpg** file on the companion CD.

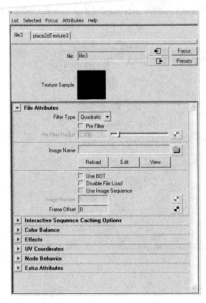

Figure 7-9

You should now have a texture ready to map onto the surface of the eye. Before we do that, however, we need to change the UV coordinates on the eye geometry. By default, when you create a polygon sphere it has spherical mapping coordinates applied to it. We are going to simplify matters by applying a planar projection instead.

165

15. With the eye selected, in a front view go to **Create UVs |
    Planar Mapping** ☐ [v7: Polygon UVs | Planar Mapping ☐].
    When the Planar Mapping Options dialog opens, make sure
    Project From is set to **Z axis** or **Camera** [v7: set Mapping
    Direction to **Camera**]. (See Figure 12-21 for the Maya 7 ver-
    sion of this dialog box.)

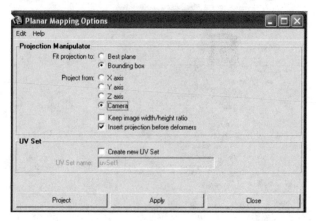

Figure 7-10

I personally prefer to set Project From to Camera because I
am assured the view I am looking through is the same as that
of the UV projection.

16. Press the **Project** button to assign the projection and close
    the dialog box. A planar mapping manipulator will pop up in
    the viewport, showing how the texture is being projected onto
    the geometry.

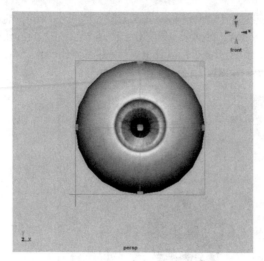

Figure 7-11

The texture is applied to the eye geometry but it is not scaled quite the way we want it. We will have to adjust the UVs to get the iris to be the proper size.

17. Open **Window | UV Texture Editor**. The UV Texture Editor window will pop up, and you should see the UV representation of the eye geometry along with the Lucy_eye texture.

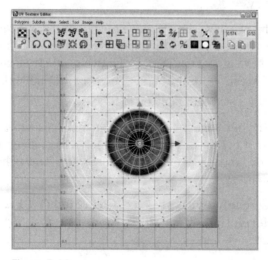

Figure 7-12

167

18. Right-click in the window and, when the marking menu pops up, select **UVs**. Select all of the UVs that make up the eye and scale them uniformly so that the edge of the iris is just outside of the two tightly spaced edge loops.

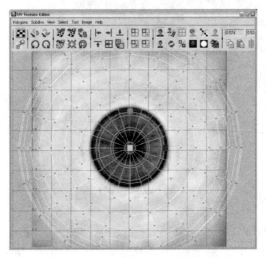

Figure 7-13

Don't be concerned if the geometry ends up outside of the texture space. Any tiling that occurs will be obscured by the head geometry.

19. Now that we have the eye geometry textured, we can prepare it to be placed inside of the head. Make sure both the cornea and the eye are visible. Select the two geometries and then choose **Mesh | Combine** [v7: Polygons | Combine].
    Name the new combined object **left_eye**.

20. Move the new object up to match the reference image, or simply align it to the stand-in eye geometry. Remember to rotate it slightly on the Y-axis. You can now safely delete the stand-in eye geometry.

21. Make sure **left_eye** is selected. Go to **Modify | Freeze Transformations**. This will zero out any translation and rotation on the geometry.

22. With the geometry still selected, go to **Edit | Duplicate Special** ❐ [v7: Edit | Duplicate ❐]. When the dialog box opens, set the Scale to **–1, 1, 1**. Hit the **Duplicate** button to mirror the geometry to create the right eye. Move the new eye geometry into position in the right eye socket. Be sure to name the geometry **right_eye**.

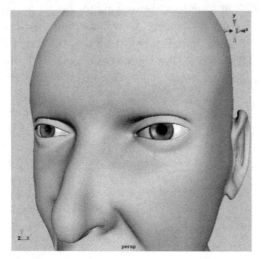

Figure 7-14

23. The last things we will do to wrap things up is apply a smooth node to the eyes and add them to their own layer. Then go to **File | Optimize Scene Size** to clear out any layers that we are no longer using.

24. **Save your file!**

Wrap-Up

In this chapter we learned how to make a realistic eye for our model. This is another geometry that you can add to your library. You will never have to build an eye again.

Our head geometry is now complete, but not finished! We will still have to do some additional tweaking to correct perspective issues and nail down a likeness. We will also add a texture and, of course, eyelashes and hair. But before all that we need to get back to our character's body, so grab some coffee, clear your head, and turn the page.

Chapter 8

Open Wide

Getting Your Chops

Refer to Chapter_8 on the companion CD.

To really capture a likeness we need to sweat the details. Every little nuance adds credibility to the model. To avoid having an emotionless character, you need to be able to represent movement of the face.

By and large, we each have our own way of expressing ourselves. The face can express a number of things without a single word. A smile, a frown — each is easily recognizable. In order for our model to best represent the person we are basing it on, we will at some point open the mouth, thus revealing what is inside.

So in this chapter we will run through the process of creating teeth, gums, and a tongue for our character. In order to capture the nuances of our model, we will be sure to address any special characteristics of the bite when we build them. Noting this will help sell the realism of our character.

The Teeth

1. Let's start by opening **Chapter8_start.mb** from the companion CD. You'll see that we have an image plane that shows the teeth from a front view. If the image doesn't show up, you can load it in from the Chapter 8\sourceimages folder. Lucky for you, I took the liberty of sizing the image so that it matches the scale of your model!

Let's take a quick moment to discuss the teeth. Teeth basically come in three shapes and sizes. We have the incisors, which are the four teeth in the front. Next are the canines, one on either side, commonly referred to as vampire teeth. Then last but not least we have the molars. Now since this isn't *Dentistry for Morons* (that will be my next book), that's really about all we need to know about the teeth. After all, we are modeling them, not drilling them.

2. Choose **Create | Polygon Primitives ▸ Cube** ◻. When the dialog box opens, set Subdivisions Along Width to **2**, Subdivisions Along Height to **4**, and Subdivisions Along Depth to **2**.

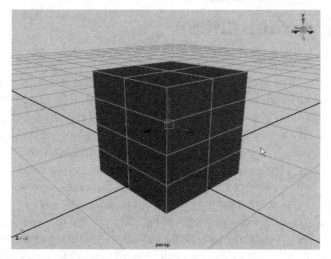

Figure 8-1

3. We start right up front with the incisors. Although there are four incisors, we only need to make one and then vary it a bit on the three copies we make. Adjust the geometry so that it looks like the front and side views in the example shown in Figure 8-2.

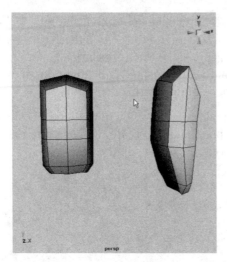

Figure 8-2

4. Once you have completed the modeling, move it up to match the position and size of the tooth in the reference image. Duplicate it and then move the new tooth over to create the second incisor. Manipulate the vertices to match the reference.

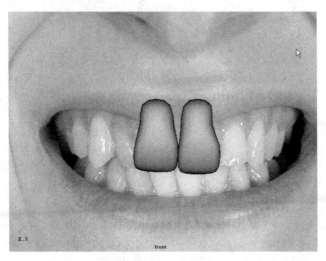

Figure 8-3

5. Ultimately the teeth will be smoothed, and thus will shrink down a bit. Apply a Smooth to the two teeth to see if there are any unwanted gaps. Make the necessary adjustments on the low-res version to compensate. This might entail overlapping some of the edges of the teeth.

6. Go ahead and make another copy of the tooth. Scale it down and shape and position it to create the incisor to the right. Make sure to rotate it slightly in the process.

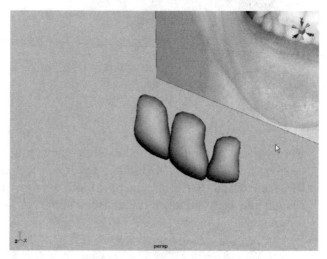

Figure 8-4

7. Before moving on, select the incisor and go to **Modify | Freeze Transformations**. Doing this will allow you to mirror the tooth with the rotation intact along the X-axis. With the tooth still selected, go to **Edit | Duplicate Special** ☐ [v7: Edit | Duplicate ☐]. When the dialog opens, set Scale to **–1, 1, 1** and Geometry Type to **Copy**. Hit **Apply**. You should now have a mirrored copy of the right incisor.

8. Move the copy to its position on the left side. Notice in the reference photo the slight variation in the incisor's position as compared to the one on the opposite side. Make necessary adjustments to match the reference.

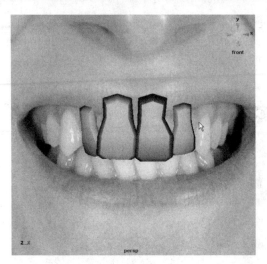

Figure 8-5

9. Again copy one of the teeth. Extrude the faces on the bottom of the tooth so as to create more of a point for the canine. Move the verts around a bit until it looks like the one shown in Figure 8-6.

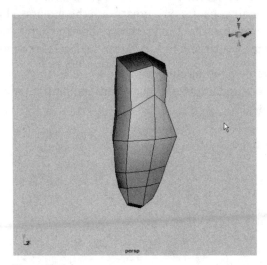

Figure 8-6

10. Position the tooth based on the reference image. Duplicate it across the X-axis as before, and match the duplicate to the canine on the left.

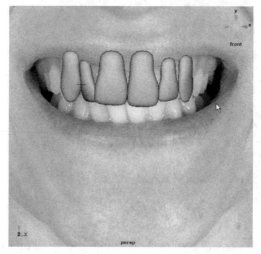

Figure 8-7

The teeth behind the incisors are the molars. They consist of two general types: the premolars and the molars. The only real difference is that the premolars have a slightly sharper surface in comparison to the flatter surface of the molar.

11. Let's create another cube with the same settings as the first one we created. Move the points around until it resembles Figure 8-8.

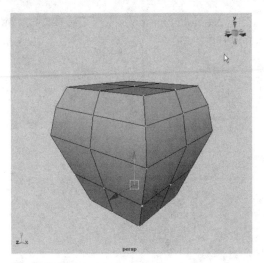

Figure 8-8

12. Select the top four faces and extrude them so the faces are inset from the original position. Form the geometry so that it looks similar to Figure 8-9.

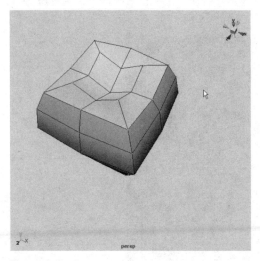

Figure 8-9

13. To create the premolar, simply select the vertices on the outside and pull them up.

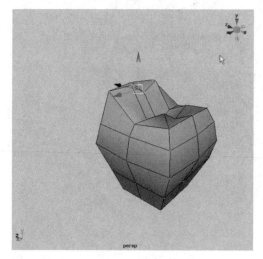

Figure 8-10

14. Rotate and scale the tooth and then move it up to match with the photo reference.

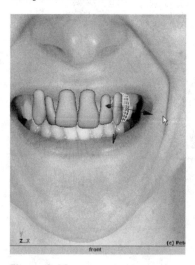

Figure 8-11

15. Rotate into a top view and, instead of mirroring the tooth right now, create three consecutive copies and position them as shown in Figure 8-12.

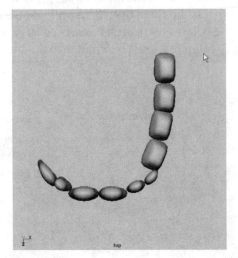

Figure 8-12

16. Select the molars and freeze the transforms. Combine the teeth by selecting them and choosing **Mesh | Combine** [v7: Polygons | Combine]. Now duplicate the teeth as we did before on the X-axis, then position them on the opposite side.

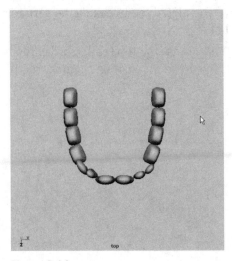

Figure 8-13

179

17. Select all of the teeth and combine them. Give them the name **upperTeeth**.

18. In order to get the lower teeth we need simply make a copy of the upper teeth and flip them over. This will involve a bit of tweaking as the bottom teeth aren't nearly as large as the top. They also have more of a level bite line than do the upper teeth.

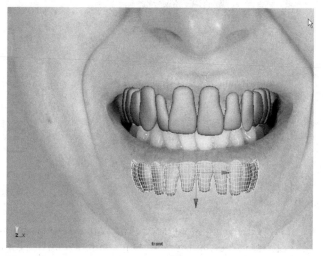

Figure 8-14

19. Once you have completed the tweaking, be sure to name them **bottomTeeth**.

Be aware of the fact that the top teeth overlap the bottom teeth in front, so be sure to position them correctly.

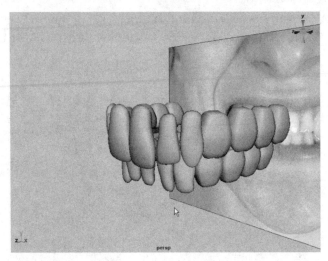

Figure 8-15

The Gums

1. Next, of course, we'll need to create gums for our teeth. Create a 20-sided cylinder with Subdivisions Caps set to **3**.

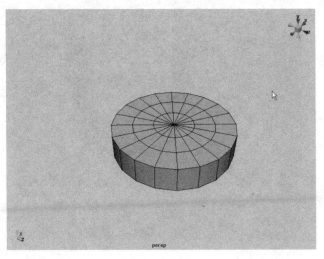

Figure 8-16

2. Name the cylinder **upperGums**. Delete the back half of the model, then in a top view, position it directly under the teeth.

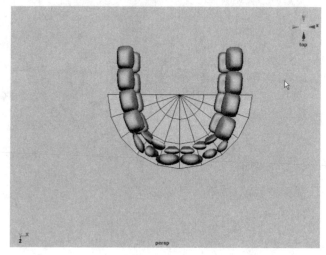

Figure 8-17

3. Scale the cylinder on the X-axis so that it matches up a bit better to our teeth. Don't worry if it's not perfect.

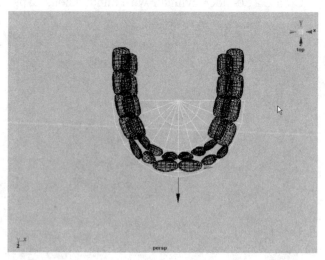

Figure 8-18

4. Move the gums up above the top teeth.

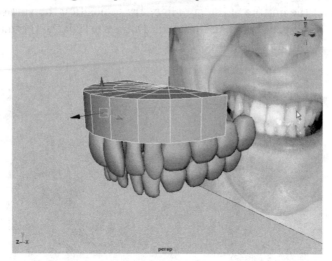

Figure 8-19

5. Select the back open edge of the gums and extrude back.

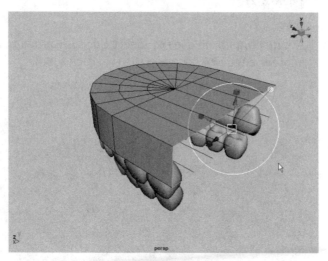

Figure 8-20

6. In a front view, move the bottom row of vertices down to meet the bottom of the gum line. Try to position the vertices so that they sit between the teeth. Don't worry if the teeth protrude through the gums at this point.

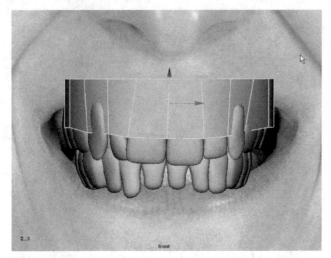

Figure 8-21

7. Rotate around and use the Insert Edge Loop tool to add another edge loop between the two back teeth.

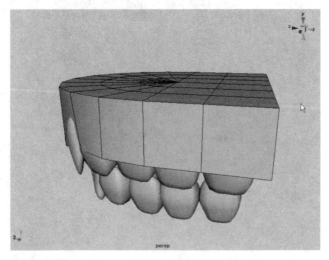

Figure 8-22

8. Once again, use the Insert Edge Loop tool to add an edge loop between each of the existing loops.

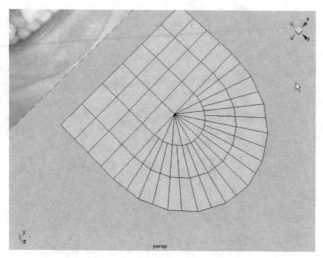

Figure 8-23

9. Rotate around and position the vertices to get a zig-zag appearance.

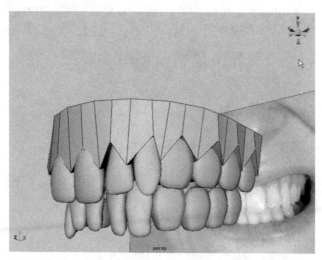

Figure 8-24

10. Use the Insert Edge Loop tool to add two edge loops around the gum line.

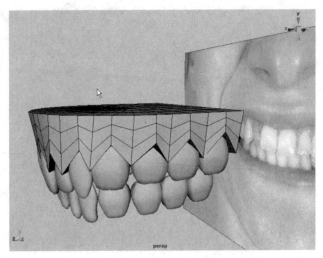

Figure 8-25

11. Go around and move the vertices to get a nice gum line. Refer to a smoothed version of the gums as well as the teeth to see if there are unwanted gaps. Feel free to add an edge loop here and there to get the right look.

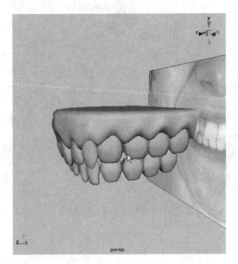

Figure 8-26

12. In a top view, select the inside group of faces and move them up on the Y-axis. Be sure the faces on the inside of the mouth are selected as well.

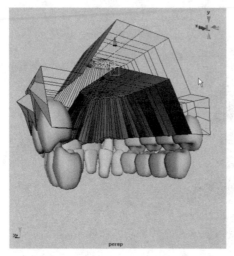

Figure 8-27

13. Select the top edge loop around the gum line and scale it on the X- and Z-axes.

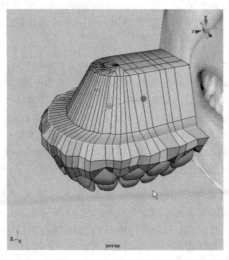

Figure 8-28

14. One more thing we want to do to the gums is delete the faces that aren't going to be visible on the final model. So select the faces on the top of the gums and delete them.

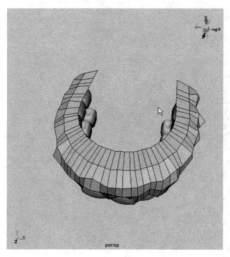

Figure 8-29

15. Duplicate the gums on the Y-axis in order to get the bottom gums. Name the new geometry **lowerGums**. We'll need to do a little massaging to get the gums in position with the bottom teeth. The best way to handle this is by using a lattice deformer.

16. First, uniformly scale the lower gums down so that they will be easier to manipulate with the deformer. In the hot box, choose **Deform | Create Lattice ☐**. (Deform is on the Animation menu selection in the hot box.) You may also access Create Lattice from the menu at the top if Animation is selected in the left box on the status line. When the dialog opens, set the Divisions to **3, 3, 3**.

17. When the lattice appears, right-click on it and select **Lattice Points** from the marking menu. Now that the points are highlighted, use them to get the gums to line up with the bottom teeth. When you finish using the lattice, select the geometry and choose **Delete History**.

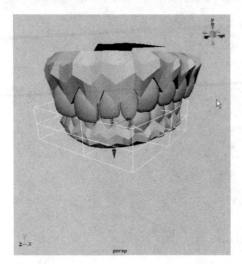

Figure 8-30

18. Where there are still issues, you can manually adjust vertices or apply the smooth node and use the Sculpt Geometry tool.

   The teeth and gums are one of the few geometry types that don't necessarily need to keep their low-resolution counterpart. Once they are done there is no need to go back and mess with them. You may, however, want to keep a low-res version handy so that the poly count won't hinder the animation process.

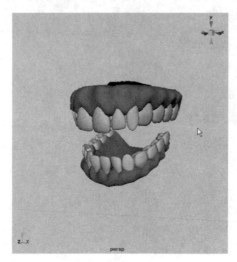

Figure 8-31

So that pretty much does it for the teeth and gums. The next thing we will do is add a very basic geometry for our tongue.

The Tongue

We can create a very serviceable tongue with very little effort. Although the tongue plays a major role in the way we speak, it is really just an added bonus when it comes to modeling a character. For the most part the tongue won't be visible, even during speech. The tongue is used primarily when an "l" or "th" sound is involved, and even then it isn't visible to the viewer. Unless you need your character to lick its lips, you really don't even need a tongue. But I always lean toward the "safer than sorry" approach.

1. So with that said, we will build a tongue using a squashed sphere. Choose **Create | Polygon Primitives ▸ Sphere** ☐. When the dialog pops up, set Subdivisions Along Axis to **20**, Subdivisions Along Height to **20**, and Axis to **Z**. Select the **Scale** tool and flatten the tongue on the Y-axis.

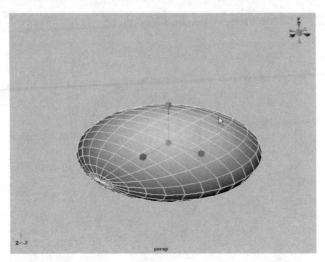

Figure 8-32

2. Now go to **Deform | Create Lattice** ☐. When the dialog box opens, set the Divisions to **3, 2, 5.** When the lattice appears, right-click on it and select **Lattice Points.** Select the last two rows of the lattice points and slide them back on the Z-axis.

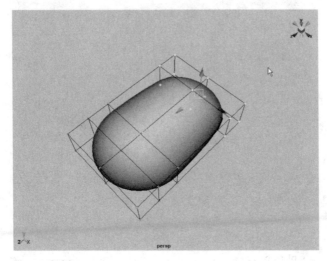

Figure 8-33

3. In a top view, scale the selected points out on the X-axis.

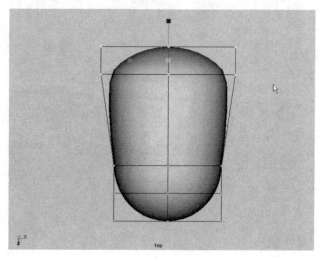

Figure 8-34

4. Select each row of the lattice points and move them so that they resemble Figure 8-35.

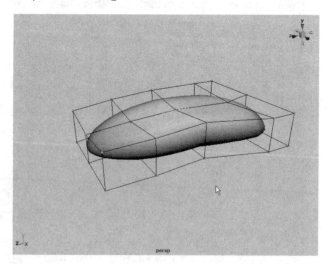

Figure 8-35

5. With the tongue geometry selected, delete the history. This will bake in the lattice deformation. Move the tongue up to position it in the mouth.

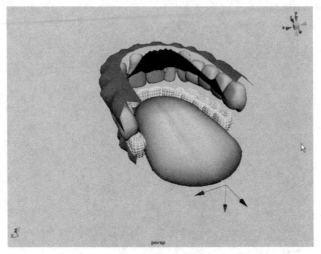

Figure 8-36

There is really no need to do any additional work to the tongue other than applying a texture. Aside from that, we are pretty well set with the inside of the mouth. The last thing we will want to do is position the teeth inside our model.

Placing the Teeth and Tongue

Let's do some final cleanup before we save the file.

1. Select the top teeth and gums and select **Mesh | Combine** [v7: Polygons | Combine]. Name the new object **UpperTeeth**.

2. Select the bottom teeth and gums and combine them as well. Name the group **LowerTeeth**.

3. Select the **UpperTeeth**, **LowerTeeth**, and the tongue, then select **Edit | Group**. Name the group something like **Teeth** or **Mouth**.

4. Select **ImagePlane1** in the Outliner and delete it. We won't be needing it for the next step.

5. Save the file as **Teeth**, then open up the file with your model and import the **Teeth.mb** file. You might need to move the teeth a bit so they fit properly into the mouth. Check the image to see the proper placement.

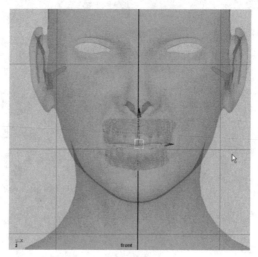

Figure 8-37

6. Once the teeth are positioned properly, create a layer and name it **Teeth_L**. Add the group to the layer and turn off the visibility before we move on to the final step.

   When we built the head we were concerned with aesthetics more than functionality, so at the time we built the lips we weren't really thinking about opening the mouth. Now that we have given our model teeth, we'll want to add some polygons to the lips so that they have a natural appearance when the mouth is open.

7. It might be beneficial to rotate in a perspective view so that the camera is inside the head looking toward the front. Select the interior open edge of the lips and extrude them farther back into the head.

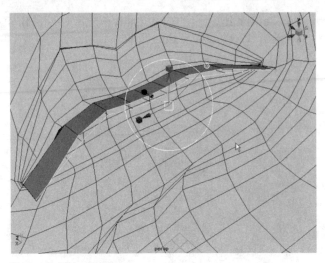

Figure 8-38

8. Extrude the edges once again and move them up or down on the Y-axis accordingly.

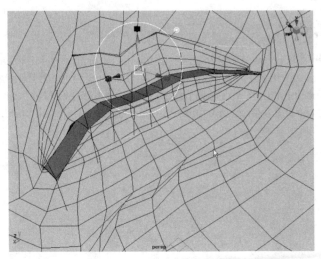

Figure 8-39

Look at the image to see roughly where the teeth should line up with the head in a side view.

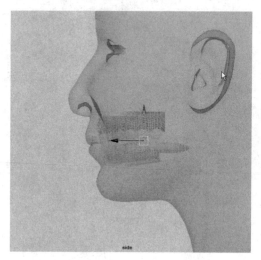

Figure 8-40

Wrap-Up

In this chapter you learned to use basic primitives to create a pretty convincing set of choppers and you set up a mouth that can be used for animation. You also have a model of the teeth that can be used over and over in any subsequent character that you build.

Fleshing Out the Body

Crafting the Figure

Refer to Chapter_9 on the companion CD.

Now that we have made it past the head, we need to focus on fleshing out the body (no pun intended!). So let's take a look at where we left off with the character. To this point we have more or less been concerned only with the mass of our figure. The majority of edge loops are there simply to dictate the general shape. So the next thing we need to do is start adding edge loops that follow more along the lines of the muscle structure. This is the stage of the modeling process that really defines your character. We are also at the point where we will rely on the photo reference considerably more than the skeleton.

So to begin with, we will want to get our figure to resemble the reference images as much as possible without adding any additional geometry. This is what I refer to as the bulking up phase. Up until this point we have been following the bone structure as our point of reference. This is a great way to get things started and it gets the general proportions of the figure squared away. However, we don't really have a sense of the figure's underlying muscle structure.

1.   Select **Mesh | Sculpt Geometry Tool** ☐ [v7: Edit Polygons | Sculpt Geometry Tool ☐]. When the dialog pops up, set Max Displacement to **.2000** and Smooth Strength to **2**.

2. Using the Pull operation, begin to sculpt the figure with short strokes. Refer to the front and side views to determine the amount of each stroke. Concentrate on the torso, arms, and legs of your character, avoiding the hands and feet for the moment.

   Don't be too concerned if the model bulges out a bit too much here and there. We will switch often to the Smooth operation in order to resolve those issues.

3. You may find it useful to adjust the Smooth Strength in order to get the results you are looking for. Just try to keep it between 2 and 9. Vary it up a bit here and there to see how it affects the Pull operation. Remember, switch back and forth between Smooth and Pull with an occasional Push thrown in here and there for the best results. Take a look at your smoothed figure to see how things are shaping up.

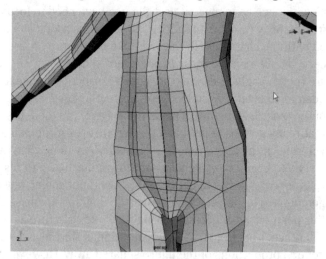

Figure 9-1

If this is new to you, give it a real chance to sink in and don't get frustrated. If worse comes to worse, you can still get the same results by manually moving the vertices about. I wholeheartedly encourage you to keep trying, and eventually it will become second nature. For additional help with the process, refer to the Sculpting avi on the companion CD.

Once you have the model following the reference as closely as possible, the next thing we will concentrate on is adding our muscle edge loops. We will begin with the stomach area.

4. Create four new edge loops that wrap around the torso using the Insert Edge Loop tool. In addition, add an edge loop around the clavicle region.

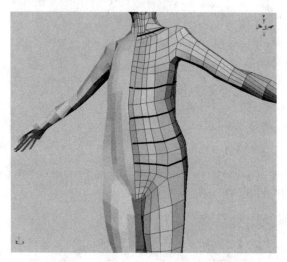

Figure 9-2

5. Starting at the center of the model, just below the rib cage, use the Split Polygon tool and draw an edge loop around the stomach area.

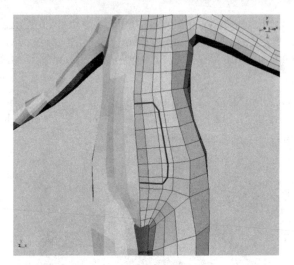

Figure 9-3

6. Draw an edge from the center of each angled edge to the corresponding vertex.

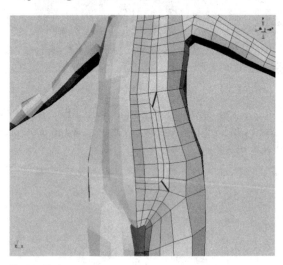

Figure 9-4

7. Create another loop inside the one you just created.

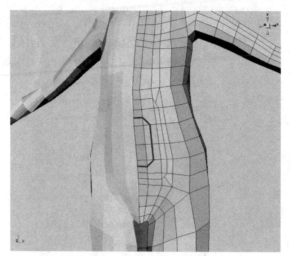

Figure 9-5

8. Select the two angled edges and collapse them.

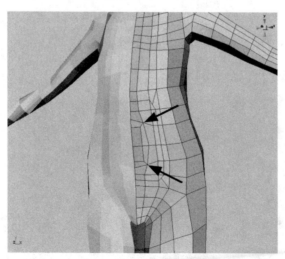

Figure 9-6

9. This next loop is a bit more complex so I will break it up into smaller steps. Make sure as you go along to keep track of the angled edges as we will be collapsing those later. Starting on the back of the model near the bottom of the buttocks, use the Split Polygon tool to draw a loop as shown in Figure 9-7.

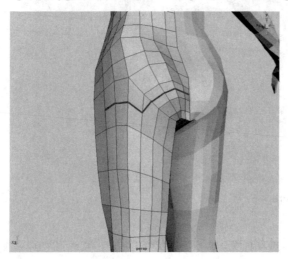

Figure 9-7

10. Now, continuing from the end of that loop, draw an edge down under the base of the pubic area.

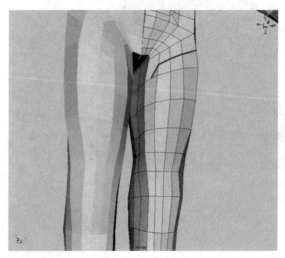

Figure 9-8

11. Continue the loop down around the front of the thigh to just below the knee.

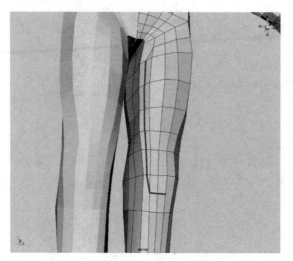

Figure 9-9

12. Then take the edge back up to the top of the hip.

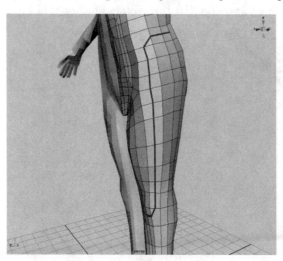

Figure 9-10

13. Continue the loop over the top of the hip and back down the thigh to just above the back of the knee.

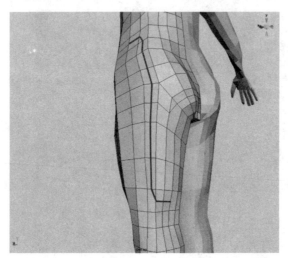

Figure 9-11

14. Okay, last one. Continue the edge back up around the back of the thigh and end it at the crotch, as shown in Figure 9-12.

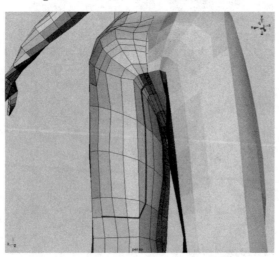

Figure 9-12

Did you get all of that? Okay, so now we need to go back and clean up all the little triangles we just created.

15. Select each of the angled edges (eight total) in the loop and collapse them. There are two behind the knee, one right where the buttocks meets the thigh, two at the top of the hips, one right beneath the pelvis, and two on the knee. We should end up with something like Figures 9-13.

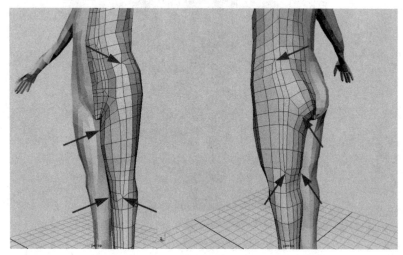

Figure 9-13

Not only do we use edge loops to define muscles, but oftentimes we will use them to define bones, especially when they are near the surface of the body. In the last step, we not only came closer to defining the muscle groupings in the front and the back of the thigh, but we also gave some form to the hip bone.

A few other examples of using edge loops to define bones would be the knees, elbows, ankles, and wrists. So with that in mind let's go ahead and define some of these bones.

16. Starting with the knee, use the Insert Edge Loop tool to add an additional edge loop above the knee and one around the center of the knee. As a change of pace, you could also try using **Edit Mesh | Offset Edge Loop Tool** [v7: Edit Polygons | Duplicate Edge Ring Tool] for the same results.

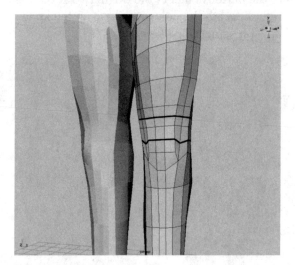

Figure 9-14

17. Use the View Compass in the upper-right corner to rotate to a back view of the model. We will now define the slight indent that sometimes occurs right above the gluteus maximus. Using the Split Polygon tool, draw two diamond shapes, one inside of the other.

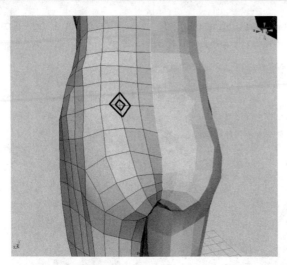

Figure 9-15

18. To finish, create and connect the angled edges to the corresponding vertices.

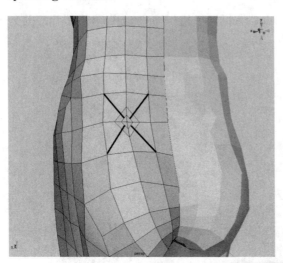

Figure 9-16

19. Let's go ahead and create two loops around the elbow using the Insert Edge Loop tool.

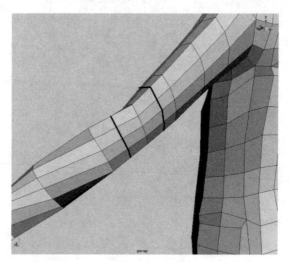

Figure 9-17

20. Now let's add an edge loop to help define the elbow.

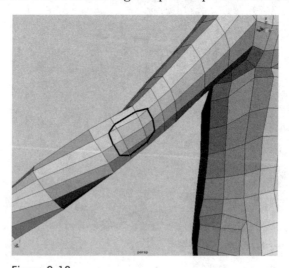

Figure 9-18

21. Go back and once again collapse the four angled edges and add an edge loop around the middle of the elbow.

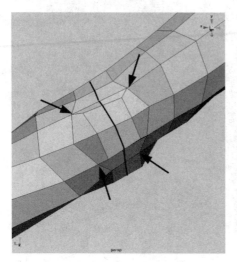

Figure 9-19

22. Rotate into a front view of the model. Using the Split Polygon tool, draw an edge loop that helps define the collarbone and bicep in one fell swoop.

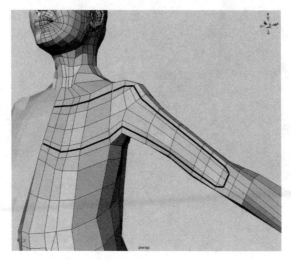

Figure 9-20

23. Collapse the two angled edges near the elbow.

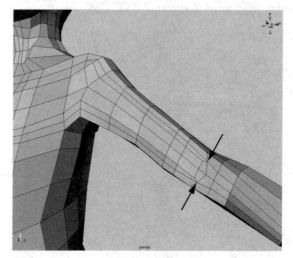

Figure 9-21

24. Moving down to the ankle, use the Insert Edge Loop tool to create two additional edge loops around the ankle.

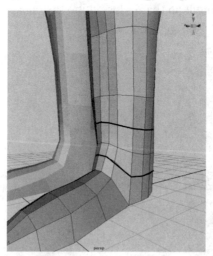

Figure 9-22

25. Now, use the Split Polygon tool to create an edge loop that circles the medial ankle bone.

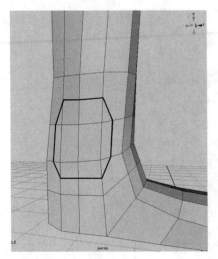

Figure 9-23

26. Once again, collapse all of the angled edges.

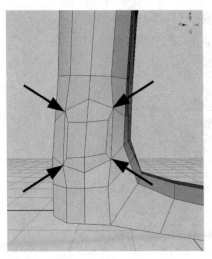

Figure 9-24

27. We also need to create an edge loop around the exterior protuberance of the ankle bone.

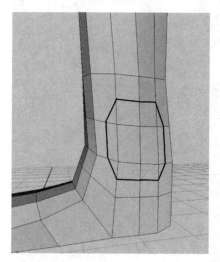

Figure 9-25

28. Collapse the angled edges.

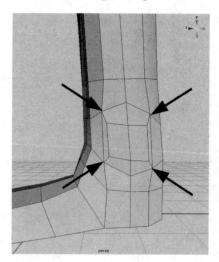

Figure 9-26

29. Create an edge loop that surrounds the ankle.

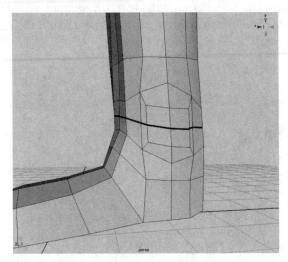

Figure 9-27

30. Add two additional loops around the calf.

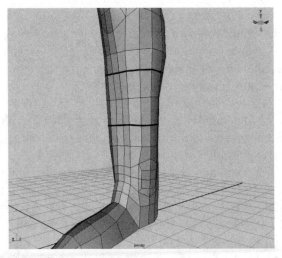

Figure 9-28

31. Using the Insert Edge Loop tool, we'll now add a few additional edge loops around the torso. Beginning near the stomach, add two edge loops that wrap around the middle of the figure.

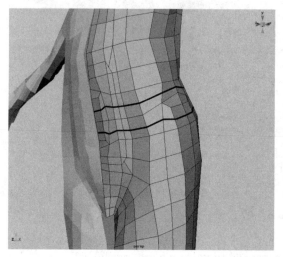

Figure 9-29

At this point, compare the geometry with the reference images to see where any adjustments are needed to get the proportions aligned. For instance, you may need to narrow the torso a bit by moving some vertices.

You can place these loops just about anywhere you need additional geometry to define your character. From well-defined muscles to horns sticking out of the character — anything is possible.

We should now have enough geometry to begin to really shape our character's body. This is where the Sculpt Geometry tool really comes into play. To begin with, we will want to add a smooth node to the geometry. Next, we will use the Sculpt Geometry tool on the higher-resolution model and then ultimately remove the smooth node to get back to our base geometry. The model will retain the shape of the sculpt, thus removing the need for major vertex tweaking. By utilizing this method you will become adept at quickly building the muscle shapes and other nuances of your character.

For lack of better terminology, I often refer to sculpted geometry areas as "bulges." This, of course, means the geometry that is pulled out from the surface of the model to define the muscles and bones.

As I stated earlier in the book, I prefer to work directly on the model, avoiding the Subdiv Proxy [v7: Smooth Proxy] altogether. I apply the smooth node directly on the base mesh and sculpt away. Then I remove the polySmoothFace node, go back to the original base mesh, and move vertices only where the Sculpt Geometry tool doesn't quite get the job done. The Go Tools toolbox contains buttons that make this process considerably easier. To delete the polySmoothFace node manually, you need to select the node in the Outliner (right-click in the Outliner and make sure that Show DAG Objects Only is deselected). Click on the polySmoothFace node and then click on Delete.

32. **Delete History and save!**

The Arm

So let's get moving. We'll begin with the arm. At this point we still want to avoid the hand.

1. With the geometry selected, choose **Mesh | Sculpt Geometry Tool** ❐ [v7: Edit Polygons | Sculpt Geometry Tool ❐]. We'll start out using the Pull operation. Set Auto Smooth to **4** and Max Displacement to **0.15**.

2. Beginning at the forearm, touch and release the geometry, trying to follow the direction of the edges. Continue around the entire forearm, making sure to rotate and check the geometry from numerous perspective views. If there are any areas you feel you've pulled out too far, switch to the Smooth operation to clean things up. In some cases where you need only minor smoothing, set the Displacement to a lower value, such as 0.005.

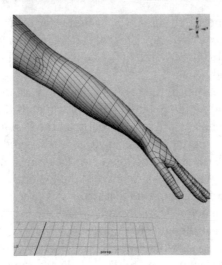

Figure 9-30

The best way to see your progress is to constantly refer to the mirrored geometry. Seeing the geometry in its shaded form without the wireframe will help you visualize the model as it will appear in its finished state.

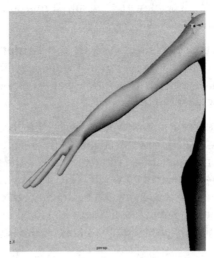

Figure 9-31

3. Try to subtly create the flow of the muscles as they wrap from the top of the elbow and around to the thumb.

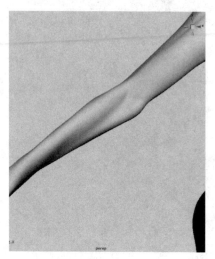

Figure 9-32

4. Also emphasize the bulge of the elbow on the bottom side of the arm.

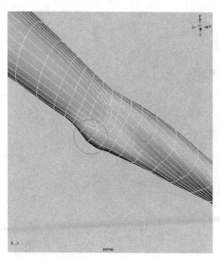

Figure 9-33

5. Move up the arm and pull the geometry to create the bicep.

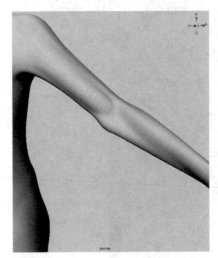

Figure 9-34

6. Move up and shape the top of the shoulder.

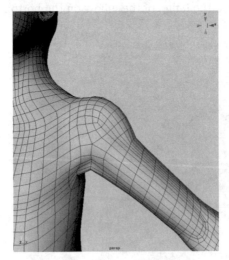

Figure 9-35

7. Subtly pull geometry along the top of the arm so that there is a slight dip at the top of the bicep.

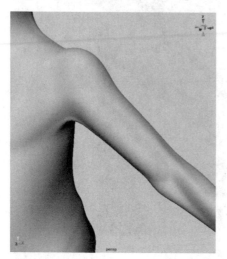

Figure 9-36

8. Rotate to the back of the figure and bulk up the arm a bit right above the elbow.

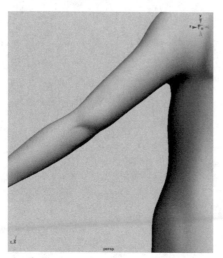

Figure 9-37

9. Move down and create a slight bulge at the back of the elbow.

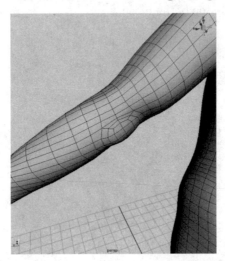

Figure 9-38

The Back

Now let's move over to address the back of our model. We'll want to give the scapula some definition. The scapula moves quite a bit in relation to the position of the arms. Because we won't set up our skeleton to animate the scapulas independently, we want to give them a natural appearance regardless of how the arms move.

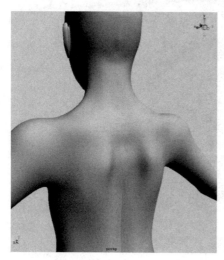

Figure 9-39

Remember as we go along that anytime the centerline of your model gets misaligned, you can go to Select | Select Border Edge Tool [v7: Edit | Select Border Edge Tool] and double-click on any center edge, then scale it back into its original position. With the Go Tools toolbox, use the Border Edge button and then Center Border Edge (right-click Border Edge) to center the edge automatically.

Now add a slight rise just left of the spine and slight bulge over the buttocks, just enough to see a glimpse of the indentation. Use the Push operation to the left of the bulge to make the bulge a bit more noticeable.

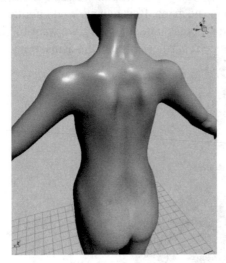

Figure 9-40

The Butt

1. Move down to the butt and switch back and forth between the Pull and Smooth operations. Be sure to refer to the mirrored side in a three-quarter view to get the form correct.

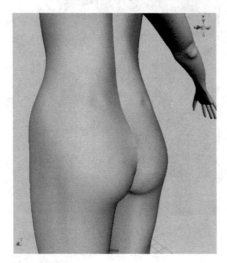

Figure 9-41

2. Take the sculpt as far as you can at this point to shape the posterior. This is an area that requires going back to the base mesh and moving points to get it to look as good as possible.

3. Let's remove the polySmoothFace node from our model. If you're not sure how to do this, refer to the section in Chapter 3 called "The Sculpt Geometry Tool." If you are using the Go Tools toolbox, (goModTools.mel) simply click on the **Delete Smooth** button under the Poly Extras tab.

4. Once you are back down to your base mesh, select the vertices at the center of the buttocks and move them into the body on the Z-axis.

Figure 9-42

5. Select the next row of vertices to the left and move them toward the center of the model on the X-axis.

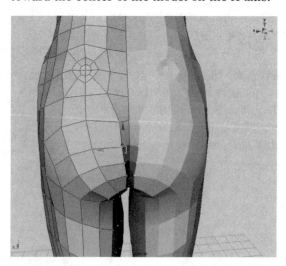

Figure 9-43

6. Move them in toward the body a slight bit on the Z-axis also.

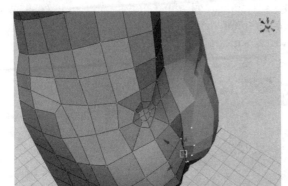

Figure 9-44

7. Adjust the vertices near the bottom of the butt so that there is a slight overlap where the cheek meets the leg on the inner part of the thigh.

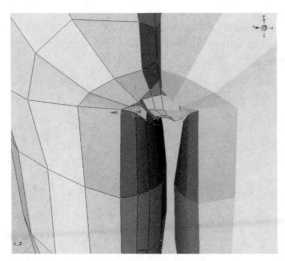

Figure 9-45

8. Switch to Object mode and then apply a new smooth node.
    Make any additional adjustments you feel necessary to get the
    buttocks to look right. It might take a bit of back and forth
    between sculpting and then moving vertices on your base
    model to get it just right.

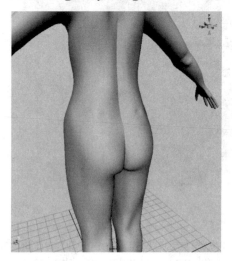

Figure 9-46

9. One important thing that adds a touch of realism is to add a bit
    of a bulge where the bottom of the cheek flows into the outer
    part of the thigh.

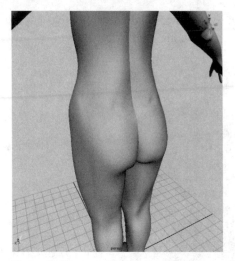

Figure 9-47

10. **Delete History and save!**

The Hips and Abdomen

1. Let's move over to the hip. The top of the pelvis (the iliac crest) will protrude slightly. Nudge it out in the front a bit as well.

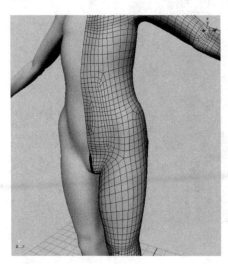

Figure 9-48

2. Move around to the lower abdomen and give it a bit of a bulge. Bulge out the pubic bone a bit as well.

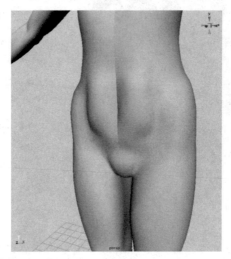

Figure 9-49

3. Moving up, define the upper abs, creating a slight indent near the right side of the stomach. Don't concern yourself with the navel at this point.

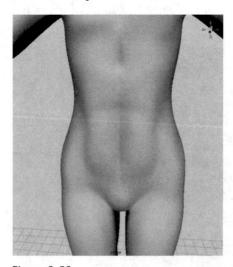

Figure 9-50

4. To accentuate the rib cage add a bulge to the right of center and then a bit in the center of the model.

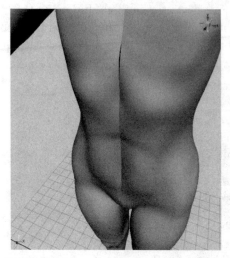

Figure 9-51

The Legs

1. Next, we'll move down to the thigh. Bulge out the front of the thigh so that it slightly overlaps the knee on the right. Also expand the thigh between the legs as well as the outer side.

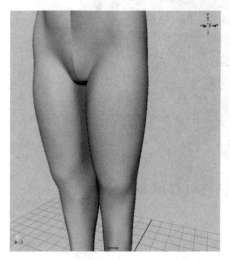

Figure 9-52

2. Now beneath that create a bulge for the knee.

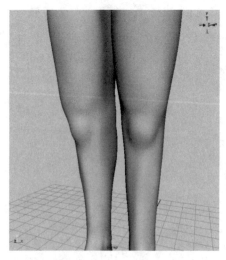

Figure 9-53

3. Give the inner thigh a slight rise, ending at a bulge on the inside of the knee.

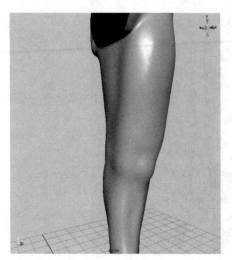

Figure 9-54

4. Expand the inside and outside of the calf.

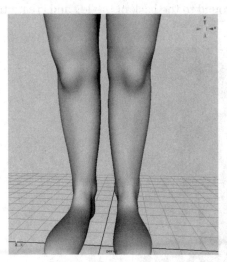

Figure 9-55

5. Create a bulge down the front of the calf to create the shin
    bone. Go back in with the Smooth operation to soften it up.

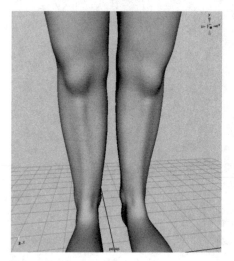

Figure 9-56

6. We'll catch up with the foot in the next chapter. Right now we
    will rotate around to the back of the leg and create the calf
    muscles.

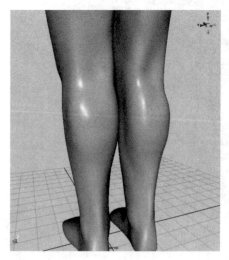

Figure 9-57

7. Directly below the calf muscle sculpt a narrow bulge down to
    the back of the heel to create the Achilles tendon. Notice from
    the image that the tendon is less noticeable near the calf and
    becomes more prominent as it flows down to the back of the
    foot.

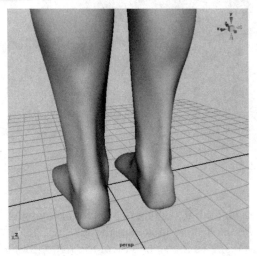

Figure 9-58

8. Working our way back up the leg, we will sculpt the ham-
    strings. The hamstrings are comprised of two muscle groups
    that extend down to wrap around the outer portion of the
    knees.

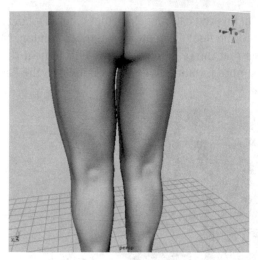

Figure 9-59

9. Also add a slight bulge along the length of the hamstring mus-
    cles on the inside and outside of the leg. Just for reference
    Figure 9-60 shows the right side of the figure (duplicate)
    moved back slightly so that you can see the interior portion of
    the thigh.

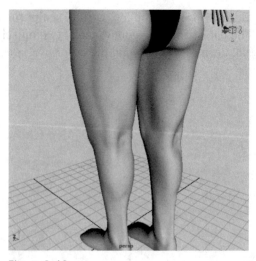

Figure 9-60

10. **Delete History and save!**

The Breasts

Now we need to go in and define the chest. We have intentionally waited to the end of the fleshing out phase to tackle this area. The breasts tend to be a difficult area to nail down. All too often we see the comic book approach to breasts. You know... the kind that defy gravity. To the dismay of some, we are going to lean toward a more natural and realistic approach for our model with a touch of artistic license. The important factor to achieving a natural look to the breasts is to remember that they overlap the rib cage. Unless the breasts are very small or surgically enhanced, like anything else they are affected by gravity.

1. Beginning with the base model, select the vertices under the arm near the pectorals and move them up on the Y-axis.

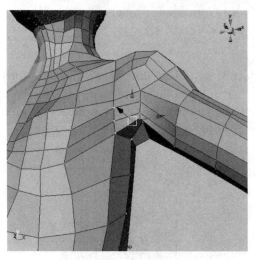

Figure 9-61

2. Select the nine faces on the chest as indicated in Figure 9-62.

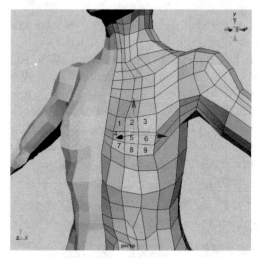

Figure 9-62

3. Select **Edit Mesh | Extrude** ☐ [v7: Edit Polygons | Extrude Face ☐]. When the option box opens, set Offset to **2.0**. Hit the **Apply** button and then the **Extrude Face** button to close the dialog. You should have two inset extrusions.

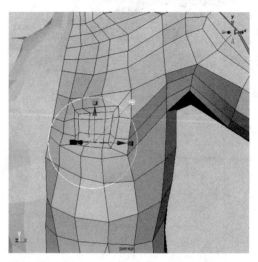

Figure 9-63

4. Switch to the Sculpt Geometry tool and use the Smooth operation to round out the spacing of the faces.

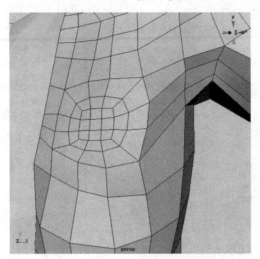

Figure 9-64

5. Select the vertices on the interior edge loops of the breast (see Figure 9-65). Select **Create | Sets ▸ Quick Select Sets** ☐. When the dialog opens, enter **breast** as the name of the set.

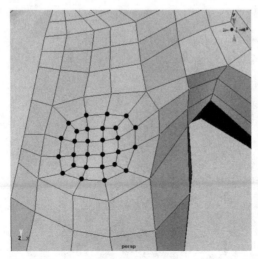

Figure 9-65

237

6. Switch to the Sculpt Geometry tool again and use it to bulge out the breast. Be sure to create a smooth transition between the upper part of the chest and the breast itself. You don't need to add a smooth node at this point.

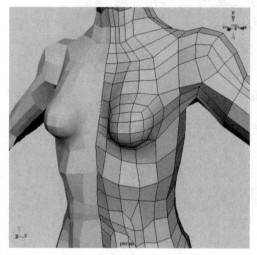

Figure 9-66

7. Select **Edit | Quick Select Sets ▸ breast**. Rotate the selected vertices on the Y-axis and then move them slightly to the right.

Figure 9-67

8. Use the Insert Edge Loop tool to add another edge loop around the breast.

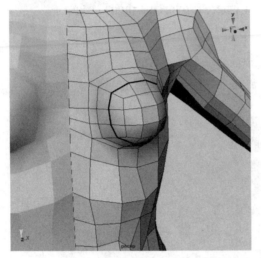

Figure 9-68

9. Select the four vertices under the breast and move them up on the Y-axis. You may need to move them back slightly on the Z-axis as well.

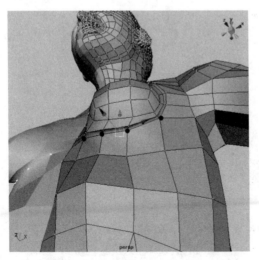

Figure 9-69

10. Now apply a smooth node to the figure. Use the Pull operation of the Sculpt Geometry tool to close the gap at the bottom of the breast where it overlaps the rib cage.

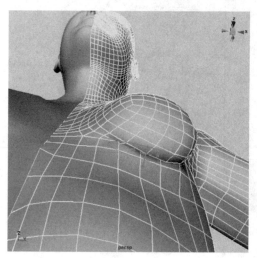

Figure 9-70

11. Use the Pull operation again to add some weight to the outside of the breast.

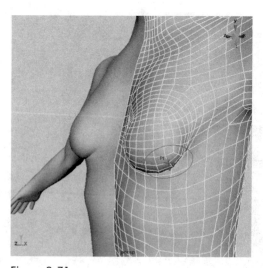

Figure 9-71

12. Rotate around so that you are looking at the side of the breast closest to the center of the model. Use the Smooth and Pull operations so that it resembles Figure 9-72.

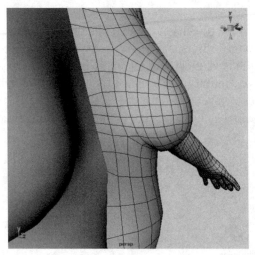

Figure 9-72

13. Continue to rotate around and look at the breast from various angles. Use the Smooth and Pull operations to continue increasing the size of the breast while keeping the geometry smooth. Be sure to refer to the shaded mirrored version of the model in the process.

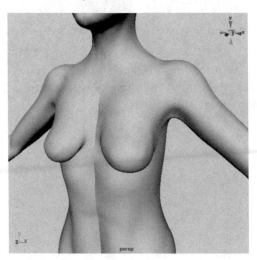

Figure 9-73

Getting a natural breast shape is surprisingly difficult, and it is important to study the breast from various positions. What may look fine from one angle will look considerably wrong from another.

14. Keep working the shape until you get a natural appearance from all angles. It may at times become necessary to switch back to the base mesh and manually move verts to get it perfect. If your intention is to make the breasts larger, build them up as much as you can with the existing geometry and then add edge loops only when the geometry no longer appears smooth.

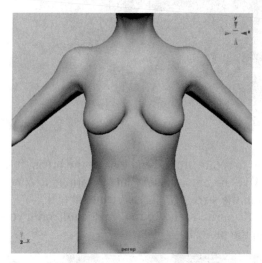

Figure 9-74

15. Once you have the breast shape completed, you can then add the nipples. Back up to your base mesh and select the nine faces on the front of the breast.

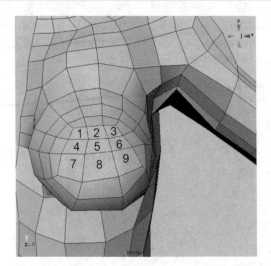

Figure 9-75

16. Select **Edit Mesh | Extrude** ☐ [v7: Edit Polygons | Extrude Face ☐]. When the option box opens, set Offset once again to **2.0**. Hit the **Apply** button three times. Leave the Extrude Face Options window open for now.

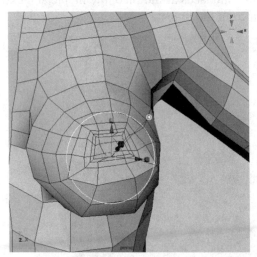

Figure 9-76

17. In Object mode, use the Sculpt Geometry tool with the Smooth operation. Set Max Displacement to **0.005**. Smooth the faces to round out the geometry.

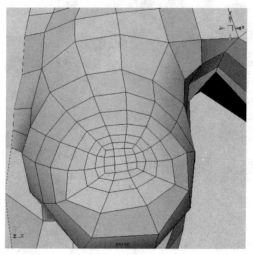

Figure 9-77

18. Select the nine faces at the tip of the nipple and extrude the faces out from the breast.

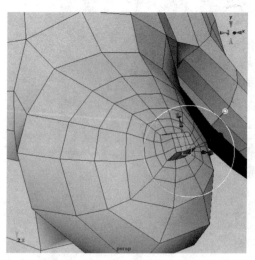

Figure 9-78

19. With the Insert Edge Loop tool, add two edge loops around the tip of the nipple.

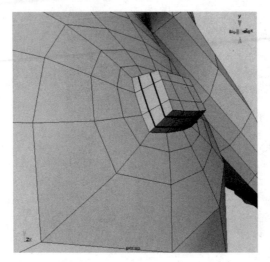

Figure 9-79

20. Apply a smooth node and then, concentrating on the tip of the nipple, use the Smooth operation of the Sculpt Geometry tool to round out the nipple.

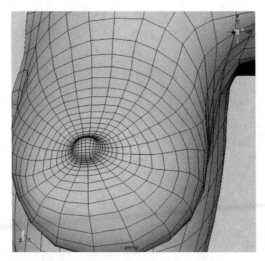

Figure 9-80

21. If you wish, you can add another loop around the outer edge of the areola to enhance the shape.

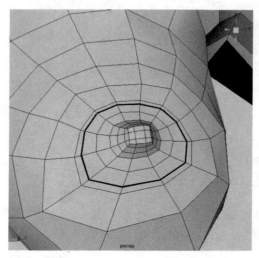

Figure 9-81

22. **Delete History and save!**

The Clavicles and Neck

When we built the head of our character we did a little preliminary work around the neck. Now, as we form the clavicles, we will address the neck in finer detail. The clavicles, in a similar fashion to the scapula, move considerably in relation to the movement of the arms. Because of that, they can be more prominently visible in certain positions and less so in others. Once again we'll take the middle ground approach and model them so that they look acceptable regardless of the position they are in.

So let's start with the base mesh and do a little preliminary work to set up the clavicles.

1. Select the seven faces that run down the side of the neck.

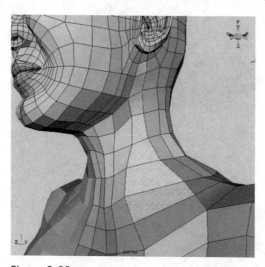

Figure 9-82

2. Select **Edit Mesh | Extrude** ⬜ [v7: Edit Polygons | Extrude Face ⬜]. Set Offset to **0.1** and then click **Apply**. Move the selected faces back into the neck of the model. Before closing the window, reset the Extrude Face settings back to the default.

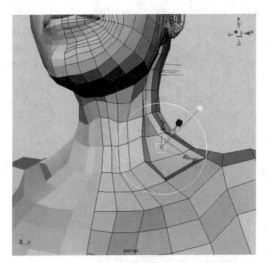

Figure 9-83

3. Next, select the two vertices near the bottom of the extrusion and pull them up a bit on the Y-axis.

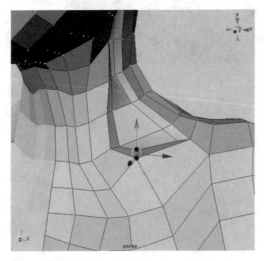

Figure 9-84

4. Select the three vertices to the right of center and pull them up a bit on the Y-axis as well.

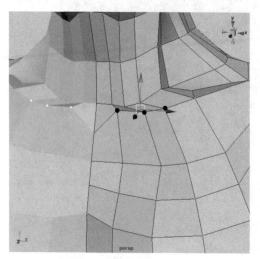

Figure 9-85

5. Move the vertex at the base of the neck down so that it lines up with the one below it.

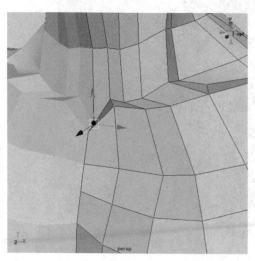

Figure 9-86

6. The next vertex should be moved up.

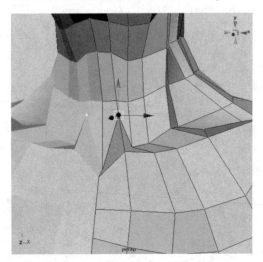

Figure 9-87

7. Add an additional edge loop right under the clavicle.

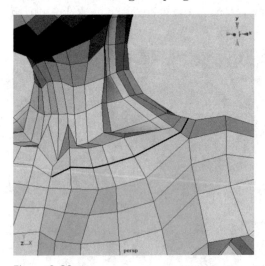

Figure 9-88

8. To create the sternocleidomastoid muscle, use the Pull operation, starting behind the jaw and ending in the middle of the base of the neck.

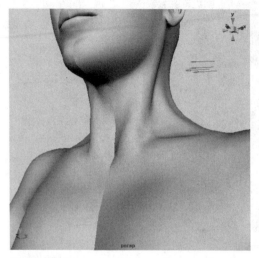

Figure 9-89

9. Now go back in and smooth the muscle, especially behind the jaw.

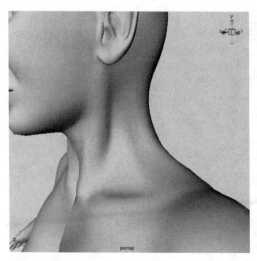

Figure 9-90

10. Continue to smooth the area between the sternocleidomastoid and the upper trapezius muscles.

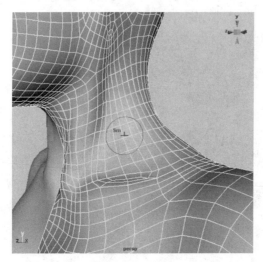

Figure 9-91

11. The clavicle has a slight bulge at the base of the neck where the two clavicles meet called the sternal facet. Use the Pull modifier to create the bulge.

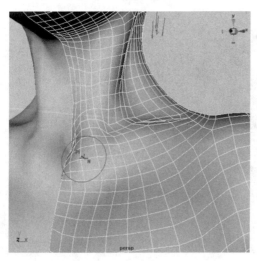

Figure 9-92

12. Use the Push operation to create a slight divot where the throat meets the sternal facet.

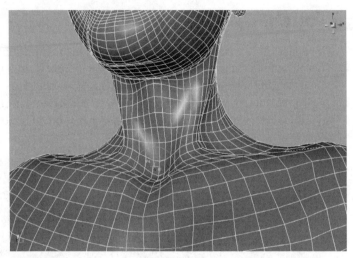

Figure 9-93

13. Beyond this you should use the Smooth operation to soften up the sternocleidomastoid and surrounding area so that they are not quite as exaggerated.

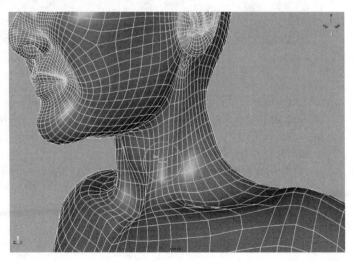

Figure 9-94

14. **Delete History and save!**

The Touch-Up

The last thing we'll do is the "touch-up." This means going back over the figure and touching up features here and there. This may include adding some additional edge loops that will help define the figure and aid in deformation. Feel free to add loops wherever you deem necessary; the butt and the upper arms would benefit from a few.

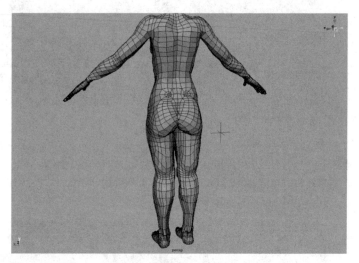

Figure 9-95

The addition of these new loops may not be necessary for your particular model. As far as I am concerned, when building a high-res model, a few extra loops here and there to make sure your surface is smooth certainly can't hurt.

You may have noticed that we have overemphasized some of the muscle groups. As a final tweak we will look to the reference images to nail down our particular model.

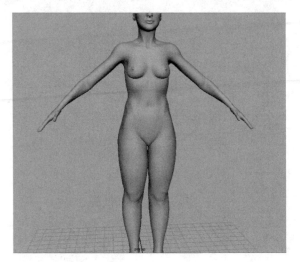

Figure 9-96

Take this step as far as you want. There is nothing written in stone that you can't deviate from your reference image. You're an artist, for crying out loud. Be artistic!

Wrap-Up

We're almost there! If you've made it this far you have good reason to be quite proud of yourself. In this chapter we used the Sculpt Geometry tool extensively to give our character a body to go along with her head. You should now realize how powerful the Sculpt Geometry tool is. You can change the look of a character in minutes — add muscle definition, give em' a potbelly, whatever.

The last thing we have to do in the modeling process is finish our model's hands and feet. From there we will combine the two halves of our character and give her the final touch-up, then it's off to texture land!

Hands and Feet

Refer to Chapter_10 on the companion CD.

Both the hands and the feet can be difficult areas to model. One thing people seem to have a lot of trouble with is adding enough geometry to create the hands and feet without adding unnecessary geometry to the arms and legs. I think once you are through this chapter you will find the process considerably easier. Remember, it's not rocket science; we just need to break things down into manageable steps.

The Hand

1. So, let's start with a little prep work. You can open Chapter10_start.mb from the companion CD. It contains a new image plane for the hand that references Lucy_hand.jpg in the Chapter 10\sourceimages folder.

2. For now we can hide the mirrored geometry and concentrate solely on the original. With your geometry selected, rotate the model 35 degrees on the Z-axis. This should put the model in a good position to work on the hand. We want the hand to be parallel to the ground plane.

Figure 10-1

3. To make things a bit easier, select all the faces that make up the hand to about midway up the forearm. Go to **Show | Isolate Selected ▸ View Selected**. The only thing showing in the viewport should be the faces you selected.

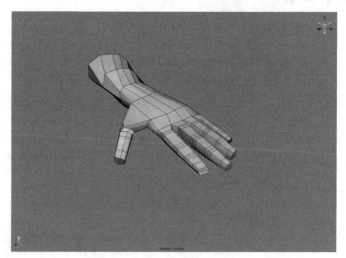

Figure 10-2

4. Because you have isolated a selected area, you may notice that the image plane is no longer visible. You can remedy this situation by first turning on the visibility of the hand_Image_L layer. The layer contains a polygon plane with the image of the hand applied. Select the plane along with the faces on the hand. When you isolate the selection you will still have the hand reference image available. Cheap, yes... but effective.

5. Begin by using the Sculpt Geometry tool to smooth the hand a bit so you have a generally clean flow of edge loops. Concentrate on the hand and not so much the fingers at this point.

6. Slide the row of vertices around the hand forward toward the fingers. Be sure to adjust the vertices on the top of the thumb as well.

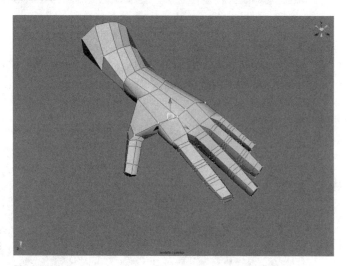

Figure 10-3

7. The next thing to do is to get the hand on our model to resemble the hand in our reference image. First add four edge loops around the thumb. After that, it is really a process of just digging in and moving vertices. Try to get your hand to resemble the image as closely as possible, but keep in mind that it doesn't need to be exactly the same. The most important thing to do is get the edge loops positioned evenly around the joints.

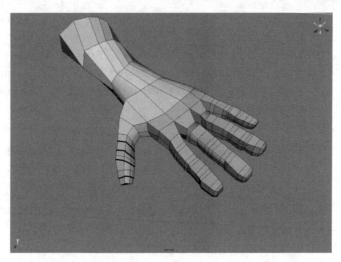

Figure 10-4

8. Getting the initial hand layout right can be tough, but once it's done, the rest should be pretty easy. If you need help with this step, look at Chapter10_template.mb.

9. Use the Insert Edge Loop tool to add a new edge loop around the wrist.

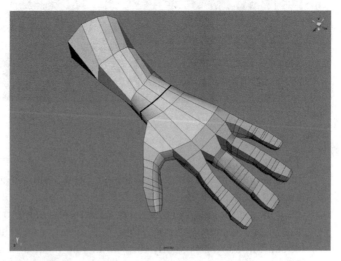

Figure 10-5

10. Add another loop that wraps around the tip of the thumb and around the hand.

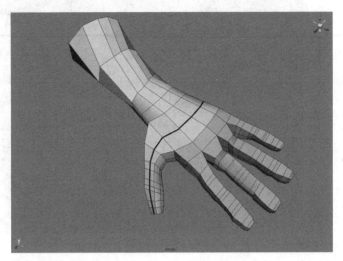

Figure 10-6

11. Select the faces on top of the index finger along with the three faces on the top of the hand. Using the Extrude tool, scale the selected faces uniformly with the center yellow cube on the manipulator so that they are inset from their original position.

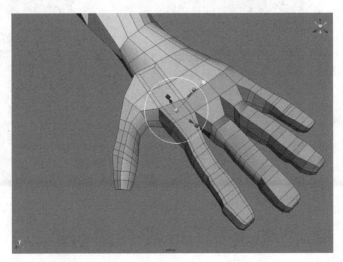

Figure 10-7

12. With the Extrude tool still selected, move the faces up a bit.

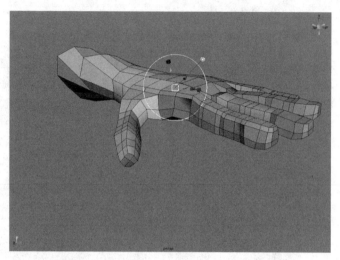

Figure 10-8

13. Repeat the process for the remaining three fingers.

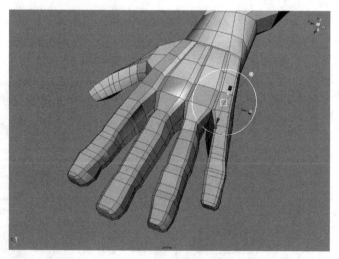

Figure 10-9

14. Use the Split Polygon tool to cut the start of an edge loop on the top of the hand near the wrist.

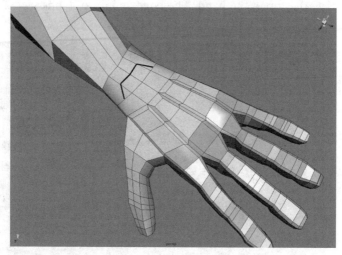

Figure 10-10

15. Create a similar cut on the palm of the hand near the wrist.

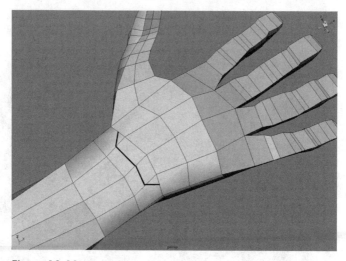

Figure 10-11

16. Use the Insert Edge Loop tool to create an edge loop that runs from the palm down around the tip of the pinky and then over the top of the hand. The edge should stop one face short of where you made the previous cuts.

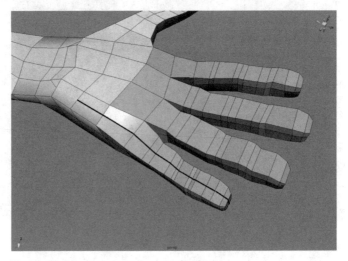

Figure 10-12

17. Create a similar loop around the tip of the index finger.

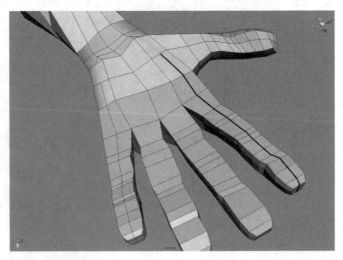

Figure 10-13

18. On the palm side of the hand, use the Split Polygon tool to connect the new edge loops to the previous cut you made.

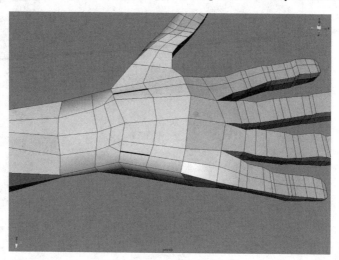

Figure 10-14

19. Cut an edge from the midpoint of each angled edge to the corresponding vertex to eliminate the triangles.

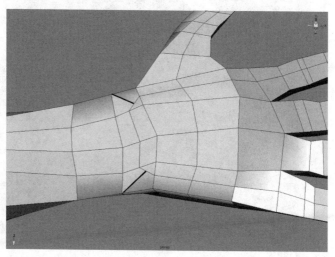

Figure 10-15

20. Flip over to the top of the hand and connect the edge loops as you did on the palm.

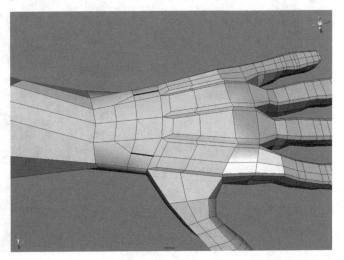

Figure 10-16

21. In this case, collapse the two angled edges.

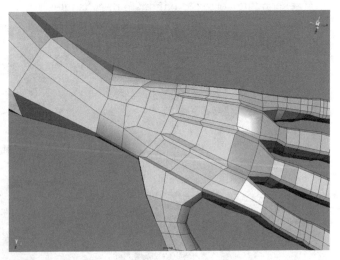

Figure 10-17

22. Next, cut a couple of new edges on the top of the hand inset from the previous loop.

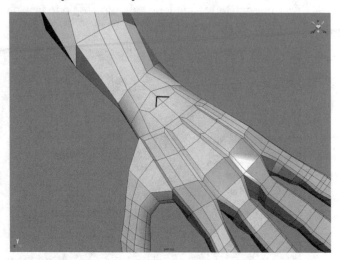

Figure 10-18

23. Do the same for the palm.

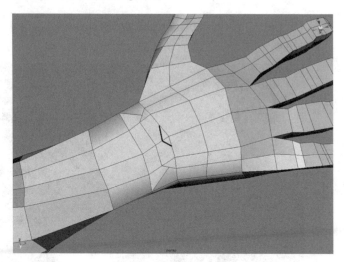

Figure 10-19

24. Create two additional edge loops — one down and around the tip of the middle finger, and one down around the tip of the ring finger. Both edge loops should stop one face short of the previous edges you created.

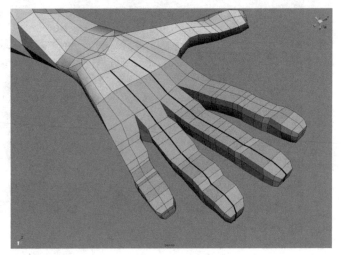

Figure 10-20

25. On the palm side of the hand, connect the ends of the edge loops.

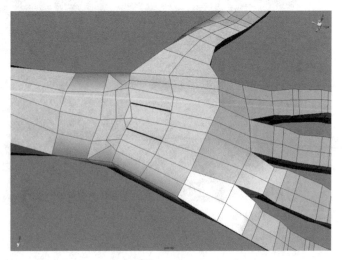

Figure 10-21

26. Cut an edge from the midpoint of each angled edge to the corresponding vertex to eliminate the triangles.

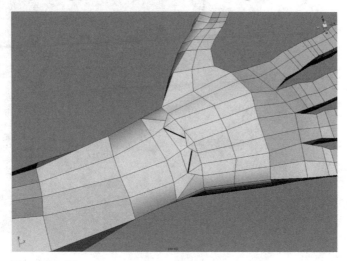

Figure 10-22

27. Flip over to the top of the hand and connect the edge loops.

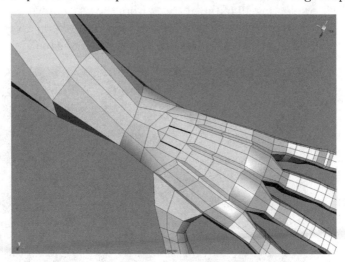

Figure 10-23

28. Once again, cut an edge from the midpoint of each angled edge to the corresponding vertex to eliminate the triangles.

29. **Delete History and save your file!**

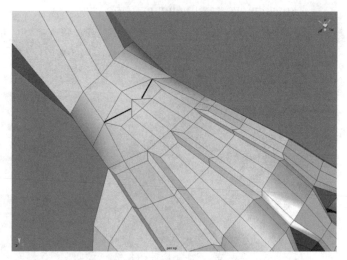

Figure 10-24

30. Now would be a good time to smooth out the geometry and shape it a bit before we add any additional geometry. Start by selecting all of the vertices from the wrist down. Select **Mesh | Average Vertices** ❑ [v7: Polygons | Average Vertices ❑]. When the options box opens, set Iterations to **2**.

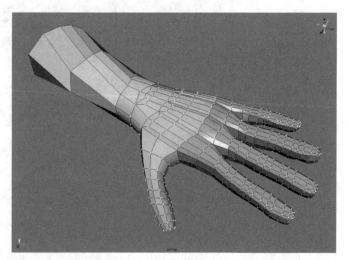

Figure 10-25

31. Next, we need to go in with the Sculpt Geometry tool. Set Max Displacement to **0.01**. Select the **Pull** operation and set Smooth Strength to **2**. It would benefit you to add a temporary smooth node to your geometry. This will make this step a bit easier.

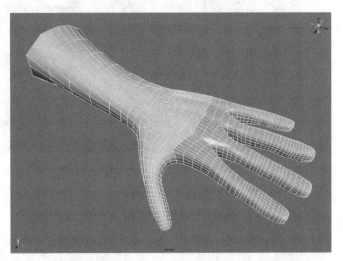

Figure 10-26

32. Start with the fingers. The amount of bulking up of the fingers will vary depending on the way you built the fingers to begin with. Regardless, work your way around the fingers with the Pull operation until you are satisfied with the size and general shape of each finger.

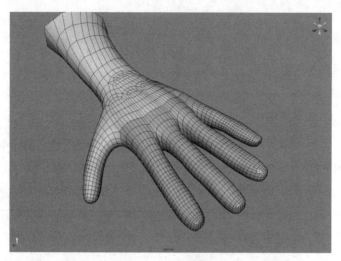

Figure 10-27

33. Move over to the thumb and bulk it up as well.

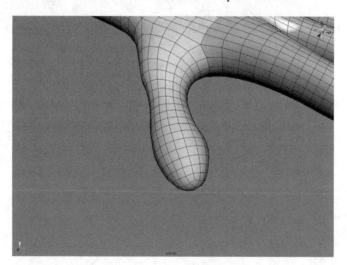

Figure 10-28

34. On the palm side of the hand, add a bit of a bulge from the base of the thumb to about the center of the hand.

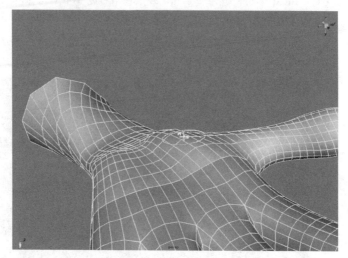

Figure 10-29

At this point the hand shape should be pretty well fleshed out. Take all the time you need to make sure the geometry looks good before we get caught up in the details.

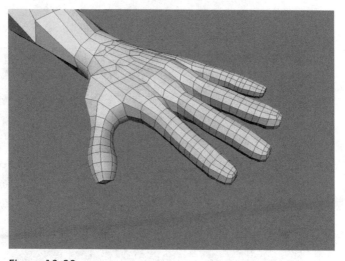

Figure 10-30

Hand Details

We want to work on the original geometry, so if you added a smooth node you will want to remove it before continuing.

1. Select the first three rows of faces on the top of the index finger along with the next row of faces below.

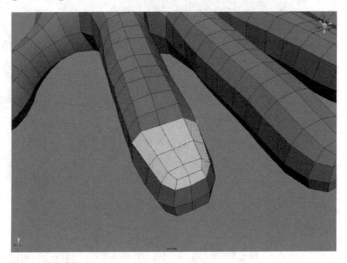

Figure 10-31

2. Use the Extrude tool to scale and inset the faces.

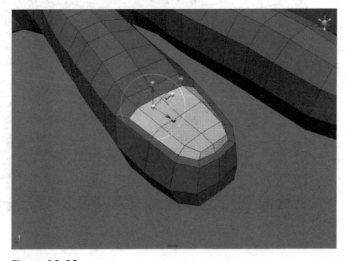

Figure 10-32

3. With the Insert Edge Loop tool, create a new edge loop around the nail bed.

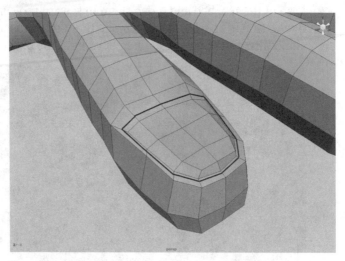

Figure 10-33

4. Select the four faces at the front of the nail and extrude them. You may need to switch the manipulator into world coordinates (little blue handle) to adjust the new geometry. You may also want to scale the faces down a bit.

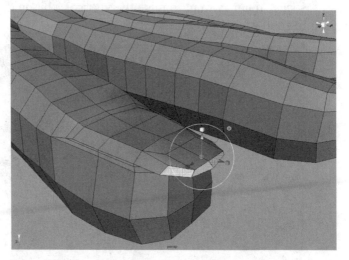

Figure 10-34

5. Now you will need to adjust the geometry a bit to give the nail its final shape. Select the two vertices on either side near the base of the nail bed and move them in toward the center of the finger. It may be necessary to move them forward as well. Generally, you are just rounding out the shape of the nail.

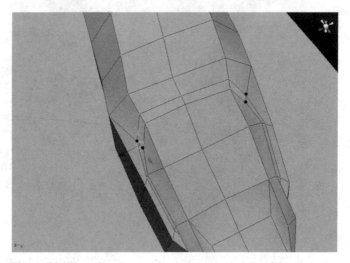

Figure 10-35

6. Move any additional vertices around to give the nail a nice shape. You may want to raise the vertices a bit on the center of the nail while you're at it.

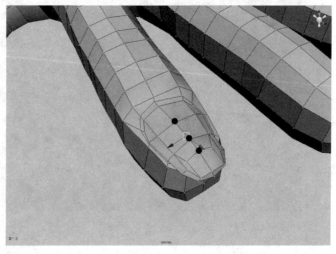

Figure 10-36

7. If you want to see a nice distinct border around the nail, you can add a few additional edge loops around it and further tweak the geometry.

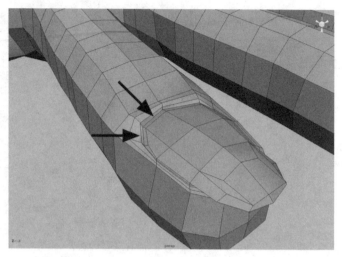

Figure 10-37

8. When you are satisfied with the nail, go back through and repeat this process for the remaining fingers.

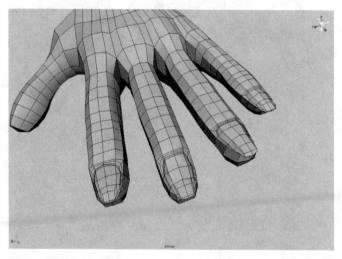

Figure 10-38

9. On to the thumb. There is a slight difference with the creation of the nail here. In this case we will only select the top faces to begin with.

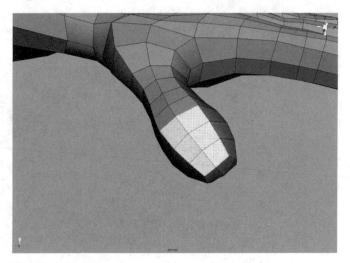

Figure 10-39

10. Extrude the selection and scale it down a bit.

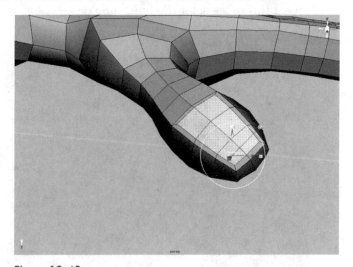

Figure 10-40

11. Create an edge loop around the nail bed.

Figure 10-41

12. Select the faces again and extrude them out with a slight inset.

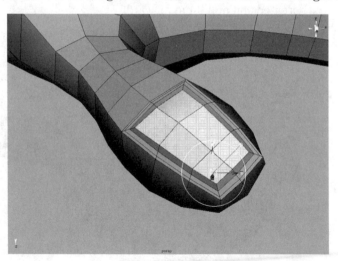

Figure 10-42

13. Create another loop around the thumbnail.

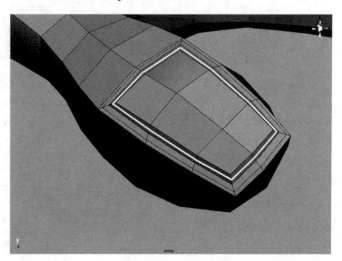

Figure 10-43

14. Select the three vertices at the front of the edge you just created and pull them forward.

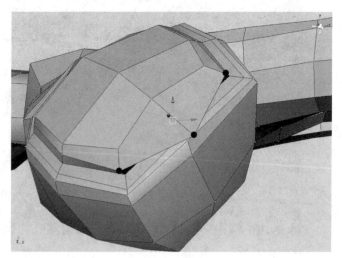

Figure 10-44

15. At this point, you need to adjust the geometry as you did with the fingernails to get the right shape. It may take a bit more tweak time because of the angle, but the same theory applies. As before, you can add additional edge loops if you want.

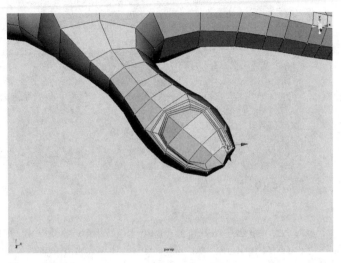

Figure 10-45

Right now we have a pretty serviceable hand, but in this business serviceable runs a distant second to cool, so we're not quite done yet.

16. Let's continue by adding another edge loop around the knuckles down around the palm.

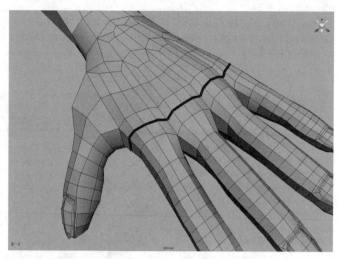

Figure 10-46

17. Next, select the edges or vertices between each of the knuckles on the hand and move them down slightly.

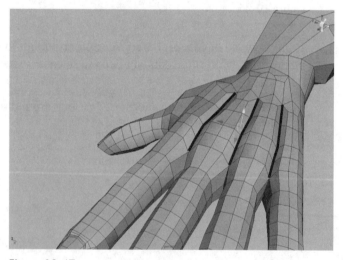

Figure 10-47

18. Select the faces along the top of each finger and use the Extrude tool to scale them inset and then up a bit.

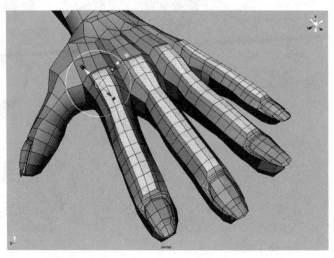

Figure 10-48

19. Use the Insert Edge Loop tool to add an edge loop at the base of each finger.

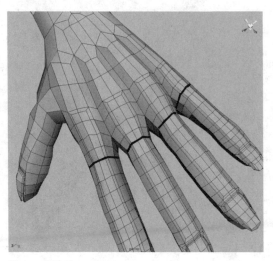

Figure 10-49

20. Add another loop around the base of the thumb.

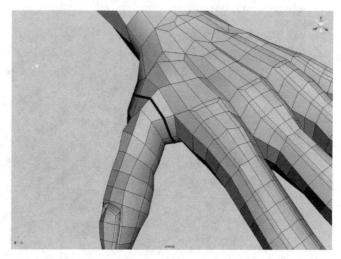

Figure 10-50

21. Continue to use the Insert Edge Loop tool to add two more edge loops through the tip of the thumb and around the hand.

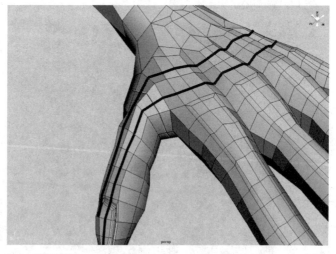

Figure 10-51

22. Add three additional edge loops around the wrist.

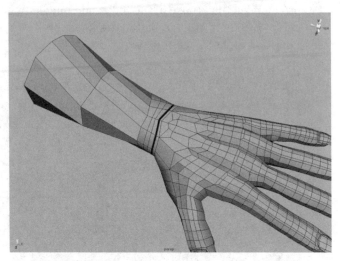

Figure 10-52

23. Let's once again use the Sculpt Geometry tool to bring out some details. Start by smoothing out the knuckles on top of the hand so that the edge loops of the knuckles are evenly rounded.

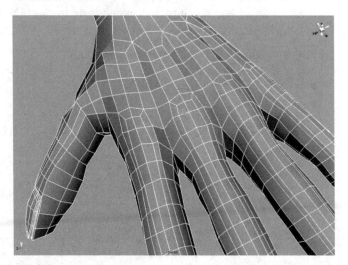

Figure 10-53

24. The knuckles for the ring and pinky fingers are generally less pronounced than those of the index and middle finger. Use the Sculpt Geometry tool to flatten the knuckles down with the Push and Smooth operations.

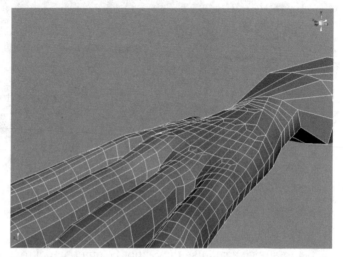

Figure 10-54

25. Bulge the knuckles up slightly on the index and middle knuckle. Then switch to Vertex mode and select the four vertices behind each knuckle and move them up slightly.

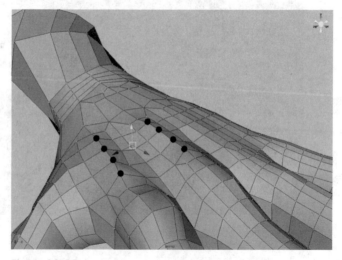

Figure 10-55

26. Flip the hand over so that we can make some adjustments to the palm. If you cup your hand you will realize that the first knuckle of each finger as well as the thumb reside more in the palm of the hand. Because of this we will need to move some of the vertices to accommodate this movement.

27. First, select the row of vertices near the fingers and slide them forward. Make sure you are not accidentally selecting vertices on the top of the hand; only select the vertices on the palm.

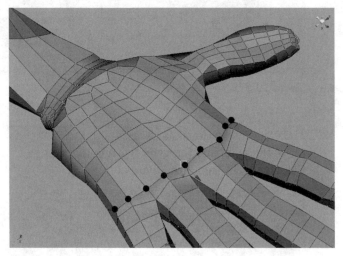

Figure 10-56

28. Adjust the next two rows down so that they look like those in Figure 10-57.

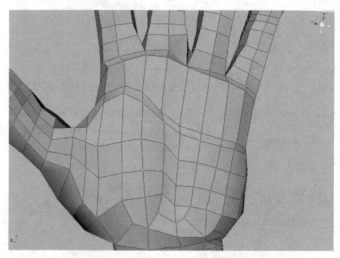

Figure 10-57

29. Make some additional adjustments to the vertices in the center of the palm and then add two additional edge loops around the palm to even out the geometry.

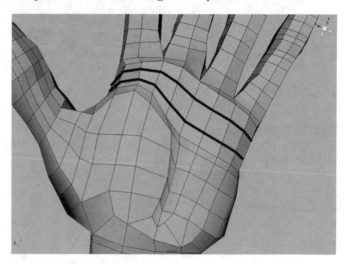

Figure 10-58

30. Next, rotate around so that you are looking at the pinky side of the hand. Select the four rows of faces on the outside of the wrist and extrude them once to give us enough geometry to create the bulge for the wrist bone.

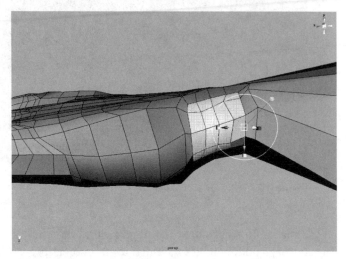

Figure 10-59

31. Let's use the Sculpt Geometry tool one last time. Just rotate around the hand and look at it from different angles. You may need to bulk up the outside of the hand near the wrist as well as round out the wrist bone. Once again, try adding a smooth node during the sculpting process.

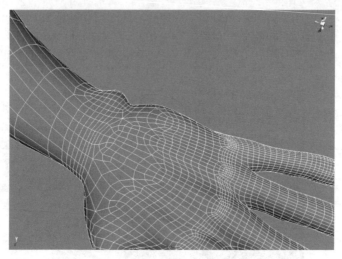

Figure 10-60

32. Take some additional time to go around the fingers as well, perhaps adding a bit of a bulge to the fingertips.

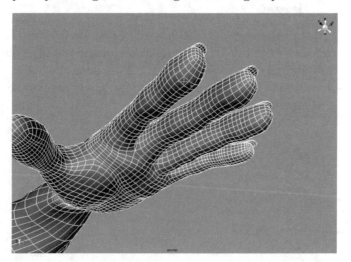

Figure 10-61

33. It's also kinda cool to add a bit of a bump here or there randomly on the top of the hand to give the impression of veins.

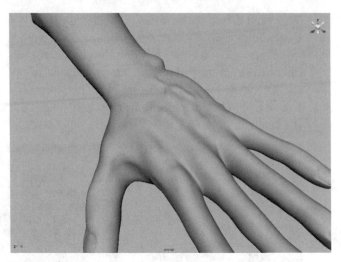

Figure 10-62

34. The last thing we will want to do is make sure the edge loops around the fingers are set up to deform properly. With all of the sculpting we have done, some of the loops may have moved. The easiest way to fix this is to simply add new edge loops around the knuckles. Don't forget about the thumb.

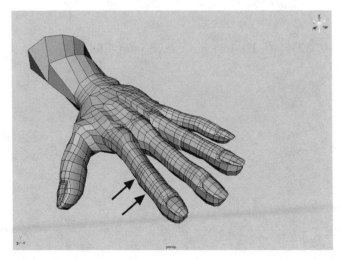

Figure 10-63

The hand is one of the areas that can vary greatly in detail depending on your needs. For example, you would have less detail on a gloved hand than one that was bare. You can go all out with geometry, adding in details such as the wrinkles on the knuckles, folds of the palm, etc. The alternative would be to use a bump or displacement map to handle the finer details; it's really up to you.

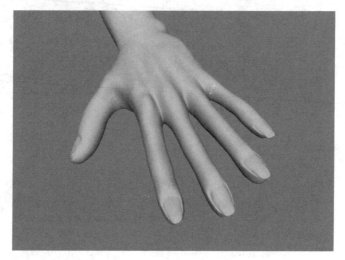

Figure 10-64

35. **Delete History and save your file!**

The Foot

Now that the hand is complete, unhide the geometry and rotate it back into its original position to begin work on the foot. We will step (ha, ha... get it... foot... step!) through the process in much the same way we did the hand. As I mentioned earlier in the book, we will be tackling the foot in more detail by adding toes.

For the most part, the characters I build have some sort of footwear. It is rare to see a character with bare feet. The exception may be some sort of creature like a woodland tree fairy or a two-toed sloth monster.

Regardless, you never know when you will need a detailed foot geometry. Because we are dealing with the classic nude figure, our model will most definitely need some feet.

1. To begin with, let's select the faces from about midway down the calf and around the foot. As we did with the hand, isolate the selection by going to **Show | Isolate Selected ▸ View Selected**. There is a polygon plane containing the foot image for reference on the CD (Lucy_foot.jpg in Chapter 10\sourceimages).

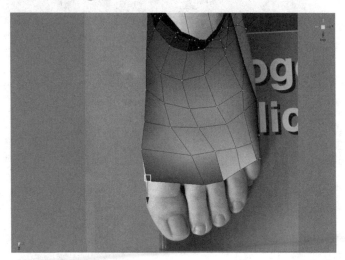

Figure 10-65

2. Remember that since we are adding toes to our model, we will more than likely have to adjust the foot geometry to accommodate the toes. Basically, we want the front of the foot to line up directly behind the toes.

3. Next, we will need to adjust the geometry to line up with the toes. Start with the big toe and the next two toes. Align the vertices so that they are in between each toe.

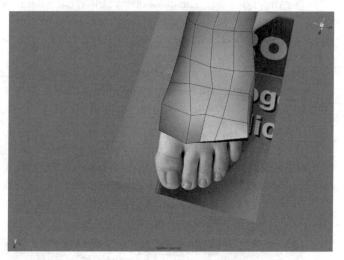

Figure 10-66

4. As you adjust the vertices, evenly space the vertices on the top and bottom of the foot as well.

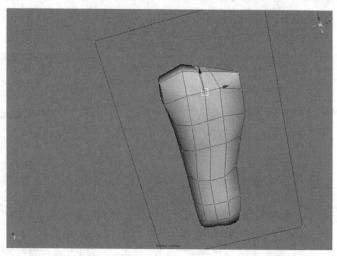

Figure 10-67

5. Select the two front vertices on the outside of the foot and slide them over so that they sit between the pinky toe and the next toe over.

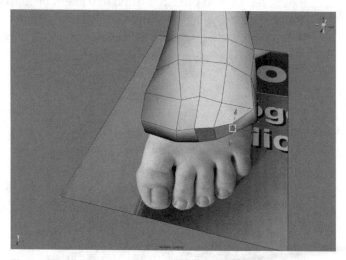

Figure 10-68

6. Select the five faces on the front of the foot and extrude them separately.

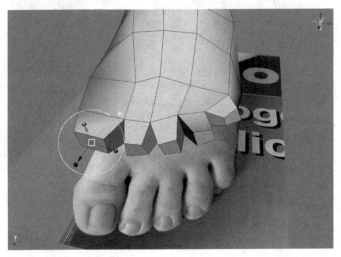

Figure 10-69

7. Select the face on the big toe and extrude it once to the knuckle, and then again to the tip of the toe. Adjust the vertices to match the reference as well as you can at this point.

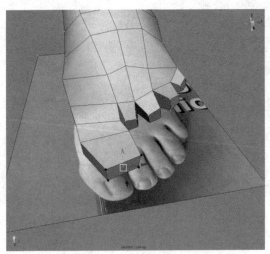

Figure 10-70

8. Repeat the process for each of the toes. First extrude to the knuckle, then out to the tip. Rotate around the foot and shape the toes a bit as well.

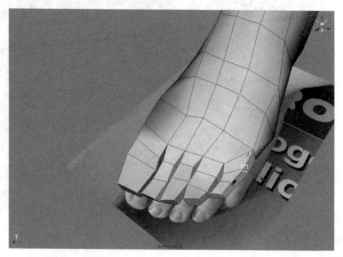

Figure 10-71

9. Use the Split Polygon tool to create a single edge on the outside of the foot.

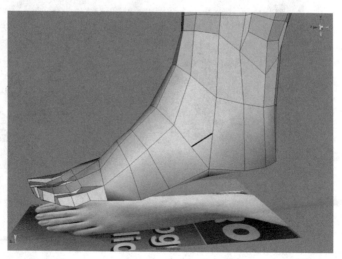

Figure 10-72

10. Create one on the inside of the foot as well.

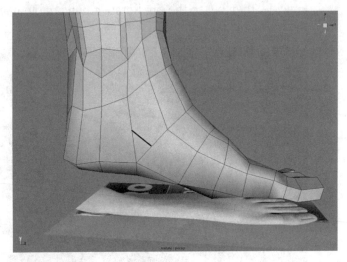

Figure 10-73

11. Use the Insert Edge Loop tool to create an edge loop that wraps around the toes and stops one face short of the edges you just created.

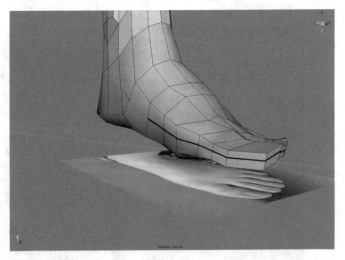

Figure 10-74

12. Create another loop that wraps around the back of the foot.

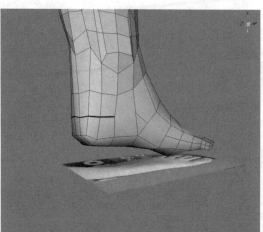

Figure 10-75

13. On the inside of the foot, use the Split Polygon tool to connect the edge loops to the single edge.

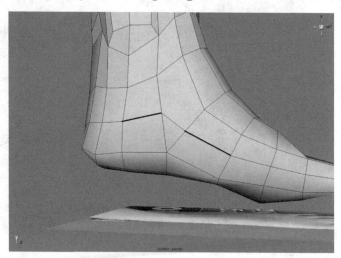

Figure 10-76

14. Collapse the middle edge to create a quad.

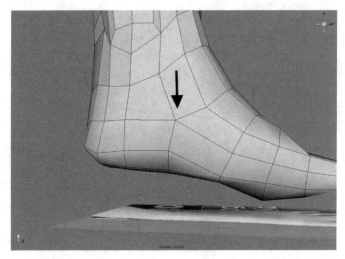

Figure 10-77

15. Repeat this process for the outside of the foot.

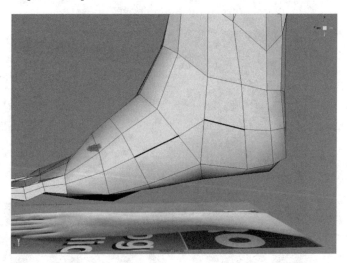

Figure 10-78

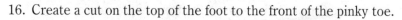

16. Create a cut on the top of the foot to the front of the pinky toe.

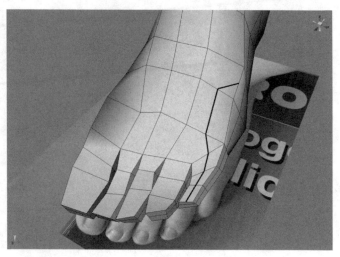

Figure 10-79

17. Create the same cut on the bottom of the foot.

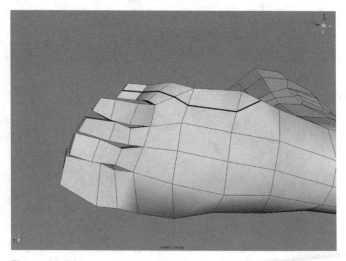

Figure 10-80

18. Connect the edge on the front of the toe.

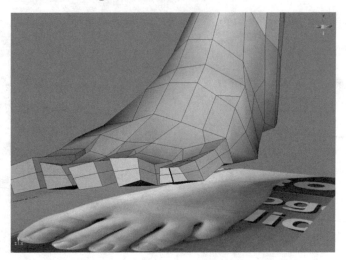

Figure 10-81

19. Connect the edge on the side of the foot as well.

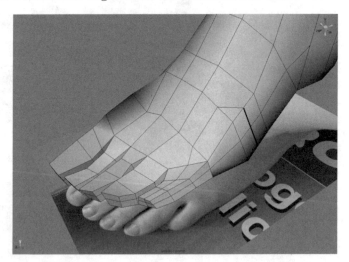

Figure 10-82

20. Select the angled edge on the front and top of the foot closest to the toe and collapse it.

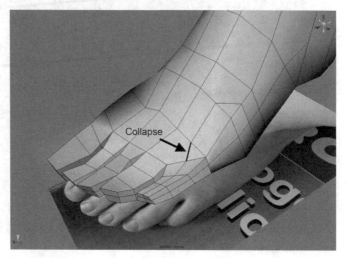

Figure 10-83

21. Collapse any other angled edges on the foot and then use the Sculpt Geometry tool to even out the geometry.

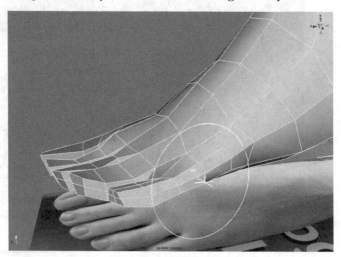

Figure 10-84

22. Create a new cut on the top of the foot.

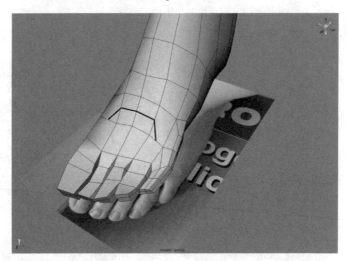

Figure 10-85

23. Create a similar cut on the bottom of the foot near the heel.

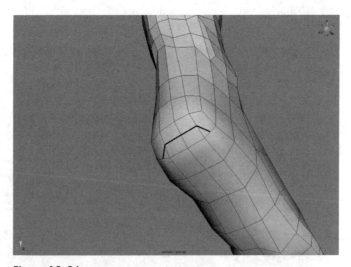

Figure 10-86

24. Use the Insert Edge Loop tool to create an edge loop over the big toe, stopping one face before the two previous cuts on the top and bottom of the foot.

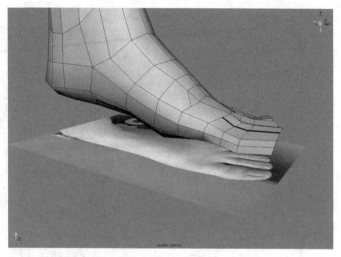

Figure 10-87

25. Create an edge loop over the toe next to the pinky toe. This should follow the same path as the last edge loop, stopping short of the edges you created.

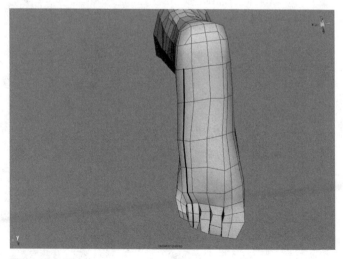

Figure 10-88

26. Connect the edge loops on the top and bottom of the foot. Once you have the loops connected, collapse those angled edges (the two on the top of the foot as well as the two on the heel).

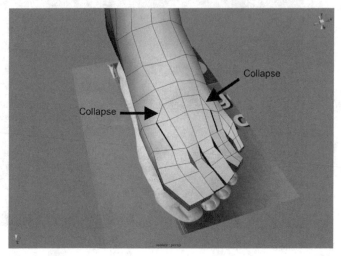

Figure 10-89

27. Create a new edge loop over the top of the second and third toes.

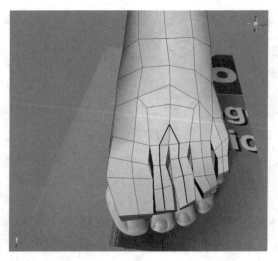

Figure 10-90

28. Add a cut to the back of the foot where you created the previous edge loop.

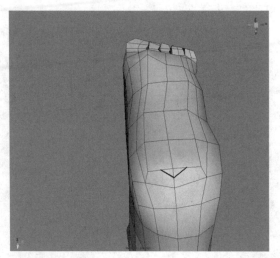

Figure 10-91

29. Use the Insert Edge Loop tool to create two loops that wrap around the two toes, stopping short of the edges.

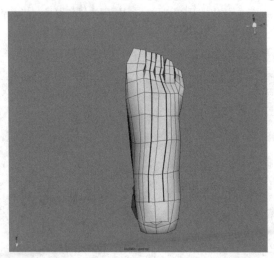

Figure 10-92

30. On the bottom of the foot, connect the edges and then draw edges from the center of the angled edges to the corresponding vertices.

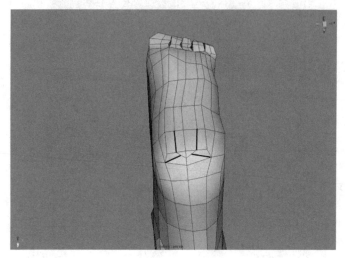

Figure 10-93

31. Back on top, connect the edges on the front of the toes and then create edges from the center of the angled edges to the corresponding vertices.

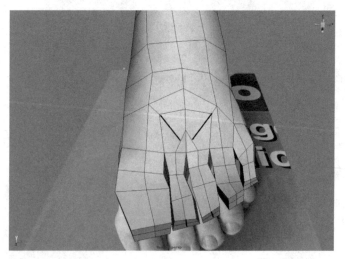

Figure 10-94

32. Add two edge loops around each of the toes, one around the middle and then one around the tip.

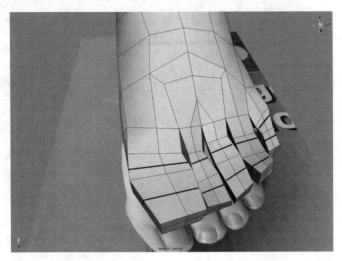

Figure 10-95

33. **Delete History and save your file!**

Foot Details

1. As we have done so many times before, let's break out the Sculpt Geometry tool and use it to smooth out and shape our foot. Apply a temporary smooth node and then rotate around and concentrate on rounding the heel as well as the ball and outside of the foot.

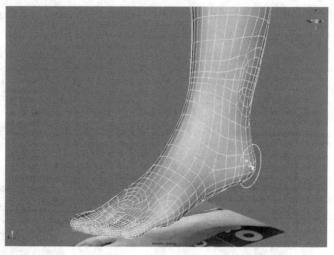

Figure 10-96

2. On the inside part of the foot, you may want to add a slight instep or arch.

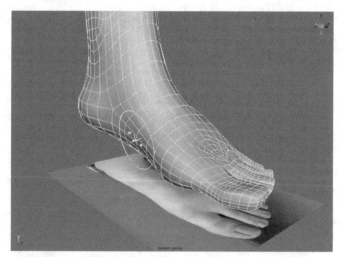

Figure 10-97

3. Approach the toes with a bit of caution. Concentrate more on the top and bottom, being careful not to intersect the sides too much. Start with the big toe and bulk up the top a bit.

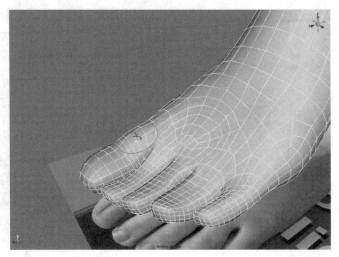

Figure 10-98

4. With the rest of the toes, try to bulk up the knuckles more than the tips.

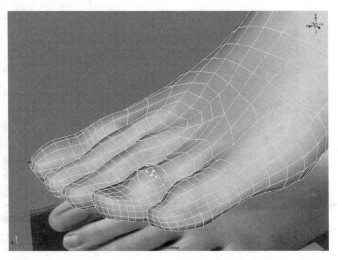

Figure 10-99

5. On the bottom of the toes, take the opposite approach by bulking up the toes and smoothing or at times pushing the geometry where it meets the foot.

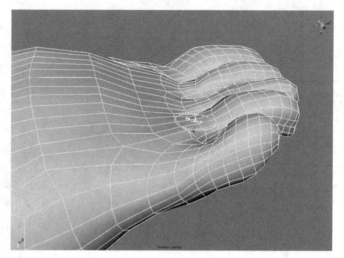

Figure 10-100

6. Bulk up the ball and smooth over any rough spots on the bottom of the foot.

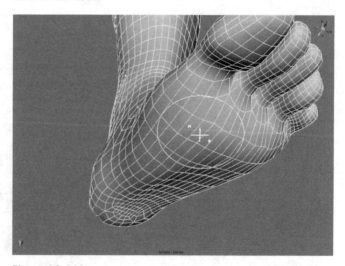

Figure 10-101

7. Remove the polySmoothFace node so that you are back to the base mesh.

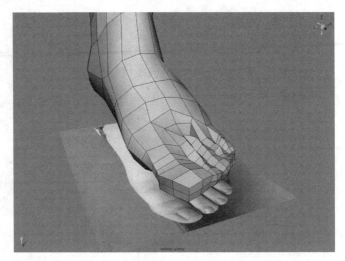

Figure 10-102

8. We'll create the toenails in the same way we did the fingernails. Start with the big toe by selecting the four faces on the top and extruding them inset from their original position.

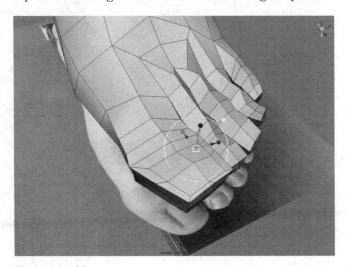

Figure 10-103

9. Create an edge loop around the nail with the Insert Edge Loop tool.

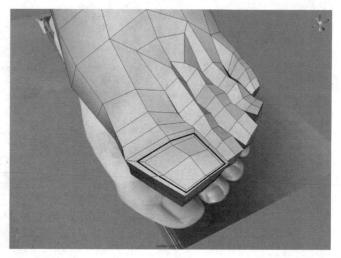

Figure 10-104

10. Select and extrude the four faces again, this time pulling them forward a bit.

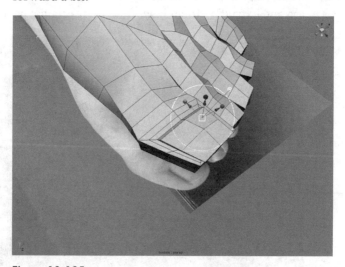

Figure 10-105

11. For the rest of the toes, select only the first two faces and extrude them in.

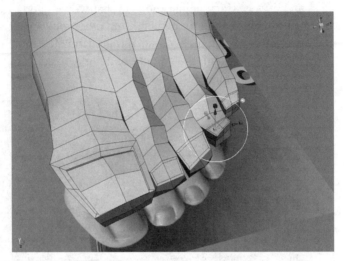

Figure 10-106

12. Extrude the faces once more, then add an edge loop around each of the nails.

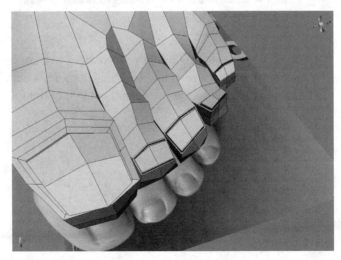

Figure 10-107

13. Take a few minutes to move the vertices to round out the toe-nails. Add a few more edge loops around the foot and ankle and, if necessary, adjust them so that we will get a clean deformation when the foot bends. From here you can add as much geometry as you feel you need to enhance the look of the foot. Just like the hand, the amount of detail you add will vary greatly from model to model.

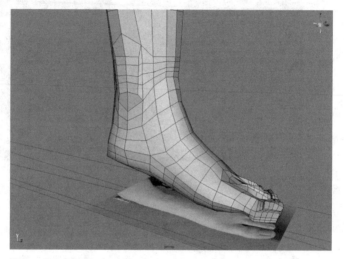

Figure 10-108

14. Because of all the sculpting we have done you may need to move the ankle down a bit. As a final step, let's bulk up the ankle bone on both the inside and outside of the foot.

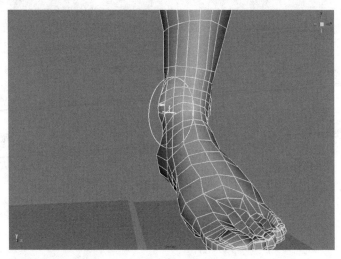

Figure 10-109

Wrap-Up

So guess what? In this chapter we added hands and feet to our figure, and that pretty much puts a wrap on the modeling phase! With the completion of nice hand and foot geometries, you have added a couple of reusable parts to your library.

The one thing that should be evident from this chapter is that we can add a lot of geometry to one part, such at the hand, without having to add any unnecessary geometry to the connecting arm. This is accomplished by redirecting the path of an edge loop so that you dictate the direction of the flow.

For additional examples of extra geometry used to enhance the hands and feet, see the file Chapter10_completeB.mb. The model contains hand and feet geometry that show what can be done in the way of adding detail.

Fine-Tuning the Model

That Perspective Thing

Refer to Chapter_11 on the companion CD.

So now we have reached the final stages of the modeling process. Up until now we have worked directly from reference images and a stand-in skeleton to get a complete character model. It would seem pretty logical that our character should have a resemblance to the reference images. This is true to a certain extent.

Somewhere back when we set up our reference I said that when using photos for reference we need to take perspective into account. Because we used orthographic view planes to create the geometry, certain features of our model may appear quite a bit larger than the reference images.

For instance, remember how we adjusted the image plane to build the ear? That was just one of the things that need to be accounted for when achieving a likeness. This is due in part to the fact that we never actually see people in an orthographic sense.

So what exactly does that mean? Well, if we exaggerate the point, it would be like looking at someone through a fish-eye lens.

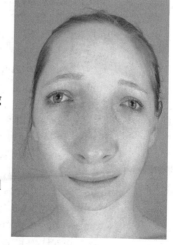

Figure 11-1

Notice how the nose looks larger and the rest of the features, such as the eyes, seem farther apart and farther away. As I said, this is an exaggeration, but the same thing occurs on the regular image to a lesser degree.

So when we created the geometry, we used orthographic views with perspective images. Therefore, our features are larger in the flat orthographic view, and when we look at the model in perspective, the features appear twice as large as they should be.

About the best way to get a head shot that has very little perspective is to stand about 30 feet away from your subject and use a telephoto lens. This obviously isn't always a possibility, especially if you are, say, trying to build a model of a famous person. You have to make do with what you've got.

So this is where your keen eye as an artist comes into play. On the companion CD you will find a variety of head shots in various positions in the sourceimages folder of Chapter 11. This, along with one little factoid, should get you through the tweaking phase.

So what I have found is this: The features in an orthographic view should be roughly half the size as they appear in a perspective view. Now this isn't written in stone, because any photo you use for reference could use any variety of camera settings, but for the most part, it is a good place to start. To make the process a bit easier, you can refer to or load up Chapter11\images\11-002.jpg in the front image plane. This will give you an idea of what the head would look like with no perspective.

There is still more tweaking involved beyond that, such as compar-

Figure 11-2

ing your model to reference images and using an artistic eye. This perception cannot be learned by reading a book; it takes practice just like anything else. If you are having trouble, try to get an opinion from someone else. When you get wrapped up in a project, sometimes it is hard to step back and take a good objective look.

Combine

When you feel satisfied with your tweaking, we will take the next giant step of combining the two halves of your model. This can always be a little intimidating. It feels so final! Rest assured that if you really need to go back and make adjustments, you can always remove one side of the body and mirror your geometry again.

1. Before we combine our model we need to make sure the center border edge is on a straight vertical path.

2. Select both halves of the geometry and select **Mesh | Combine** [v7: Polygons | Combine]. You now should have one piece of geometry.

    There is one more thing to account for though. There is a seam directly down the center of the model.

3. In a front view, zoom in and go to **Select | Select Border Edge Tool** [v7: Edit | Select Border Edge Tool] to select an interior edge from each half of the model. The entire border edge will be highlighted.

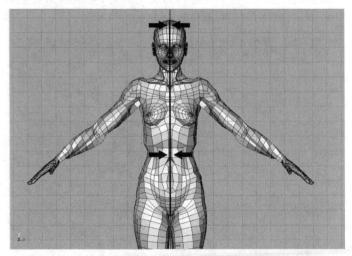

Figure 11-3

4. Select **Edit Mesh | Merge** [v7: Edit Polygons | Merge]. The separate halves of the geometry are now sewn together as one.

Congratulations! You have a complete model.

Finishing Touches

Our model at this point is perfectly symmetrical. If you look closely at the face of our reference, however, you will notice that there are distinct differences between the right and left sides. This asymmetry needs to be evident in our model as well to really make her look realistic. This is another area where observation is key. If it helps, you can bring the front image into a photo editing program and draw horizontal guidelines to see how the features differ from one side to the other.

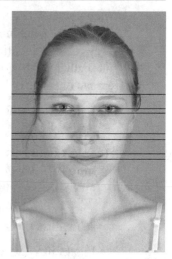

Figure 11-4

Make adjustments as necessary. This will help to sell the likeness. Even if you created a model that appears to have symmetrical features, you should still go in and add a few asymmetrical touches here and there.

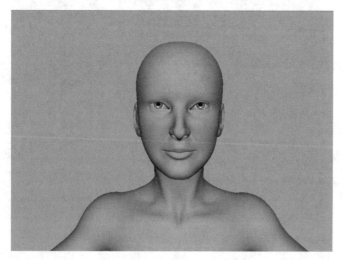

Figure 11-5

Wrap-Up

So that's it. We have completed the modeling process. Hopefully, you are satisfied with the results. In this chapter we learned the very important lesson of compensating for perspective and using an artistic eye to get a likeness. Obviously, textures play a major role in selling your character, so we will be discussing that in the next chapter.

Once again, it is beneficial to have someone else look at your model to give you an outsider's perspective on things. (Notice how I managed to squeeze perspective in there one last time... very important!)

UVs and Textures

A Bit about Advanced Shaders

Refer to Chapter_12 on the companion CD.

Now that we have a completed model we can move on to the next step — adding textures. There are many ways in which to approach the UV layout as well as the creation of the texture itself.

Characters these days are looking more and more lifelike due to the development of advanced shaders. In Chapter 3, "A Modeling Primer," we briefly discussed normal mapping. When used in Maya, the normal map is a somewhat elaborate shading network that is then applied to the geometry and rendered to achieve the desired results. Remember our example from Chapter 3?

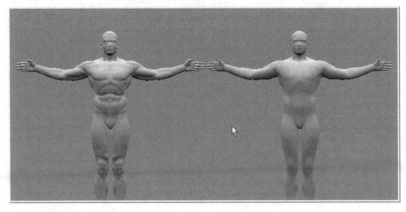

Figure 12-1

Another advancement in shaders is the use of subsurface scattering (SSS). This shader creates the appearance of light that is absorbed into the surface of an object, then bounces around the underlying layers and is reflected back out, or diminishes, as it is absorbed. Whoa! That sounds pretty complicated!

When lighting characters, the subsurface scattering effect is most prevalent in skin where the layers are thinnest. You will notice it on the ears when there is a light source coming from behind. To get a good look at SSS, hold a flashlight under your hand. It should almost appear as if your hand is glowing under the skin.

Creating this shader takes some amount of work. There are a few different means by which you can approach SSS, some more complex than others. Achieving real SSS will increase render times dramatically, but there are ways to cheat the SSS that will keep your render times a bit more manageable.

We don't have enough room here to explain the use of these advanced shaders, but there are numerous tutorials on the Internet to walk you through these methods. Because this book is geared more toward beginners, I have to assume that creating UVs and textures is daunting enough.

Our Approach to UVs

Getting good UVs is a pretty involved task when it comes to characters. As I stated in Chapter 3, pelt mapping is really coming into its own and can be used to simplify the process quite a bit. The problem I find with this approach is the fact that the pelted geometry bears very little resemblance to your actual model.

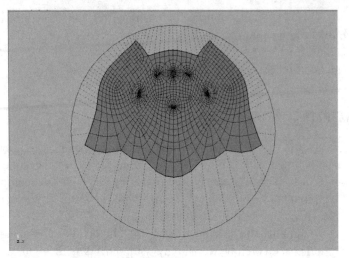

Figure 12-2: A pelt map.

This simplified UV process can save you a boatload of time, but the trade-off is the difficulty in comprehending the UV layout that results from pelting when you bring it into a paint program.

Even though I recommend learning to use pelt mapping, the approach we will focus on here is the old tried and true method of creating your own UV layout, primarily because Maya doesn't include the pelting, and also because understanding UVs is an important part of the modeling process.

We will step through the process of creating UVs for the entire character and then focus on creating textures for the head. This should give you enough of an understanding of the process so that you can continue on and texture the body yourself. The companion CD contains the completed textures for the head as well as the rest of the body so that you can see how they are constructed.

The model we created has edge loops laid out in a manner that is conducive to laying out proper UVs. In other words, it can be split out into sections that will allow for a uniform layout.

The example I usually give when creating UVs is to look at an article of clothing. Take any shirt, for instance. There are seams where different pieces of material are stitched together. If you remove the stitches you can lay each individual piece out flat. The front of the shirt is separate from the back, and the sleeves, which are essentially cylinders, can be laid out flat as well.

This is the same approach we take with UVing. Sections of the model can be split out and more or less flattened to get an accurate layout. Each section has a unique UV map projected on it, and then can be stitched together in the UV Editor.

Preparing the Model

UV layouts can be very confusing, especially if it is something you are unfamiliar with. The worst thing you can do to your model is to lay out the UVs improperly. Bad texturing can ruin the best model. My opinion is if you aren't going to spend the proper time laying out UVs, then don't texture the model at all.

To simplify the process we will start by dividing the model into sections based on how we will divvy up our UVs. To begin, we will simply apply temporary separate materials to different sections of the model. Eventually we will stitch some of the sections back together to create one continuous UV flow.

1. Select **Window | Rendering Editors ▸ Hypershade**.

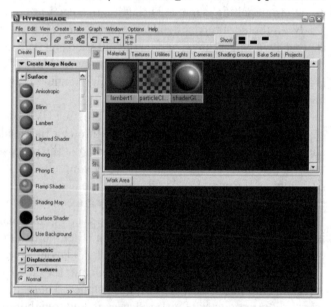

Figure 12-3

2. When the Hypershade window opens, create a new Blinn material and name it **Head**. Double-click on **Head** to open the attribute panel shown in Figure 12-4.

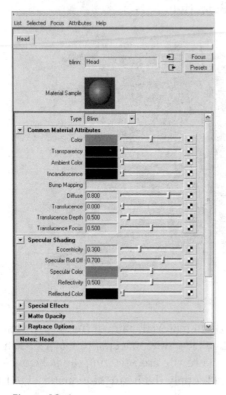

Figure 12-4

3. Click on the gray swatch next to Color to open the Color Chooser. Pick any color you like. As we go through this process you will choose different colors for each material so that it is easier to see how the UVs should be applied to your model.

4. Let's take a moment to adjust some of the settings on our Blinn material. Under Specular Shading, set Eccentricity to **0.3**, set Specular Roll Off to **0.5**, leave Specular Color alone for now, and set Reflectivity to **0.05**.

5. Select all of the polygons that make up the face of your character. Look at the example to make sure you are selecting the right faces. Right-click the **Head** material and choose **Assign Material to Selection**.

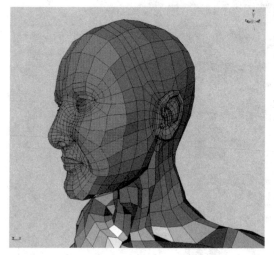

Figure 12-5

6. Create a new Blinn material, name it **head_side**, and give it a unique color. In a side view, select all the faces on the side of the head. Make sure you are selecting the polygons on both sides of the head. Apply the **head_side** material to the selected faces.

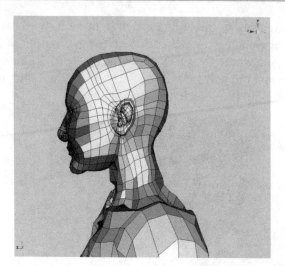

Figure 12-6

7. Create a new Blinn material, name it **head_top**, and give it a unique color. Select all the faces on the top of the head. Apply the **head_top** material to the selected faces.

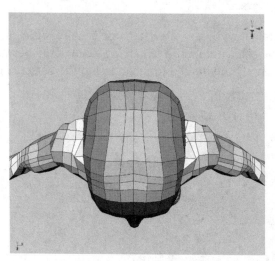

Figure 12-7

8. Create another new Blinn material, name it **head_neck**, and give it a unique color. Select the faces at the front of the neck, stopping where the neck meets the torso. Make sure you are selecting the polygons of the neck. Apply the **head_neck** material to the selected faces.

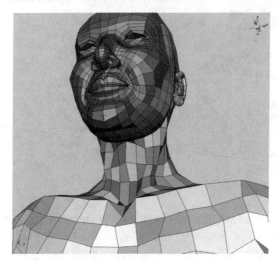

Figure 12-8

9. Create a new Blinn material, name it **head_chin**, and give it a unique color. Select the remaining faces of the head under the chin. Apply the **head_chin** material to the selected faces.

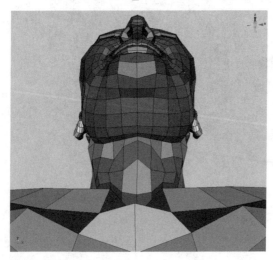

Figure 12-9

10. Finally, create a new Blinn material, name it **head_back**, and give it a unique color. Select the remaining faces on the back of the head. Apply the **head_back** material to the selected faces.

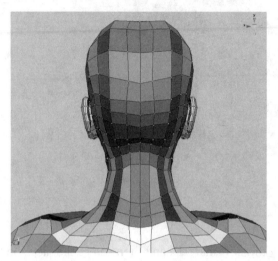

Figure 12-10

You should now have a pretty good idea as to where we are going with this. As we continue to split out the figure, we make new materials for each new section. Next, we will move down to the torso.

11. Create a material named **torso_front**. Select the faces on the front of the torso, stopping at the imaginary seams on the side of the model and near the shoulders. It should look something like a one-piece bathing suit.

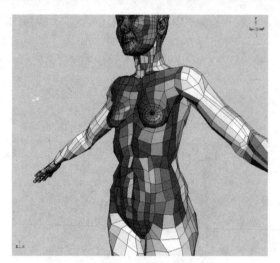

Figure 12-11

12. Apply the new material and then select the faces on the back of the torso in a similar fashion to the front.

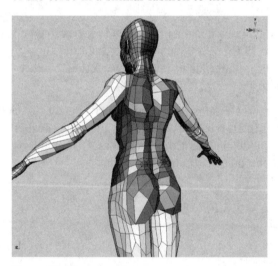

Figure 12-12

13. Apply a new material named **torso_back**.

14. Next, we will move to the arms. Select the left arm from the shoulder down to the wrist. Assign a material named **arms**.

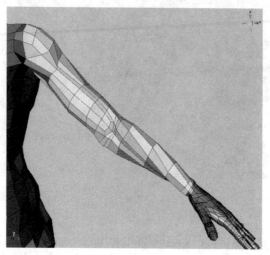

Figure 12-13

15. Repeat the previous step on the right arm. You can assign the same material you used for the left arm.

16. The hands require a bit more effort. Select the faces that make up the top of the left hand. To make it a bit easier, you can select **Display | Custom Polygon Display ☐**. When the options window opens, set Backface Culling on. You can now use the Selection tool to select only the polygons visible to the camera.

17. You will more than likely have to add and remove faces from the selection around the seam. When you are finished, your selected polygons should look like Figure 12-14. Assign a new material named **hand_top** to the polygons.

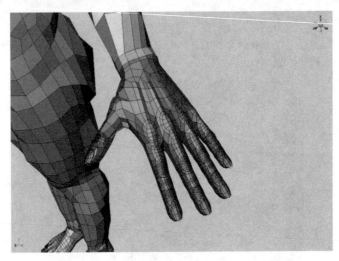

Figure 12-14

18. Repeat this process by selecting the faces on the palm side of the hand and assign a material named **hand_palm**.

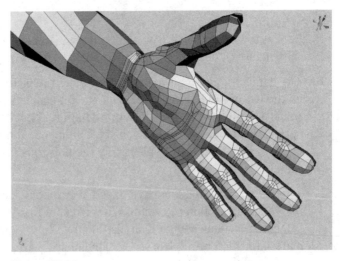

Figure 12-15

19. Repeat the process for the right hand, using the same material assignments that you used for the left hand.

20. Move down and select the polygons that make up the legs from the hips and butt down to the ankles, as shown in Figure 12-16. Assign the material **legs** to the selected faces.

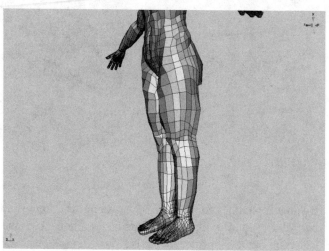

Figure 12-16

21. Select the faces on the top of the feet and assign **foot_top** as a material.

22. Repeat for the bottom of the foot and name the assigned material **foot_bottom**.

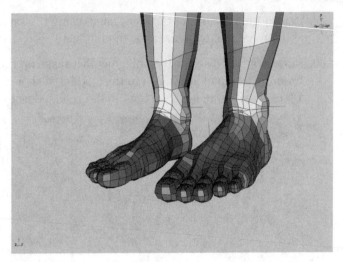

Figure 12-17

If you are so inclined, you can separate out the fingernails and toe-nails with separate materials. This is not a necessity and is really based on personal preferences. For our example, we will keep the nails as part of the hands and feet UVs.

Assigning UV Coordinates to the Head

Now that we have our figure divided into sections, we can step through the process of assigning UV coordinates to our model. Splitting out sections by material assignment now makes it easier to select the particular section we want to UV.

If you are not familiar with the UV Texture Editor, take the time to get acquainted with it by looking through the Maya help documents. Don't worry, I'll wait for you.

Got it? Alright then. By default when you open Window | UV Texture Editor, Maya will display all of the geometry of the selected mesh in a jumbled mess, as shown in Figure 12-18. As you build an object, Maya keeps track of the faces and generates UVs as you proceed.

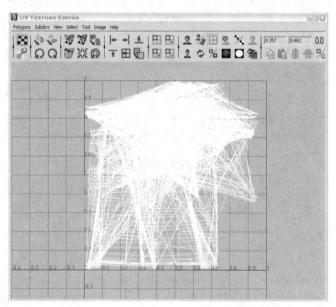

Figure 12-18

You would never use them in this state. We need to assign proper UVs in an organized manner. First, however, we want to clean up the UVs so that as we proceed we can keep the unassigned portion of our UVs out of our way.

1. With the geometry selected, go to **Polygons | Layout UVs** in the UV Texture Editor. After a few moments, the faces should display in the editor window. Right-click in the editor and choose **UVs**. Select all of the geometry and move it off to the right, outside of the grid.

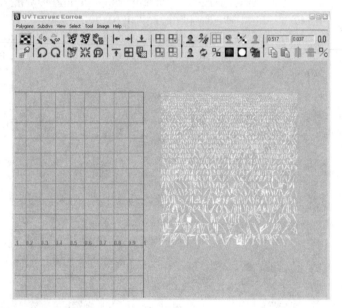

Figure 12-19

Now we are ready to assign UVs to our head. One way of applying UVs to the head is by using cylindrical mapping, as shown in Figure 12-20. This will give you a relatively good UV layout except for the top of the head and under the chin, where it will be difficult to prevent stretching of the texture. So we will put a bit more work into the head because it is really the most important part of the character.

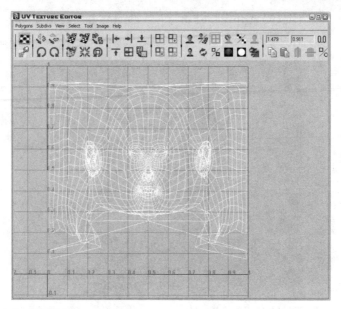

Figure 12-20

2. Let's start right at the top by right-clicking on **Head** from our list of materials. Choose **Select Objects with Material** from the marking menu. The polygons on the face of your model should now be selected in the viewport.

3. In a front view, select **Create UVs | Planar Mapping** ☐ [v7: Polygon UVs | Planar Mapping ☐]. When the options box opens, make sure Project From is set to **Z axis** or **Camera** [v7: set Mapping Direction to **Camera**]. (Figure 12-21 shows the dialog box in Maya 7. See Figure 7-10 for the Maya 8 version.)

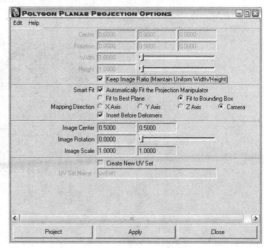

Figure 12-21

4. Hit the **Apply** button. The selected faces should be surrounded by the planar mapping manipulator.

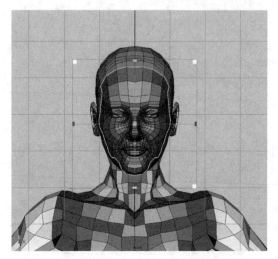

Figure 12-22

5. The selected faces now have UV coordinates assigned to them. Select **Window | UV Texture Editor**.

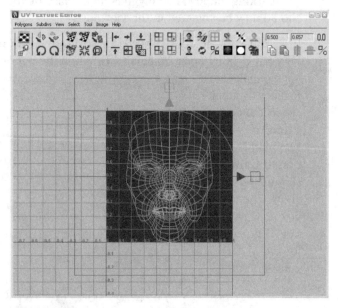

Figure 12-23

The face of your model should be visible in the editor window. Initially, there should be a manipulator that allows you to scale and move the selected faces.

You should also note that the selection resides within the grid from 0 to 1 in both directions. It is common for all UVs to reside within the 0 to 1 parameters. This is not absolutely necessary, as any texture you apply to any given selection will repeat itself over and over in all directions. So your texture would sit at 0 to 1 and repeat again at 1 to 2, and 2 to 3, and so on. This will become more apparent as we start creating textures.

6. We ultimately want to apply one texture to the entire head, so we will want to combine the separate UV projections into one layout. Let's start by selecting the face in the UV editor and scaling it down.

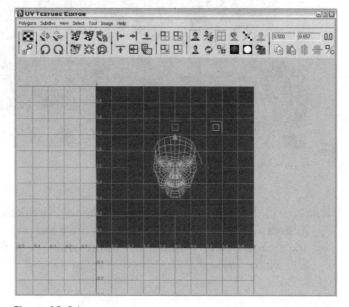

Figure 12-24

If you inadvertently turned off the UV manipulator, right-click in the editor window and choose **UV** as the selection type. Be sure to select all of the UVs, and then you will be able to use the scale manipulator to scale your selection. Maya will also show you the current UVs you are working with in the viewports.

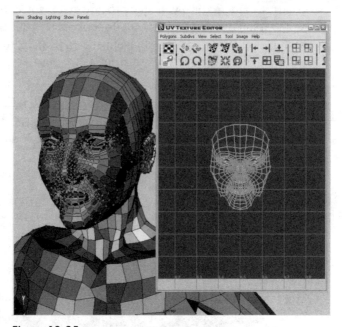

Figure 12-25

7. Back in the Hypershade window (Window | Rendering Editors ▸ Hypershade), right-click on the **head_side** material and choose **Select Objects with Material**. The new selection will be evident in the viewport.

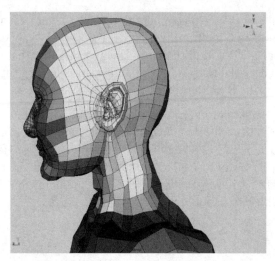

Figure 12-26

8. Rotate to a side view and select **Create UVs | Planar Mapping** [v7: Polygon UVs | Planar Mapping]. Once again, your selection is surrounded by the planar mapping manipulator. Go back to the UV Texture Editor to see the new projection.

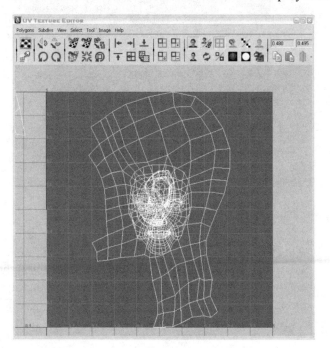

Figure 12-27

345

You should notice a couple of things when you look at the editor window. The first thing is that the new UVs appear right on top of the UVs from the face. The second thing that will be evident is that both sides of the head are right on top of each other. This is not a problem.

9. First, select both halves of the side of the head and scale them down in the editor window so that they are close to the size of the face. Now, select any one UV on the side of the face. Go to **Select | Select Shell** at the top of the window. All of the UVs that are part of that side of the head should now be selected. Use the Move tool to separate the two halves.

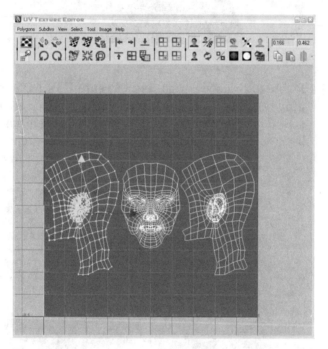

Figure 12-28

10. Check the viewport to verify on which side of the head the UVs you have selected are located. We want the right side of the head selected. If you have the left side of the head selected, select the right side UVs instead.

11. With the right side UVs selected, go to **Polygons | Flip UVs**.
By default, the UVs will flip horizontally, which is what we
want. Move the selection over to the right side of the face
(screen left in the editor).

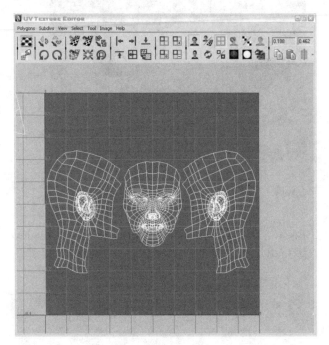

Figure 12-29

12. Go back into Hypershade and right-click **head_top**. Rotate to
a top view and assign planar mapping to the selection.

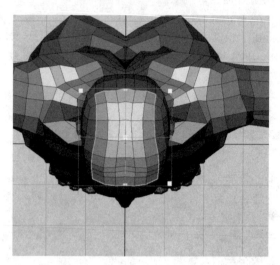

Figure 12-30

13. Back in the UV Texture Editor, scale the new selection down to match the size of the rest of the head.

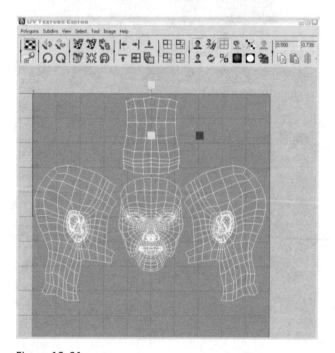

Figure 12-31

14. Repeat the process for the chin, assigning planar projection. You can rotate to a bottom view or you can stay in the top view to create the new UV map. If you remain in the top view, you will need to vertically flip the chin UVs in the UV Texture Editor. Scale the chin in the UV Texture Editor down to match the rest of the head.

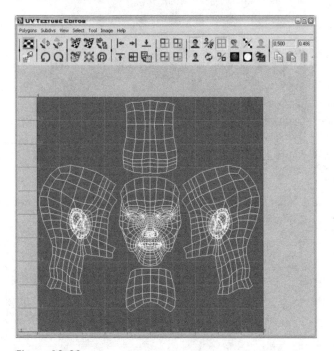

Figure 12-32

15. Select **head_neck** to select the neck section of your model. In a front view, apply a planar projection to the selection.

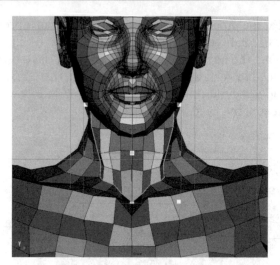

Figure 12-33

16. Go back to the UV Texture Editor and scale the neck selection down to match the rest of the head.

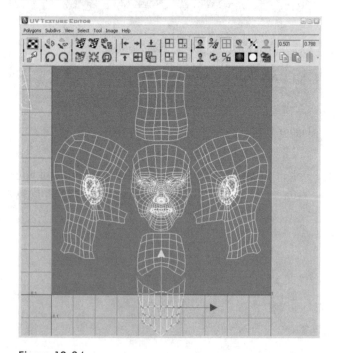

Figure 12-34

17. Finally, rotate to the back of the model and assign a planar map to the back of the head. Scale it down to match the rest of the head.

    Now that we have all of the coordinates laid out for the head, we can clean up the UVs by stitching sections together. So at this point we will assign a single material to the head.

18. We can use one of the materials we have already created. Double-click on **Head** in the Hypershade window to bring up its attributes. Click the checkered button to the far right of Color. When the Create Render Node window pops up, select **Checker**. Since by default the UV Texture Editor displays the geometry in white, we should alter the checker color to make our lives easier. Select the **checker1** tab in the Head attributes. On the Checker Attributes, click on the white color swatch and change it to any color other than white.

19. In the UV Texture Editor, select all of the UVs. Go to **Select | Convert Selection to Faces**. Right-click the **Head** material in Hypershade and choose **Assign Material to Selection**. If the checker texture does not show up on the model in the viewport, hit the number **6** key on your keyboard to see it. If the checker pattern appears blurry, select **Shading | Hardware Texturing** ☐ and select **Unfiltered** under Texture Filter.

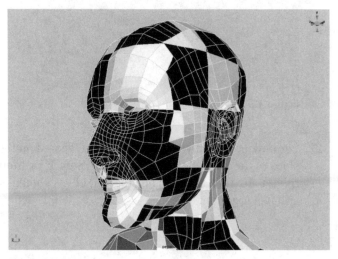

Figure 12-35

So the idea here is to get the checkers on the geometry to look as square as possible to eliminate stretching that may occur in the final texture. We do this by adjusting the UVs.

20. We will start by adjusting the positions of the different sections of the head UVs. Scale the sections so that the checker pattern is roughly the same size when you look at the head in the viewport.

21. There are noticeable seams in the checker pattern that will be taken care of as we stitch the UVs together. We start by stitching the sides of the head to the face. In the editor window, right-click and choose **Edge**. Select the edges along the side of the face. As you do, you will see the corresponding edges on the side of the head highlight as well, indicating that they are shared edges on your geometry.

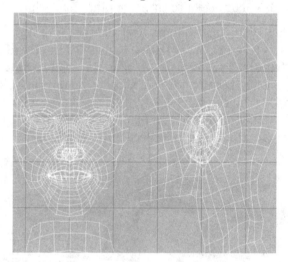

Figure 12-36

22. For now, select only the edges that are shared on the face and sides of the head. Select **Polygons | Sew UVs** from the top of the UV Texture Editor. The selected edges should now be stitched together.

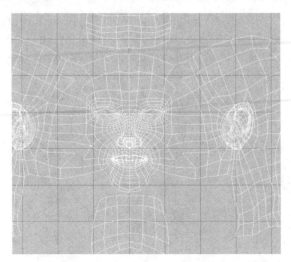

Figure 12-37

You should notice that the checker pattern around the stitched areas is looking a little smoother.

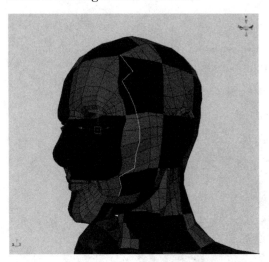

Figure 12-38

Don't worry if the checker pattern looks stretched on the geometry; we will address that issue as we move along.

23. Select the edges along the bottom of the face until the top edges of the chin are selected in a similar fashion to the way we did the side of the head. Select **Polygons | Sew UVs** to stitch the chin to the face.

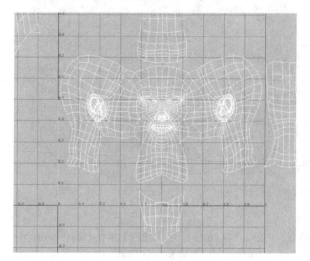

Figure 12-39

Once again, you should notice that the checker pattern around the stitched areas is a little smoother.

Figure 12-40

24. Stitch in the top of the head just as you did the chin.

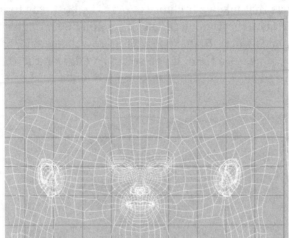

Figure 12-41

25. Select the edge down the center of the faces for the back of the head section. Select **Polygons | Cut UVs** in the editor. This will create two separate halves. Select the edges along the right side of the head and then go to **Polygons | Move and Sew**. The piece from the back of the head will be stitched to the right side of the head. Repeat the process for the other side.

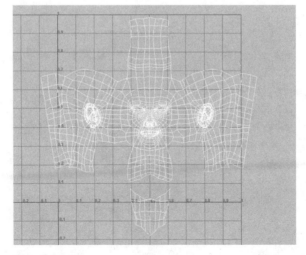

Figure 12-42

26. As a final step, we will sew in the neck. This is one of the areas that takes a bit more effort. The best way to handle the neck is to first move the neck section down to give yourself room to work. To make it a bit more manageable, sew just a few edges at a time. If you select an edge on the right side, be sure to select the same edge on the left.

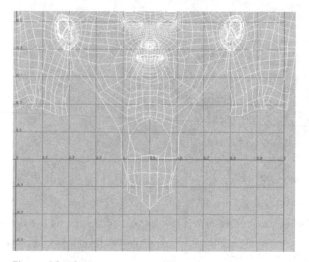

Figure 12-43

Once the edges are sewn you should have something similar to Figure 12-44.

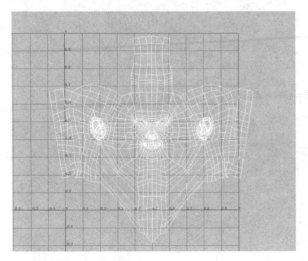

Figure 12-44

Next, we will need to adjust some of the UVs to get the checker pattern flowing correctly.

27. Concentrate on the area around the chin first. Manually move the UVs and refer to the model to see how your adjustments are affecting the checker pattern.

    In addition, you may want to relax the UVs to make them a bit more uniform.

28. Select the UVs below the chin and select **Polygons | Relax UVs** ◻. When the Relax UVs Option dialog box opens, make sure Pin UVs is set to **Pin Unselected UVs**, and Max Iterations is set to **2** in the Stopping Condition area. Your UVs should look something like Figure 12-45.

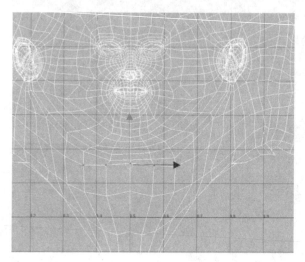

Figure 12-45

29. Next, select the UVs on the upper edge of the eyelids. If it
    makes it easier, select them in the viewport. Move the UVs
    down in the editor so that there is more surface space for the
    eyelid.

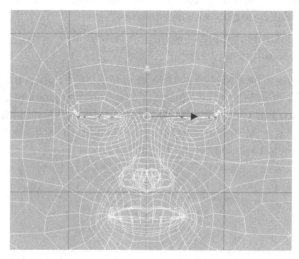

Figure 12-46

There are a couple of other areas we need to concentrate on: the nose and the ears. Both these areas are troublesome because of overlapping geometry.

30. Select the UVs around the nose in the editor and select **Polygons | Relax UVs** ☐.

31. You may need to repeat the relax a few times to get it right.

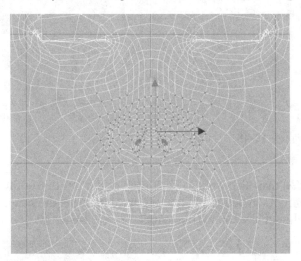

Figure 12-47

32. Select the UVs of both ears. Make sure that you have the same UVs selected on each side. Repeat the relax process until the UVs resemble Figure 12-48.

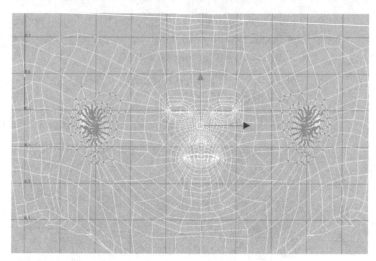

Figure 12-48

33. You may also want to separate out the interior of the mouth into its own UVs. When you are done with the head, you should have something similar to Figure 12-49.

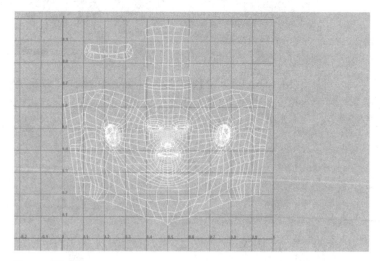

Figure 12-49

You should now have a pretty decent UV layout for the head. At this point, you can continue the process of UVing the rest of the body or move right along to the texturing part of the lesson.

Here are some tips for UVing the body:

▶ Use planar mapping for both the front and the back of the model and the hands and feet.

▶ Use cylindrical mapping for the arms and the legs.

▶ Use the relax process on the breasts to remove any overlap issues.

Figure 12-50 shows the finished UVs for the body. The UV layout is available on the companion CD, along with the textures.

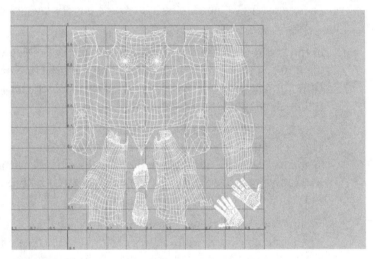

Figure 12-50

Texturing the Head

Now that we have our UVs, it's time to create some textures for our model. We will be creating three standard textures: a color map, a bump map, and a specular map. Short of subsurface scattering, these three textures combined create a pretty convincing-looking character.

For this particular section you will need a pretty decent paint program. I will be referring to the Photoshop tool set exclusively. If there is one universal tool in this industry, it's Photoshop. For the most part, I will assume you have a good understanding of Photoshop.

So for starters we need to be able to see our UV layout in Photoshop.

1. In the UV Texture Editor, be sure that your UVs reside within the 0 to 1 section of the grid. Select **Polygons | UV Snapshot** ⬜. When the UV Snapshot box opens, select a location and file name for your image.

2. The default settings for Size X and Size Y are 4096 x 4096. This is a rather large image size, but will give you the ability to add a great amount of detail. If you want a more manageable size to work with, set Size X and Size Y to **2048 x 2048**. This will still get you a fairly detailed texture.

3. Finally, make sure Image Format is set to **Targa**. This image type is the most preferable to work with because it can manage a great wealth of color information without any loss due to compression of the file. It is a good idea to steer clear of the ever-popular JPEG due to the fact that the color information it stores can be compressed, which could result in artifacting (jagged pixels). Hit **OK** to save the image. Name the image **Head_Template** or anything you like. If you have not created a new project folder, the texture will be in the My Documents\maya\projects\default\images folder.

4. Now open the image in Photoshop, then open **Lucy_Front.jpg** from the companion CD. **Select All** and copy **Lucy_Front** and paste it into the UV texture. This should create a new layer. Turn the opacity down a bit so that you can see the UV layout underneath, as shown in Figure 12-51.

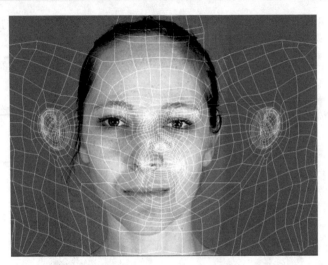

Figure 12-51

5. You may need to scale the image nonuniformly to match the UVs. You also may need to move some of the features to match up with the UVs. You can do this by cutting and pasting or by using the Liquify tool (see Figure 12-52). When the features are aligned, open **Lucy_Side.jpg**.

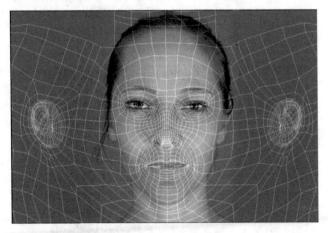

Figure 12-52

6. Copy and paste **Lucy_Side.jpg** into the UV layout. Move the image so that it is aligned to the left side of the front view image. Move and scale it until you are satisfied with the layout.

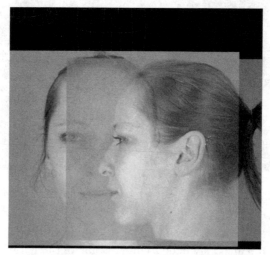

Figure 12-53

7. Now you will need to blend the side image into the front image. Erase the unwanted areas of the side of the head. Use the Clone tool to blend the two layers so that there are no noticeable seams.

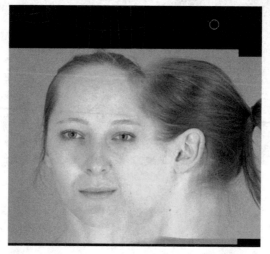

Figure 12-54

Eventually we will copy the side layer and flip it, but for now we will continue to work with only one side of the head. For the sake of simplicity, our texture will contain the hair as well. Later, we will add some additional geometry for the ponytail and stray hairs. This is not necessarily the best approach to creating hair, but it will contain the elements used to create a hairpiece using geometric strips and alpha maps. The other alternative would be to use Maya's Hair system, which unfortunately is only available in the Maya Unlimited version. I wanted an approach that could be used with Maya Complete as well.

8. Use the Clone tool as well as cutting sections of hair and pasting them. Be sure to follow the flow of geometry. Using the Liquify tool will enable you to curve portions of the hair to match the geometry.

Figure 12-55

9. The next thing we will do is remove some of the details from the image. First, we will remove the nose. Essentially we want to take out the nostrils and any shadows around them. Use the Clone tool and sample areas around the nose. Be sure to avoid any repeating patterns.

365

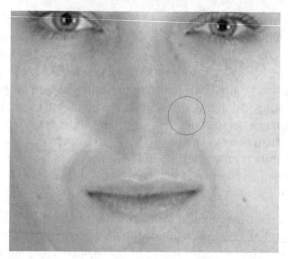

Figure 12-56

10. Next, we will concentrate on the ear. Eliminate all of the details and shadows.

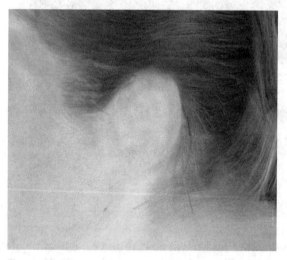

Figure 12-57

11. The eyes are another thing that we want to remove from our texture. Once again, use the Clone tool to remove the eyes. When you are through cloning, use the Paintbrush to add a subtle pink tone to the eye area.

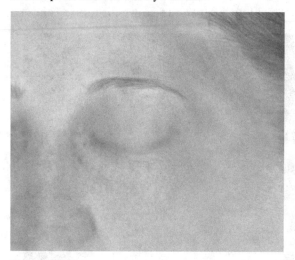

Figure 12-58

12. We will also want to remove any shiny spots that tend to occur on the oilier parts of the skin, like the forehead and nose, along with any shadows in the image. Use the Clone tool to remove them.

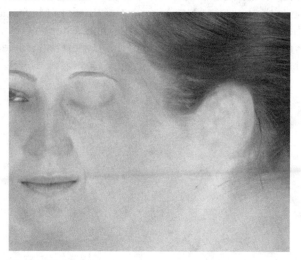

Figure 12-59

13. You can now copy and flip the side of the head over. Make sure there are no noticeable seams or other issues. Once you have adjusted the layer to match up with the UV layout, you can collapse the color map down into one layer. Be sure to keep the UV layout on a separate texture for future reference.

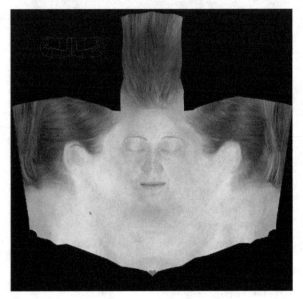

Figure 12-60

14. Now would be a good time to check the texture on our model. Save the image as **head_color.tga**. Back in Maya, right-click the **Head** material in the Hypershade. Choose **Graph Network**. In the Work Area tab of the Hypershade, select the checker texture and delete it.

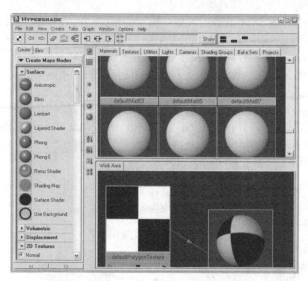

Figure 12-61

15. Double-click the **Head** material to open the attributes. Click the checker button next to Color and choose **File** from the Create Render Node box. The File Attributes should pop up. Click the folder next to Image Name and browse to where you saved head_color.tga. You should now see the texture on the geometry.

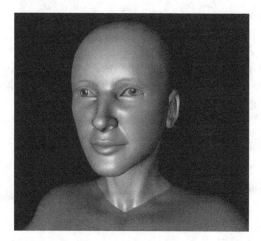

Figure 12-62

16. Rotate around the model to see if the texture is lining up to the geometry correctly. Also look for any noticeable seams. If you need to make adjustments to the UVs, right-click on the **Head** material in the Hypershade and choose **Select Objects with Material**. Open the UV Texture Editor. The texture should be visible underneath your UVs (see Figure 12-63). Move the UVs where you need to so that the texture is properly aligned with the geometry. When you are satisfied, save the file and go back into Photoshop.

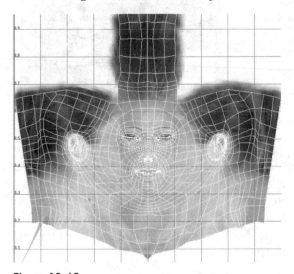

Figure 12-63

17. Add a new layer so we can add a bit of detail to our color map. First add a bit of a red hue to the nose and ears. This should be very subtle. You may want to adjust the opacity of the layer to get the right effect.

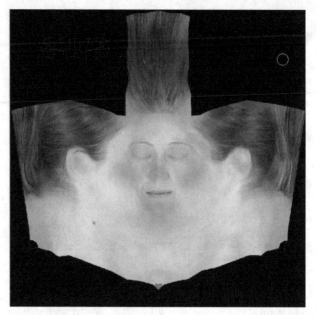

Figure 12-64

18. Add another layer. On this layer we will add some small spots
to simulate pores, freckles, and other little details visible on
the skin. One easy approach to this is to use a rather large
brush and set the mode to **Dissolve**. Turn the opacity down to
about **10**. Paint on random parts of the texture, varying the
color from pink to light brown and red. Now erase any
overspray on the lips or other areas you don't want affected.
Add a Blur filter to the layer to soften it up, then adjust the
opacity of the layer so that it doesn't appear overpowering.

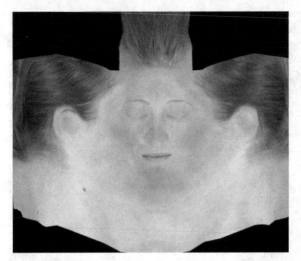

Figure 12-65

19. As a final step, use a small brush size to add additional strands of hair. You may use a brush that contains a series of dots or even create your own. I have found that a small standard brush is effective as well. Use the Eyedropper tool to randomly select color values from the hair as you go along. The hair in a photo is often somewhat blurry. Adding additional hair strokes will alleviate some of that.

    That should about do it for the color map. You can collapse the layers down or, if you want, save a PSD file for any future tweaking. Check out the texture in Maya and make any other adjustments you deem necessary.

20. The next thing we will do is create our bump map. The bump map will give the texture the appearance of having a 3D quality. We will start by saving our color map as a new image. Name the new image **head_bump.tga**. The first thing we will do is desaturate the image by converting it to grayscale.

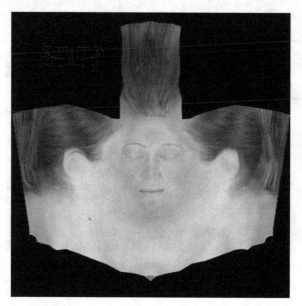

Figure 12-66

A bump map will use the light and dark values to give the impression of raised and receding areas on the texture. So the lighter areas are raised and darker areas become recessed. The bump map for the face should be subtle, with a limited range in the grayscale values. In other words, we would rarely use true black or true white as they would appear a little too extreme. The hair in this image should contain about as close to the extremes as we would ever get.

21. As a grayscale image we have a pretty good start with the tonal values we need; we just need to level them out a bit. The first thing we will do is make a copy of the image onto a new layer and then invert it. This way areas that would be recessed on the grayscale image will now protrude instead. The exception would be the lips and the creases near the mouth. Erase the lips from the inverted layer, revealing the grayscale lips. Use the Burn tool to darken the creases on the sides of the mouth.

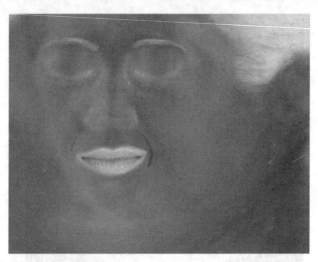

Figure 12-67

22. Level out the image by adjusting the contrast. In this case we are looking for less contrast so that the values are a bit more even. The lips may need some additional work as well. Use the Dodge and Burn tools to add a few creases but remember — be subtle!

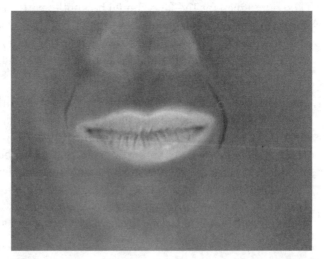

Figure 12-68

23. You can also add a few lighter spots here and there to create slightly raised bumps or beauty marks. Save the image.

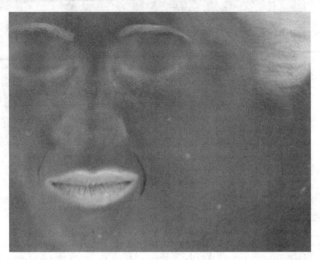

Figure 12-69

We now have our bump map, so let's take a look at it back in Maya.

24. Double-click the **Head** material to open the attributes. Select the checker button next to Bump Map and select **File** from the Create Render Node window. Browse to select the **head_bump.tga** file from its saved location.

25. The bump is now assigned, but the default bump will not work for our model. In the Hypershade, right-click **Head** and choose **Graph Network**. There is an icon that represents the bump node of our shader.

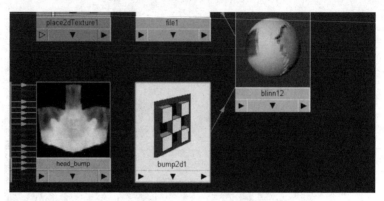

Figure 12-70

26. Click on it to open the bump attributes. Set the Bump Depth to **0.035**.

27. Now we need to render our scene in order to see the results of the bump map. Apply a smooth node and zoom in relatively close to the head in a perspective view. Select **Window | Rendering Editors ▸ Render Settings**.

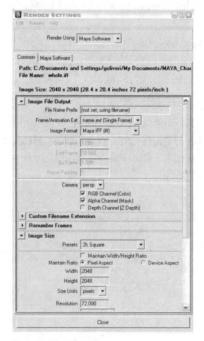

Figure 12-71

28. From the Render Using list, select **Maya Software**. In the Image Size area, select **1k Square** from the Presets list. You can now close the Render Settings window.

29. Select **Render | Render Current Frame**. You should see a render of your model in a few seconds. Take a look at the way the bump map rendered in order to make necessary adjustments to the Bump Depth setting. Go back and forth between rendering and adjusting the Bump Depth until you are satisfied with the results. The bump shouldn't be glaringly obvious and should only really be visible at a very close range.

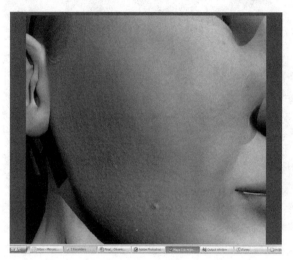

Figure 12-72

You should consider adding lights to the scene. A direct light with Raytraced Shadows turned on and a couple of additional lights with lower intensity levels should suffice for now.

This brings us to the final map. We need to create a specular map for our model. Right now, if you take a look in the renders the specular highlights are apparent on the entire model. As I mentioned before, some areas of the skin are more apt to receive specular highlights than others. These are generally the areas of the skin that tend to be more oily.

30. Back in Photoshop, begin by copying **head_bump.tga** and call it **head_spec.tga**. To create the specular map we will lighten areas of the texture along with giving it a slight hint of a bluish tint. Once assigned to the specular node of our shader, hotspots will only appear on the areas that are dictated by the specular map.

31. So let's begin by eliminating light areas that are left over from the bump map and won't apply to the specular map. The first thing to do is to get rid of the eyebrows.

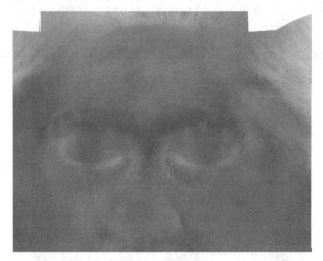

Figure 12-73

32. The next thing to do would be to tone down any other areas that shouldn't receive concentrated specular highlights. Some areas to hone in on would be the neck and the lower cheek area.

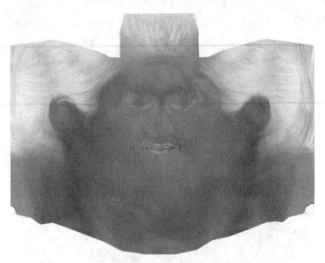

Figure 12-74

33. Now we will step through and add lighter values to the areas that should be affected by the specular highlights. Concentrate on the forehead, the tip of the nose, the crease at the corner of the nose, the chin, and, to a lesser degree, the cheeks. The ears should also receive a fair amount of specularity.

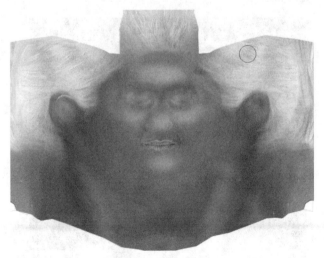

Figure 12-75

34. The hair should also receive some amount of specularity. Add some various light tonal streaks randomly through the hair.

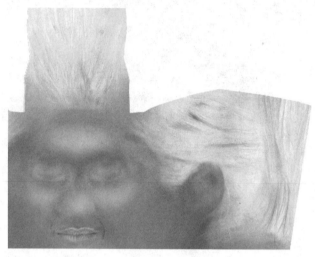

Figure 12-76

35. Save the texture and assign it to the Specular color channel of the Head material. Now check the specular map by rendering the scene.

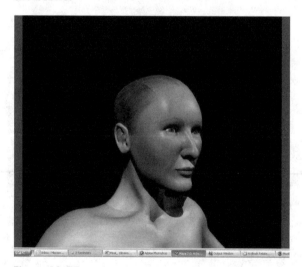

Figure 12-77

As with the other textures, you may find it necessary to bounce back and forth between Maya and Photoshop to get the results you want.

Finishing Touches

Adding eyelashes and some additional geometry for hair will add more realism to your model. Here is a quick run-through on the subject.

There are a couple of ways to add eyelashes to your character. The first is to create tiny cones and position them around the eyes. You can then apply a simple black material to complete the effect.

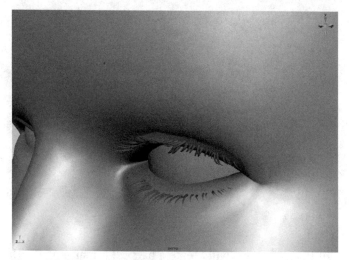

Figure 12-78

Another method is to create strips of geometry and paint the eyelashes using a transparency map. Simply paint the map in Photoshop and then save a negative to use as the transparency map.

As a final step we will add the ponytail and some flyaway hair to our character.

1. Create a plane in Maya that is three units wide and eight units long. Assign a planar map and then make several copies; roughly six to eight should do.

2. Create a new phong material and name it **Hair**. Assign the material to the strips of geometry.

3. Now move the geometries to the back of the head and then bend and shape each strip to create the ponytail shape It is not a major concern if the geometry intersects. Using a lattice deformer might make things a bit easier. Add a few additional strips here and there on the head itself. When you have the geometry in place, combine the individual strips together and name the geometry **ponytail**.

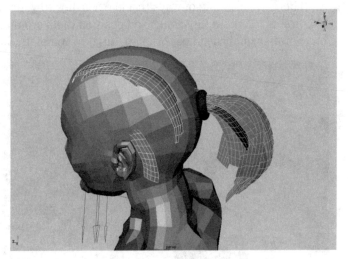

Figure 12-79

In Photoshop we will create a hair color map along with a bump map that will stand in for the specular and transparency maps. Like the bump map, a transparency map will use light and dark values to achieve levels of opacity, with the lighter values being more opaque and the darker values increasingly transparent.

4. Start with a new targa image that is 1024 x 512. Cut sections of hair from your head map or any of the other textures available on the companion CD and add them to a new layer. Repeat this a few times by creating individual strips on the texture, as shown in Figure 12-80. Save the image as **ponytail_color.tga**.

5. Save an additional copy and desaturate it. Name it **pony-tail_bump**.

Figure 12-80

6. In the ponytail_color texture, hold down **Ctrl** and click on the layer in the Layers Editor. Select the **Channel** tab and, at the bottom, select the gray box with a circle in it. This will save the selection as an alpha channel. Turn off the RGB color channels, leaving just the alpha channel on. Save the image as **ponytail_trans.tga**.

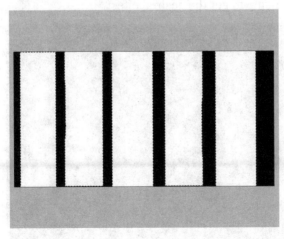

Figure 12-81

7. We want to give the illusion of strands of hair, so in the transparency map we will paint some negative lines as well as soften the edges of the strips.

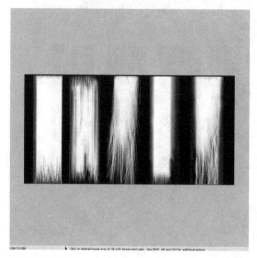

Figure 12-82

8. Back in Maya, add the **ponytail_color** file in the Color channel. Add the **ponytail_trans** file in the Transparency channel, and add the **ponytail_bump** file in the Bump channel as well as the Specular Color channel. You will need to render the scene in order to view the transparency map at work. Adjust the bump to get the desired effect.

Figure 12-83

9. In the UV Texture Editor, randomly assign the UVs to the various strips of hair.

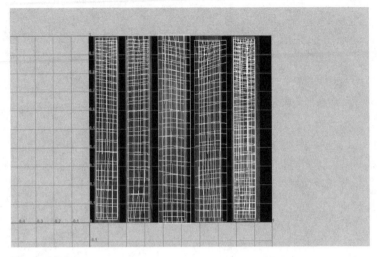

Figure 12-84

Wrap-Up

This chapter took you through the creation of textures and how to use textures to create the little nuances that bring a character to life. We also learned how to effectively add UVs to our model. Like I said, we did it the hard way but this should give you a more complete understanding of how UVs work.

Adding believable textures, although time consuming, will really give your model that finishing touch it so deserves. Take your time when creating your maps, and your efforts will pay off.

Character Rigging

Understanding Joints

Refer to Chapter_13 on the companion CD.

In most cases, when we build a character model we expect to be able to animate it. Luckily, we have taken that into consideration during the modeling process. How, you ask? Well, to a great extent we have tried to get our model geometry to follow the natural shape of the muscles, as well as provide enough geometry around areas that will bend and rotate. Even if you don't plan to animate the model, it would still benefit you to use a skeletal system to pose your model in something other than the current default pose. I think you will agree it would look a lot better on your demo reel.

Now let me warn you that no matter how hard we try, we will never get the model to move perfectly by just throwing some joints inside. The human body is quite an amazing machine. We have reached a point in the world of 3D characterization where actual muscle systems are being used in models in order to achieve human motion.

In this book, however, we aren't going to go there. The skeleton setups I show you here are meant to give you a quick orientation into the rigging process. For the most part, the gaming industry still uses a relatively simple skeleton setup. So I will go through this setup initially and then describe a more advanced setup using controllers and set driven keys.

Maya itself provides a skeletal rig that contains full body IK and provides you with a more than adequate setup. If you are pretty well versed in rigging and wish to skip this chapter, by all means go ahead. For those of you who are not at ease with the rigging process, you might want to follow along.

Something to understand right up front is that in order to get the most out of our joints, we will generally not place the joints exactly where they would line up with their skeletal counterpart. A good example for this would be the spine. If you know nothing else about human anatomy, you know that your spine runs down your back. But if you were a 3D model, your spine would run right down the center of your torso. Kinda creepy, huh? The reason for this is that the closer we are to the center of the torso, the more evenly the points will move when a spine joint is rotated. So the points on the stomach and on the lower back are equidistant to the joint.

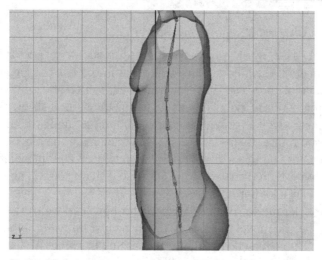

Figure 13-1

Some joints will give you trouble no matter what you do, specifically the hips and, worse yet, the dreaded shoulder! Both of these areas consist of a "ball joint" setup. They are able to rotate in all directions, making weighting an absolute nightmare.

The shoulder has additional issues to deal with. Aside from the ball joint, shoulder motion also involves movement of the clavicles and scapula. Try this: With your arm down at your side, note the position of your clavicle. Now, slowly rotate your arm up. See how the clavicle rotates up as well?

Okay, try this one: Stick your arm straight out with the palm of your hand facing down. Notice that the elbow is facing back. Now, without rotating your wrist, rotate your arm so that your palm is facing forward. This rotation is happening at the shoulder.

Now picture your model. You get the weighting all tight with the arm moving up and down. Then you go to rotate it like you did with your own arm in the previous example. More than likely the points on the shoulder will end up on the back of your model. Not exactly what we are shooting for. You see, on the human body there are many areas where bone movement is coupled with muscle movement in a way that is hard to recreate in a computer model. Fortunately, we have a number of tricks up our sleeve to compensate for most of these issues.

Some of these tricks involve adding extra joints into our character's skeleton that aren't present in the human body. So in order to compensate for this wacky shoulder rotation, we would add what is commonly called a "roll bone." The roll bone would be placed about midway between the shoulder joint and the elbow joint, as shown in Figure 13-2.

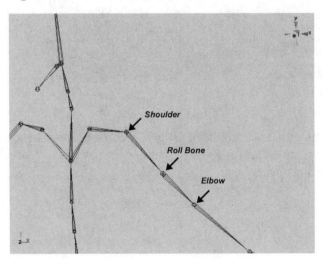

Figure 13-2

This bone would be used only for the purpose of the rotation we have been discussing here. Instead of the rotation happening exclusively at the shoulder, the roll bone would be used instead to give the arm the look we want, which is keeping the shoulder muscle where it belongs. This is not the only place we would use a roll bone. It is also used to create radius rotation in the forearm. If you remember, we set up our arm during the modeling process in the position where the radius is twisted over so that the palm faces down.

The wrist is kinda funky in that you can bend it up and down and back and forth, but its rotation emanates from the elbow region. Because this book deals more with modeling than animation, we will only use the roll bone for our forearm to keep things simple.

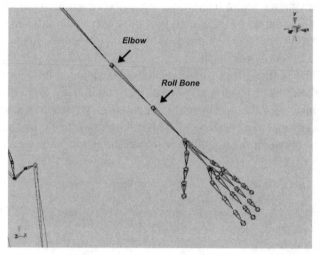

Figure 13-3

Sometimes a more advanced setup is preferred. For instance, there is a joint layout for the forearm that uses two bones to represent the radius and ulna.

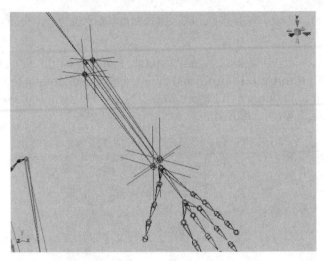

Figure 13-4

Other areas that can benefit from the roll bone are the thighs and, to a lesser degree, the lower leg. For our purposes, we will stick to a standard leg setup, which consists of the thigh, knee, and shin joints.

The fact is there are so many different approaches to setting up a skeleton that it's hard to keep up. Suffice it to say that what you learn in the pages to follow will give you a pretty comprehensive understanding of the standard process. From there, you can pursue other alternatives to creating skeletal rigs.

Sometimes the skeleton by itself is not enough; in these cases, a rig is required. A *rig* is a group of controllers that make moving the character much easier than just rotating joints manually. In its simplest form, a rig might just be inverse kinematics (IK).

So let me explain kinematics. *Forward kinematics* (FK) refers to the standard way that joints rotate. You select it and you rotate it. Any joint that is parented to the joint you rotate will rotate as well. Pretty simple. *Inverse kinematics* creates a chain of joints that move together, where the child joint will inversely control the rotation of the joints it is parented to. Both types of kinematics have their place in animating your character.

Let's take a look at a couple of examples of how you would use IK and FK.

1. In a side view, let's create a simple leg joint setup. Select **Skeleton | Joint Tool** and create a chain containing four joints, as shown in Figure 13-5. These joints will represent the thigh, knee, ankle (heel), and toe.

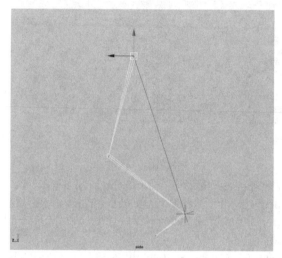

Figure 13-5

Now we certainly know that the rotation of the hip joint in turn rotates all of the joints attached to it. The knee, shin, and ankle are *children* of the thigh joint. The thigh joint is considered the *parent* in this string of joints. This is forward kinematics. All rotations emanate from the parent joint.

Now let's say we want to make our character climb up steps. In an FK world, we would need to rotate the thigh, then the knee, and then the ankle to get our leg to rotate properly so that the foot rests on the first step. As the character moves to take a second step, we would need to account for the rotation that would take place on the pelvis, thigh, and knee, while keeping the foot planted. This is incredibly hard to do with FK.

This brings us to inverse kinematics.

2. Go to **Skeleton | IK Handle Tools**. Click on the heel joint and then the thigh. You should now have an IK link. Grab the IK handle at the heel and move it around a bit. You will notice that the thigh stays stationary but the rest of the chain corresponds to the movement of the IK handle.

    Now our IK handle needs one more thing to get the effect we want: a *constraint*.

    Constraints fall into the rigging category. Normally it is a device that dictates how a particular joint or object moves. In the case of our leg, we want the foot to stay planted as we move the rest of the leg.

3. So let's create a constraint for our foot. First off we will create a *locator*. If you've never used a locator before, it is pretty much as the name states. Go to **Create | Locator**. The locator should appear in your scene at the origin. Select the locator and, while holding down the **V** key, snap it to the position of the IK handle.

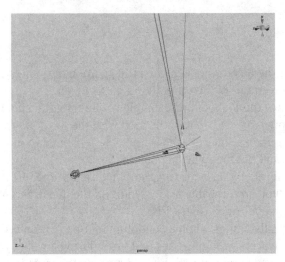

Figure 13-6

4. Select the locator and then Shift-select the IK handle. Select
    Constraint | Point (located under the Animation menu).
    Move the thigh joint and notice that the foot will remain
    planted until it is stretched beyond the length of the joints.

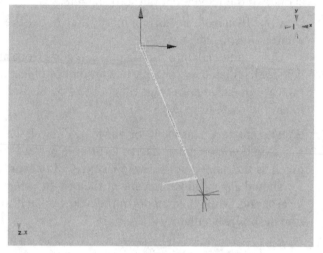

Figure 13-7

In effect, the locator now dictates the position of the foot in relation
to the movement of the other joints in the chain.

So now think about our example of climbing the stairs. With IK,
you simply move the foot to the step with the locator. When the
character goes to take another step, you only need to move the parent joint and the foot will stay put.

So this should give you a general idea about the effectiveness of
IK. Now you are probably asking yourself the question, "When
would you ever need to use FK?"

FK really shines when a pendulum motion is required. For anything from arms swinging back and forth during a walk cycle to a
character swinging a sword, FK is definitely the right way to go.
Luckily, Maya makes it relatively easy to switch between IK and
FK.

Another thing to take note of is the way that Maya handles joint orientation. When you set up a skeletal chain, ideally the same axis should always point to the next joint in the chain.

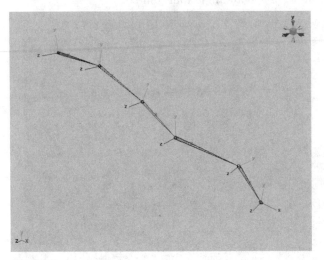

Figure 13-8

In the case of a standard bipedal character, the bones in our skeleton will only rotate and never actually translate. In other words, you wouldn't move the joints in the arm to get the hand straight up in the air; instead you would rotate the joints.

Now here comes the tricky part. Whenever you draw out a joint chain, Maya will automagically point the selected axis (by default the X-axis) to the next joint in the chain. This is exactly what we want. So here is the problem: Say you need to move a joint to get it to line up with your character. Maya doesn't account for this and leaves the axis pointing to where that joint used to be. Are you lost yet?

Let's do a quick experiment to show you what I mean.

1. In a front or side view, open **Skeleton | Joint Tool** and create a new chain containing four joints.

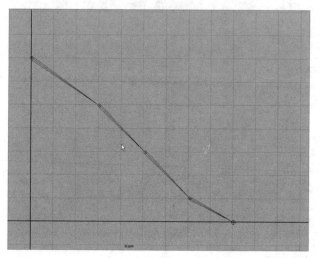

Figure 13-9

2. Select all of the joints by clicking on each one individually while holding down the **Shift** key. Now select **Display | Transform Display ▸ Local Rotation Axes** [v7: Display | Component Display ▸ Local Rotation Axes]. You should see the local rotational axis of each joint. You should notice that indeed, each axis is pointing to the next joint as it should.

3. Now select one of the joints in the middle of the chain and move it. See how the joint axis didn't reposition itself when you moved the joint?

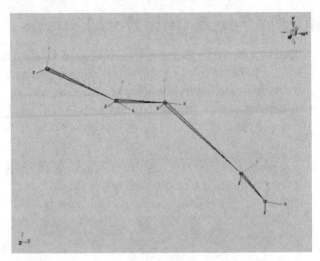

Figure 13-10

Before we actually fix the problem, let's do one more thing. Try rotating a joint. Notice how the axis will rotate as well. So what have we learned from this little example? Quite simply — rotate good, translate baaaad!

4. So how do we fix it? Well, the way to adjust the axis would be to use **Skeleton | Orient Joint** ▢. When the dialog pops up, select the orientation you want by selecting in most cases **XYZ**, where X is the axis pointing to the next joint in the chain. This is something that should be done once all of the joints are placed and lined up to your character.

So this chapter will tackle the process of setting up proper joint placement for your character skeleton. We'll also take it a bit further and create a rig for our skeleton. The next chapter will actually address the proper way to attach the model to the skeleton. So let us begin, shall we?

Placing the Torso and Head Joints

1. Begin in a front view and select **Skeleton | Joint Tool**. We are not going to create a joint to account for each and every segment of the spine. We are just adding enough joints to give us a pretty good range of motion on the torso. You can now begin to place the joints that will represent the spine.

2. Begin at the center of the torso between the hips and place the first joint. Hold down the **Shift** key and create another joint above the first, just below the hips. Holding down the Shift key will keep the joints running in a perfectly straight line.

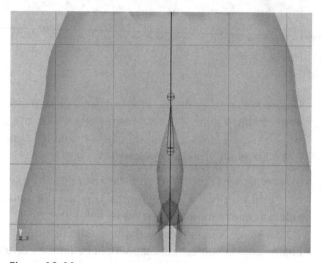

Figure 13-11

3. Still holding the **Shift** key, create another joint right at the navel and another midway between the navel and the base of sternum. Continue by creating one at the base of the sternum, another joint midway up the sternum, and then one at the base of the neck (see Figure 13-12). Starting at the first joint at the bottom of the chain, name them **pelvis, spine_1, spine_2, spine_3, spine_4, spine_5**, and **spine_6**.

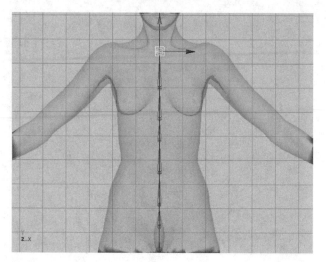

Figure 13-12

4. Select **pelvis** and then choose **Modify | Freeze Transforma-tions**. The pelvis should now have zeroed coordinates, meaning that the translations of the selected object (or joint in this case) will replace its world space x, y, z coordinates with zero values. What does that mean exactly? Well, think of it this way: You can move the joint wherever you want in 3D space and then return it to its default position by typing **0** for the x, y, z translation values.

    This is a very effective means of being able to return the joints to their original positions once controllers are attached, as we will see later in the chapter.

5. Rotate to the side view and position the joints as shown in Figure 13-13.

    Select **pelvis** and then **Modify | Freeze Transformations**. The pelvis should once again have zeroed coordinates.

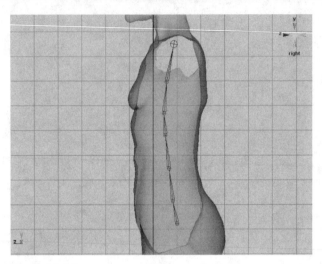

Figure 13-13

6. Create a joint about midway up the neck and then another at the base of the jaw just below the ear. Create one more joint at the top of the head. Name the new joints **neck, head,** and **head_end**.

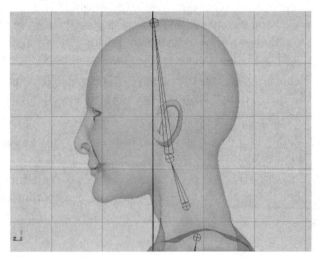

Figure 13-14

7. Select **neck** and Shift-select **spine_6**. Hit the **P** key or choose **Edit | Parent** to parent the joint.

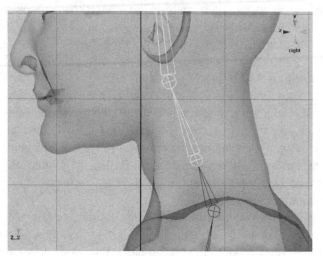

Figure 13-15

8. Create a joint right about where the jaw meets the ear. Now place one more at the chin. Name them **jaw** and **jaw_end**. Select **jaw** and Shift-select **neck_2**, then hit **P** to parent **jaw** to **neck_2**.

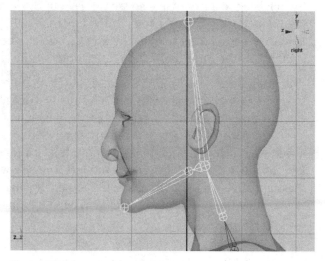

Figure 13-16

Before we go any further, let's take a few minutes to talk about the joint names. There are a number of conventions used when it comes to naming joints and it is ultimately up to the animator on any given project to decide what each joint should be named. We are using a pretty standard naming convention here for our joints. Maya has its own built-in method for naming joints under Skeleton | Joint Labeling ▶ Add Retargeting Labels.

Sometimes it is better to adapt a certain convention when a particular animation program is involved. For example, MotionBuilder is an animation program that is used extensively throughout the industry. It uses its own standardized names, which allow for quicker setups when using MotionBuilder to animate. As an example, MotionBuilder uses the word "Hips" as opposed to "pelvis" in its naming convention.

Because we aren't using MotionBuilder here, it really isn't necessary to go that route, but I wanted to give you the option. When it comes right down to it, you can name the bones pretty much whatever you want as long as it doesn't affect other people in the pipeline. Since at this stage you are the only one in the pipeline, I guess it doesn't really matter. ;)

Placing the Leg and Foot Joints

1. Switch back to a front view so we can lay out the joint placement for the leg. Create a joint at the hip, then hold the **Shift** key and place another joint at the knee. Place another joint right below the knee joint, and then another at the ankle.

2. Still in the front view, create a joint at the heel, then continue to create more joints straight down for the ball of the foot and the tip of the toes. Don't worry about the position of the last two joints. We will properly position them when we rotate into a side view. Name the joints **left_thigh**, **left_knee**, **left_shin**, **left_ankle**, **left_heel**, **left_ball**, and **left_toe**. We won't be making individual joints for each of the toes. If you don't plan on wiggling the toes, this setup should be fine for most animations.

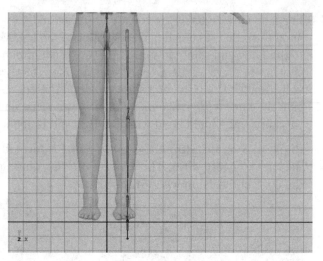

Figure 13-17

If the leg of your model is not perfectly straight, that's okay. For now just approximate the location of the knee and ankle. We will rotate the joints to fit the legs in the next step.

3. So I guess you can figure out what we are going to do next. That's right, we're gonna rotate the joints to fit our leg. Start at the top joint at the hip and rotate it so that the joints are centered in the leg.

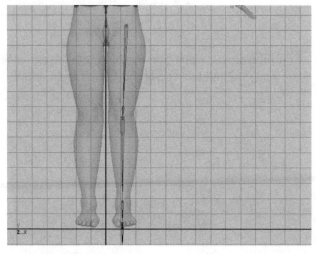

Figure 13-18

4. In a side view, start at the top joint. Rotate and move it if you need to so that it runs down the center of the leg. Move down to the knee and rotate it so that there is a slight bend, as shown in Figure 13-19. Even if your leg is perfectly straight, you should be able to get a slight angle to the knee. This will give the knee a *preferred angle*. Basically, it tells Maya which way the joint should bend when an IK chain is applied.

5. Right-click on **left_knee** and select **Set Preferred Angle.** Do the same for **left_shin.** This will ensure that our leg bends in the correct direction when IK is applied.

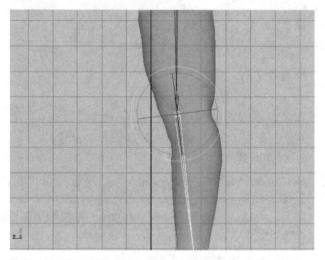

Figure 13-19

6. Continue down to position the foot joints. Remember to rotate and scale the joints to position them. Do not move the joints!

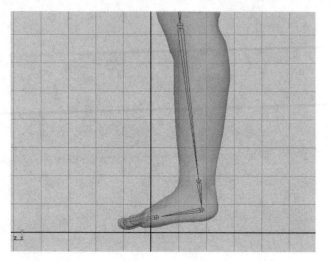

Figure 13-20

7. When you are done with the foot, select **left_thigh** and then **Modify | Freeze Transformations**. We are only concerned with the rotation values here, so don't worry if you see values other than 0 in the Translate XYZ.

8. In a front view, create a joint directly below the pelvis and then create a second midway between the pelvis and the thigh. Name the joints **pelvis_2** and **left_hip**. The second pelvis joint can be used to rock the pelvis of our character and also aids in posing the character in a seated position.

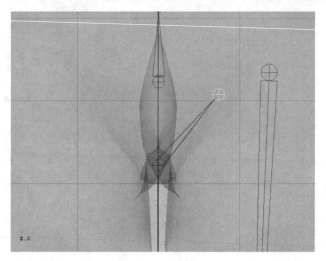

Figure 13-21

9. Select **pelvis** and then **Modify | Freeze Transformations** to zero the rotations on the upper joint structure. Select the thigh joints and **Modify | Freeze Transformations**. This will zero out the rotations on the leg joints, which will come in handy later on. This must be done prior to adding the IK chains.

10. Now that the joint rotations have been zeroed, rotate each of the knee and shin joints on the Z-axis. Right-click on the joint and select **Set Preferred Angle**. Return the joints to their original position by typing **0** for Rotate Z setting in the Channel Box.

11. Parent **left_thigh** to **left_hip** and then parent **pelvis_2** to **pelvis**.

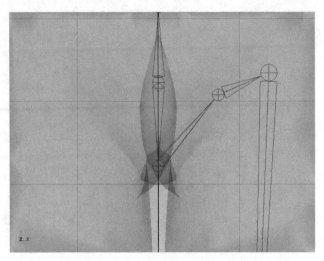

Figure 13-22

12. **Delete History and save!**

Placing the Arm and Hand Joints

We will take a little different approach in laying out the joints for our arm. Ideally, we want to make sure that the joints are in a straight line. Obviously, the arms of our model were built at more or less a 45-degree angle. So, in order to get the arm joints as straight as possible, we will rotate both the skeleton and the geometry so that we can accurately place the arm joints in a straight line.

First off, we will temporarily group the skeleton and the geometry to ensure that we are rotating them together from the same pivot point.

1. Select the geometry and the pelvis of the skeleton and go to **Edit | Group** or press **Ctrl+G** on the keyboard.

   The skeleton and the geometry are now grouped together. You will notice that the pivot of the group should be right at the origin, or 0 on the XYZ axes.

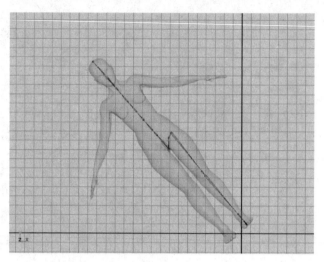

Figure 13-23

2. Rotate the group roughly 35 degrees on the Z-axis. The arm should be parallel to the ground plane. We should now be set up to add the arm and hand joints.

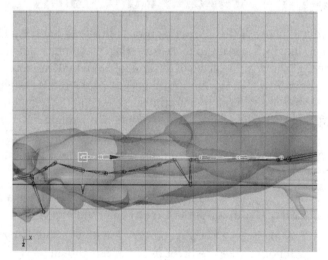

Figure 13-24

3. Starting in a front view, create a joint midway between the center and left shoulder of the character. Continue by creating a joint at the shoulder of the character. Now, hold down the **Shift** key and create a new joint for the elbow, one for the forearm roll bone, and one for the wrist. Name the joints **left_clav, left_shoulder, left_elbow, left_forearm,** and **left_wrist**.

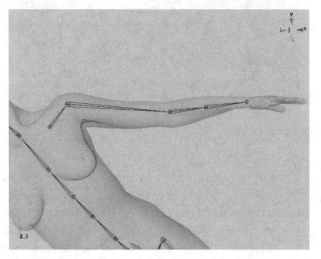

Figure 13-25

4. Rotate into a top view. Most likely you will need to adjust the position of the arm joints so that they are centered to the arm of your character. Select the joint representing the clavicle and move it so that the joints are centered. Note that the bottom half of the model and skeleton have been removed in Figure 13-26 to make it easier for you to see the joints. (Don't do this with your model!)

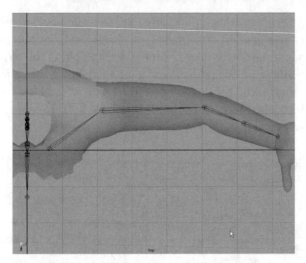

Figure 13-26

You will probably need to do some additional tweaks, such as rotating the elbow joint to fit your model. Be careful not to move the joints in the chain. As a rule of thumb, the only joint you should actually move is the first one in the chain. All other joints should only be rotated and scaled to properly line up to the mesh. Doing this will ensure that the local axis always points toward the next joint in the chain. Remember our example from earlier in the chapter?

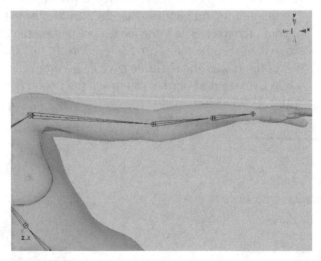

Figure 13-27

5. In a top view we will begin to lay out our hand joints. Begin by creating a single joint directly at the center of the palm. If it helps, you may want to hide the faces on the lower portion of the body, as shown in Figure 13-28, while you work on the hand.

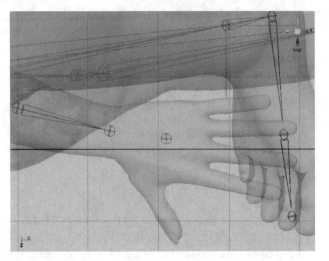

Figure 13-28

6. In a similar fashion to the way we created the actual fingers of our model, we will create the finger joints. Start at the first knuckle of the index finger and create a joint for each of the knuckles, ending with a joint at the fingertip. Be sure to hold down the **Shift** key to keep the joints in a straight line.

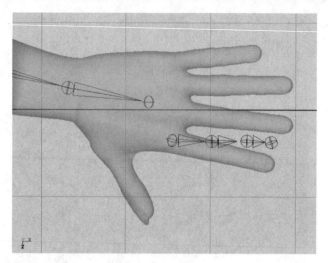

Figure 13-29

7. Select the first joint of the finger and select **Edit | Duplicate**.
    Move the joints over to the middle finger, then rotate and scale
    them to fit the geometry. Repeat the process until you have all
    of the fingers completed.

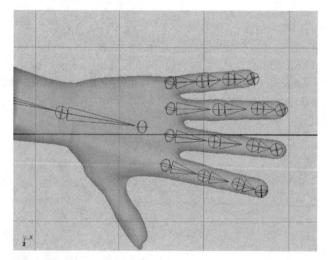

Figure 13-30

8. Copy the finger one last time and move it over for the thumb.
   The thumb is unique because the first joint resides more or less in the palm of the hand. It is also unique in the fact that it rotates in more of 45-degree angle, so we will have to account for that as well when we attach the fingers to the hand.

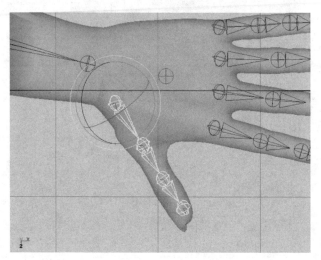

Figure 13-31

9. Create one final single joint on the pinky side of the hand.

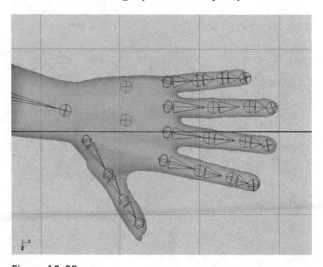

Figure 13-32

10. When we create our joints, by default they are positioned on the ground plane. Select the two single joints and then the root joint of the fingers and the thumb. Rotate into a front view and move the selected joints up to the hand of your model.

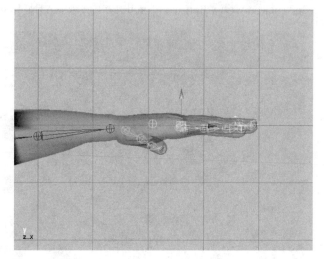

Figure 13-33

11. Before we parent the joints we will want to make sure that they are all in their proper position. Start by selecting the root joint of each of the fingers and adjusting them so that they are centered to each finger of your character.

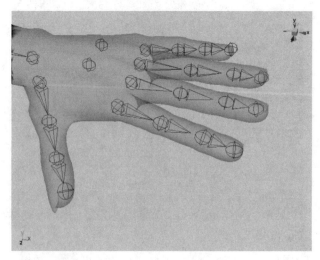

Figure 13-34

12. Once you have them positioned correctly, we can move on to the thumb. Start by selecting the root joint of the thumb. Shift-select the rest of the thumb joints and then select **Display | Transform Display ▸ Local Rotation Axes** [v7: Display | Component Display ▸ Local Rotation Axes]. You should now be able to see a local axis for each of the thumb joints.

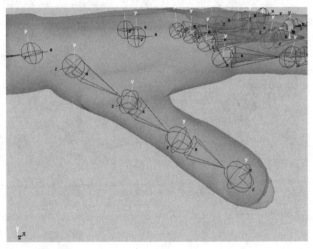

Figure 13-35

13. Select the root of the thumb and rotate it so that the local axis is at a 45-degree angle. Rotate and scale the joints so that they are aligned with the thumb of your model.

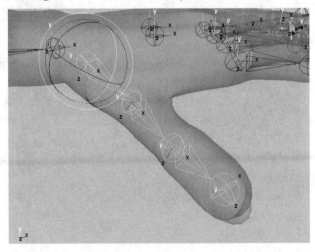

Figure 13-36

415

14. Now we can parent all of our hand joints to the wrist of our model. Begin by selecting the root joint of the pinky finger and then Shift-selecting the single joint on the outer part of the hand. Hit the **P** key to parent the pinky joints.

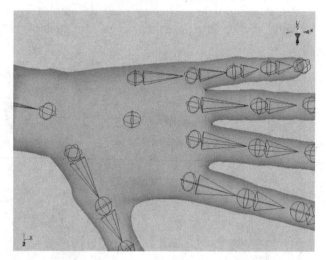

Figure 13-37

15. Select the root joint of the three remaining fingers and then parent them to the single joint in the center of the hand.

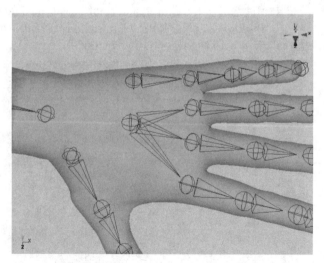

Figure 13-38

16. Select the root joint of the thumb and the two root joints in the hand and then parent them to the wrist joint.

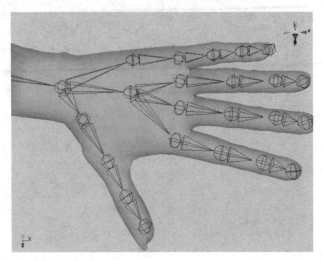

Figure 13-39

17. Now that all of the joints are parented, let's perform a simple test to check if all of our axes are correct. Select the first knuckle of the index finger. Shift-select the rest of the index finger joints. Continue to add the rest of the fingers and thumb joints to your selection. Don't select the joints in the hand itself.

18. Once you have all of the joints selected, use the rotate manipulator to check them out. If all is well, the fingers should begin to make the shape of a fist as you rotate them on the Z-axis.

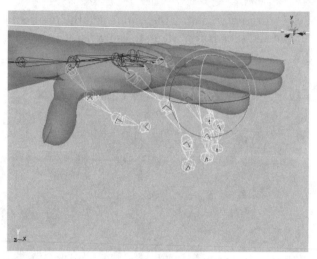

Figure 13-40

After you are through playing around, make sure you return the fingers to their original positions.

19. Before we go any further we will need to name the joints in our hand. Name the joint in the center of the palm **left_hand_1**. The joint on the outer part of the hand should be named **left_hand _2**. Name the rest of the joints as follows: **left_thumb_1, left_thumb_2, left_thumb_3, left_thumb_ end, left_index_1, left_index_2, left_index_3, left_index_ end, left_middle_1, left_middle_2, left_middle_3, left_ middle_end, left_ring_1, left_ring_2, left_ring_3, left_ring_end, left_pinky_1, left_pinky_2, left_pinky_3,** and **left_pinky_end**.

20. We still have one last joint to connect. Go back and select **left_clav**. Zero its rotations by selecting **Modify | Freeze Transformations**, and then parent it to **spine_5**.

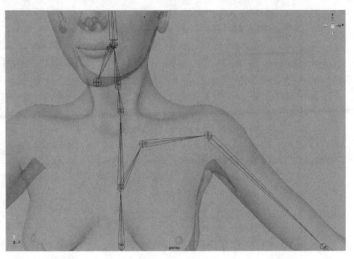

Figure 13-41

21. Now that we have our arm completed we will rotate the group to its neutral position by setting the Z-axis rotational angle back to **0**. At this point we can get rid of the group by selecting the pelvis joint and the geometry and then selecting **Edit | Unparent**.

We now have the joints laid out for the left side of our character. In order to get the right side joints, we will simply mirror our joints from the left side over to the right.

22. Select the **left_clav joint**, then select **Skeleton | Mirror Joint ❑**. When the dialog box opens, verify that Mirror Across is set to **YZ**.

23. When you hit **Apply**, the right-side arm joints will appear and will also be parented to the spine joint. Also note that all of the joints have been renamed using "right_" automagically!

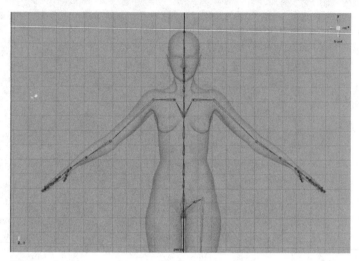

Figure 13-42

24. Select **left_hip** and mirror it to get the right leg. Once again, the renamed joints should appear parented to pelvis_2.

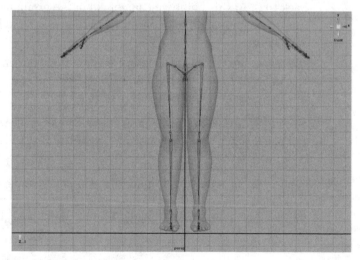

Figure 13-43

25. We now have our complete skeleton and are ready to move on to setting up a rig. Before moving on though, verify that all of the joints are oriented correctly. If a joint does not have the proper orientation, select **Skeleton | Orient Joints** to make the proper adjustments. Set Orientation to **XYZ** and Second Axis World Orientation to **+z**. In some cases, Second Axis should be set to –z. Make sure the joint orientation resembles the following figure.

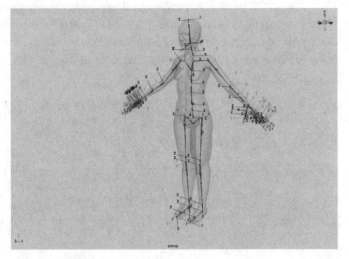

Figure 13-44

26. **Delete History and save!**

Creating Controls for the Pelvis and Torso

With our skeleton complete, our next step will be to set up our character to be animated. The base skeleton itself is really only useful for motion capture where all of the joints are driven by motion capture data.

In a nutshell, *motion capture* involves the placing of reflective markers on the joints of a live actor. As the actor moves, the data is captured and applied to the joints of your skeleton.

In our case we will be setting up our character to be hand animated. When we animate our character manually we want to make the process as easy as possible. That means adding a "rig" to our skeleton. A rig consists of handles or shapes that will "control" the movement of our skeleton.

1. The first step in creating a rig is setting up the controllers for our torso. Start by selecting **Create | NURBS Primitives ▸ Circle**. Scale the circle so that it is about the size of a hula hoop in comparison to your character. Name the circle **pelvis_control**.

2. Move the pelvis_control up and press the **V** key to snap it to the pelvis. Select **Modify | Freeze Transformations**. Your pelvis_control now has zeroed local coordinates. This will make it easier to return it to its default position as you progress.

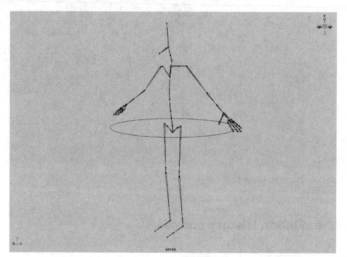

Figure 13-45

3. Now we will create a more advanced setup for the spine. Select **Skeleton | IK Spline Handle Tool ▢**. When the dialog opens, leave the default settings except for Number of Spans, which you should set to **1**, and then check the **Root Twist Mode** option. Select **spine_1** and then **spine_6**. A spline IK handle will appear at the neck, as shown in Figure 13-46.

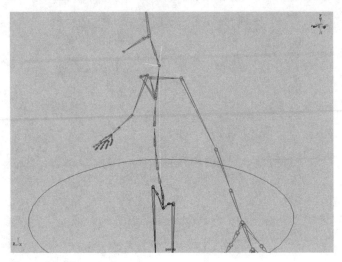

Figure 13-46

4. In the Outliner, Shift-select **pelvis** to show the entire hierar-
   chy. Select **curve1** from the list.

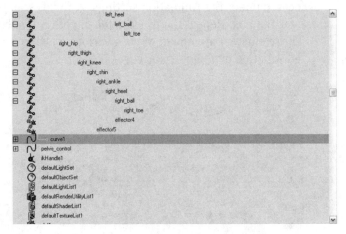

Figure 13-47

5. With curve1 selected, switch to component mode. You should
   see a total of four tiny purple boxes. There should be two solid
   boxes and two wireframe boxes.

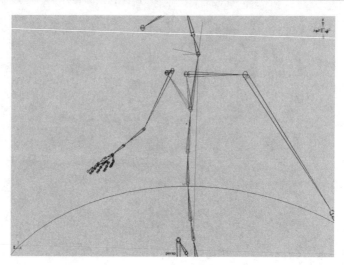

Figure 13-48

6. Ignore the first box at the base of the spine and then select the next box up the spline. Select **Deform | Create Cluster** located under the Animation settings. A tiny C should appear over the box. Repeat the process for the other two boxes. These clusters are one of Maya's various ways to control the deformation of geometry or curves.

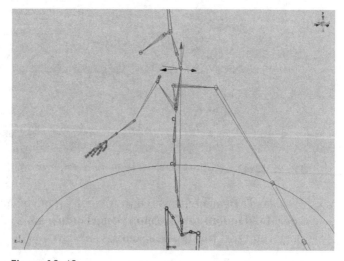

Figure 13-49

7. Create a polygon cube and move it up and behind the spine. Duplicate the cube for each of the corresponding clusters. You should have a total of three cubes. Position the cubes so that they are directly behind each of the clusters. Select the middle cube and duplicate it once more. Move it back behind the other cubes.

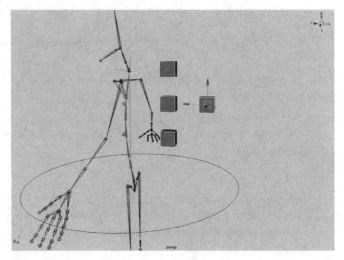

Figure 13-50

8. Select all four cubes and go to **Modify | Freeze Transformations** to zero the translation values on the cubes. Name the cubes **spine_control1, spine_control2, spine_control3**, and **spine_control_master.** In the Outliner, select the three cluster handles, one at a time, and use the **P** key to parent each to the cube directly behind it. Select each of the cubes and parent them to **spine_control_master.**

9. Now if you move the cubes you will see the spline IK at work. Either undo your moves or type **0** in the appropriate spine_control Translate XYZ to return the cubes to their original positions.

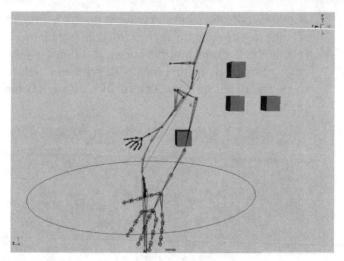

Figure 13-51

The last thing we need to do for the spine is to have spine_control_master control the twist of the spine. For this particular situation we will create a new attribute to do just that.

10. With **spine_control_master** selected, go to **Modify | Add Attribute ☐**. When the dialog box opens, type **SpineTwist** in the Attribute Name box. Under Numeric Attribute Properties, type **–45** for the Minimum value and **45** for the Maximum value, then press **OK**.

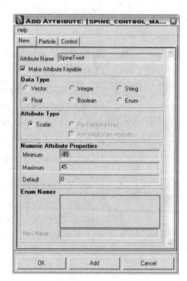

Figure 13-52

Now when you select the spine_control_master, the SpineTwist attribute will appear at the bottom of the list in the Channel Box. Right now the attribute does absolutely nothing. We have to connect it to something — namely the Twist attribute of the spline IK.

11. Select **Window | General Editors ▸ Connection Editor.** When the dialog box opens, make sure **spine_control_master** is selected and then click **ReloadLeft** at the top of the window. Next, select the spline IK handle and click the **ReloadRight** button. Then you simply select **SpineTwist** in the left column and **Twist** in the right. These attributes are now linked and the spline IK twist is now driven by the SpineTwist attribute.

12. Now select the **pelvis** and Shift-select **pelvis_control.** Hit the **P** key to parent the pelvis to the controller. Now all movement of the pelvis is accomplished by translating and rotating the pelvis_control.

Figure 13-53

Now we will set up a control for the lower pelvis. Basically, the lower pelvis is used for rocking the pelvis forward and backward. This makes it easier to animate your character in a seated position, as well as help convey weight distribution when the model stands in a relaxed pose.

13. Create a new polygon cube and move it up to rest behind pelvis_2. Select **Modify | Freeze Transformations** to zero out the cube's translations. Name the cube **pelvis_tilt.**

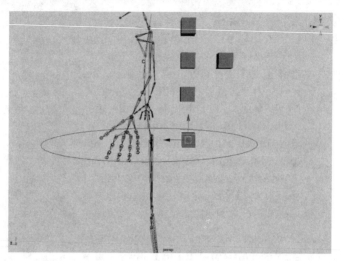

Figure 13-54

14. We'll once again use the Connection Editor to set up the motion for pelvis_2. Open **Window | General Editors ▸ Connection Editor** and enter **pelvis_tilt** in ReloadLeft and then **pelvis_2** in ReloadRight. Select **Translate Y** in the pelvis_tilt column. Now select **Rotate Y** in the pelvis_2 column. The rotation Y of the lower pelvis is now controlled by pelvis_tilt. Move pelvis_tilt up and down to see the effects.

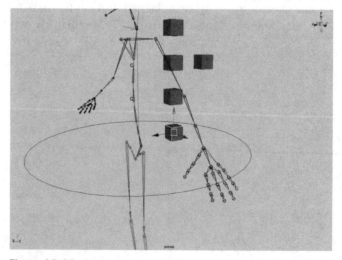

Figure 13-55

15. With **pelvis_tilt** selected, press **Ctrl+A**. When the Attribute Editor panel opens, make sure the first tab is selected. Click on the **Limit Information** panel. Under Translate, click the check boxes next to each of the Trans Limits on both the Min and Max sides. Click on the arrow to the right of the Min column and to the left of the Max column for Trans Limit X and Trans Limit Z. The X and Z boxes should now be set to **0.00**.

16. Set the values for the Translate Y to **–0.5**, **0.00**, **0.5**. This will prevent you from moving the pelvis too far. It should have a subtle motion. We now have our torso pretty well rigged, so it's time to move on to the next step, which is to rig the head.

Creating Head Controls

The setup for the head is pretty much identical to that of the pelvis, only on a smaller scale.

1. Create a new NURBS circle and name it **head_control**. Rotate the circle 90 degrees on the Z-axis. Move the head_control up so that it either encompasses the head joints or sits above them. Freeze the transforms on the circle.

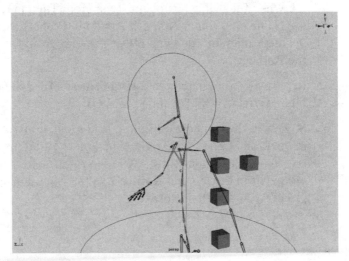

Figure 13-56

2. With **head_control** selected, press **Ctrl+A**. When the Attribute Editor panel opens, make sure the first tab is selected. Click on the **Limit Information** panel. Under Translate, click the check boxes next to each of the Trans Limits on both the Min and Max sides. Click on the arrow to the right of the Min column and to the left of the Max column for Trans Limit X, Y, and Z settings. The X, Y, and Z boxes should now be set to **0.00**. Check all of the boxes under the Rotate panel. Set the Rot Limit X, Y, and Z to **0.00** as well.

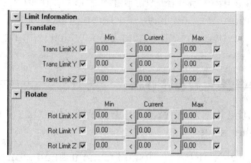

Figure 13-57

3. With **head_control** selected, go to **Modify | Add Attribute** ❏. When the dialog box opens, type **HeadTurn** in the Attribute Name box. Under Numeric Attribute Properties, type **–60** for the Minimum value and **60** for the Maximum value. Click the **Add** button.

4. Repeat the process to create **HeadTilt** at **–45, 45** and **HeadTwist** at **–35, 35**, then press **OK**.

5. So now in the Connection Editor, load **head_control** in the left side and **head** in the right side. Select **HeadTurn** in the left column and then **Rotate X** in the right. Next, select **HeadTilt** in the left and **Rotate Z** in the right. Finally, select **HeadTwist** and then **Rotate Y**.

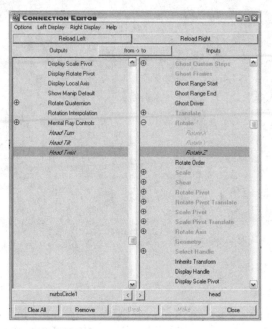

Figure 13-58

So the head should be in pretty good shape. If you want to be a Mr. Fancypants, you could add other attributes that control the jaw movement, rotate the neck, etc.

Creating Arm and Hand Controls

In this step we will set up the controls for our arm and then controls for the hands. When we get to the hand portion of the setup I'll show you two common methods for controlling the fingers, one using IK and the other utilizing the Connection Editor.

1. Let's get started with the arm. Select **Skeleton | IK Handle Tool** ☐. When the dialog opens, set the Current Solver to **ikRPsolver**. Select the **left_forearm** joint and then the **left_shoulder**. You now have an IK link for your left arm. Grab the IK handle and move it around a bit. Make sure to return it to its original position. Name the handle **left_arm_IK**.

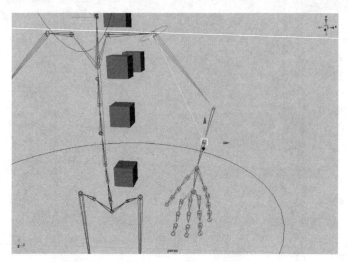

Figure 13-59

Now because we are using an extra bone in the forearm to rotate the wrist, we didn't begin the IK chain on the wrist bone. This would lock the ability to freely rotate the forearm during animation. Placing the IK chain one joint up will leave the forearm free to be rotated.

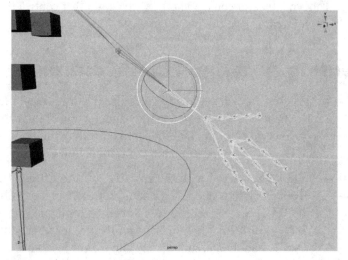

Figure 13-60

2. The next step will be to set up a controller for our arm. In our example we will use a locator for our control. Select **Create | Locator**. A locator will appear at the origin. Hold the **V** key and snap the locator to **left_wrist**.

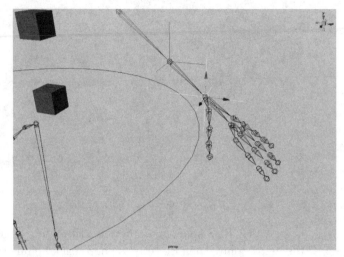

Figure 13-61

3. With the locator selected, go to **Modify | Freeze Transformations**. Your locator now has zeroed local coordinates. This will make it easier to return the locator to its default position as you progress. Name the locator **left_arm_control**.

4. Next, we need to enable our locator to control the IK handle. Select **left_arm_control** and then **left_arm_IK**. Hit the **P** key to parent the IK handle to the control. The IK handle is now being controlled by the locator.

    In addition to the arm_control, we can add a few other controls to make sure our arm moves the way we want it to.

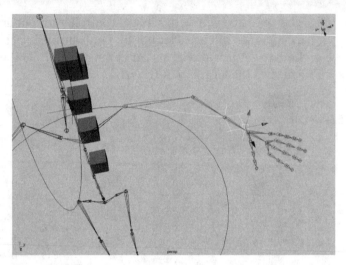

Figure 13-62

5. Create a NURBS sphere and then use the **V** key to snap it to the elbow joint. Then move the sphere back behind the elbow.

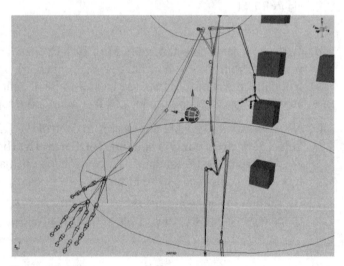

Figure 13-63

6. Select **Modify | Freeze Transformations.** Name the sphere **left_elbow_control.** With **left_elbow_control** selected, select the **left_arm_IK** handle. Then go to **Constraints | Pole Vector.** The sphere will now dictate the direction that the elbow points. If you want, you can parent the elbow control to the arm control. Try moving the left_arm_control along with the left_elbow_control.

7. Create a new NURBS sphere and place it directly behind the left shoulder. Call the sphere **left_shoulder_control.**

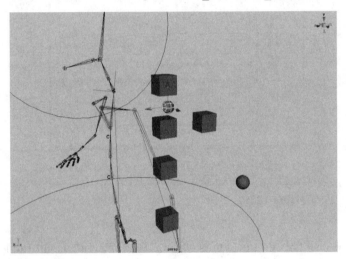

Figure 13-64

To get a really cool setup for the arm we will use expressions. *Expressions* are simple lines of code that connect attributes. The reason we want to use expressions here instead of the Connection Editor is because we want to be able to create situations where if you move one object 10 units, the second object may move 20 units. There is an alternative method using the Connection Editor that we will get to later.

Just a quick note here. Because of the angle of this joint, you need to verify that you are setting up the right rotation. In this case, the rotate attribute of the clavicle may be Z or Y.

8. Open **Window | Animation Editors ▸ Expression Editor**. In the box labeled Expression at the bottom, type **left_clav.rotateZ = (left_shoulder_control.translateY) *10.**

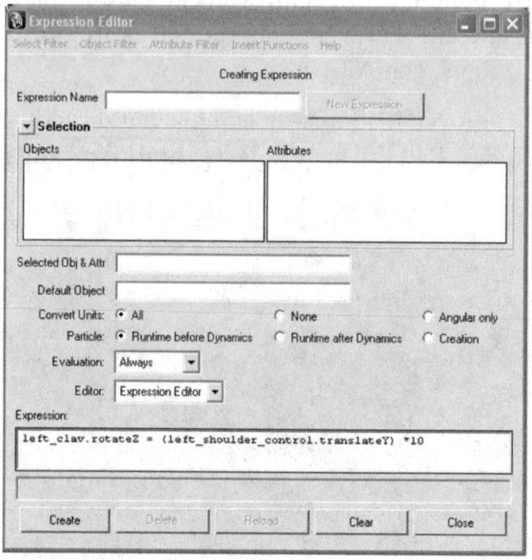

Figure 13-65

This expression is stating that for every 1 unit the left_shoulder_control is moved along the Y-axis, the left_clav will rotate 10 units on the Z-axis. This will prevent us from having to move the shoulder controller too far away from the rig in order to rotate the clavicle.

It is important to note that the controller is being moved in world space while the joints are rotating on their local axis, hence the reason a translation on the Y-axis could control the rotation on a Z-axis.

Another thing to note is that the only part of the Expression Editor you need to concern yourself with is the box under Expression near the bottom of the window. Once you create the expression, Maya knows to assign the values to the proper nodes in the scene.

9. Create a new expression and type **left_clav.rotateY =
   (left_shoulder_control.translateZ) *10.**

   This expression will rotate the clavicle forward and backward
   when the shoulder control is moved on the Z-axis.

10. Let's go in and limit the translations. With **left_shoul-
    der_control** selected, hit **Ctrl+A** on the keyboard. Under
    Limit Information, check all of the boxes under Translate. Set
    the Trans Limit X to **0.00**, Trans Limit Y to **−2.00, 0.00, 3.50**,
    and Trans Limit Z to **−1.00, 0.00, 3.50**.

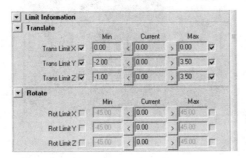

Figure 13-66

Like I said before, there is an alternative approach to what we
have just done that allows us to use the Connection Editor and
some of Maya's other fancy doo-dads.

11. First off, open up the **Hypershade.** In the Create Maya Nodes
    dialog box on the left, scroll down under General Utilities and
    select **Multiply Divide.** You will see the node pop up in the
    Work Area to the right.

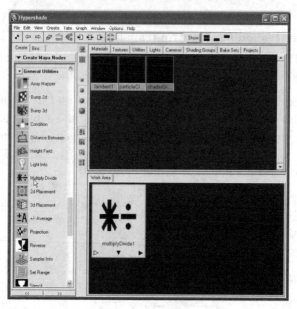

Figure 13-67

12. Keep the Hypershade open, and select **Window | General Editors ▸ Connection Editor.** Select the **left_shoulder_control** in your viewport and then select **Reload Left** in the Connection Editor. Select the **multipyDivide** node from the Work Area of the Hypershade. Select **Load Right** in the Connection Editor.

13. In the left_shoulder_control Outputs, scroll down and select **TranslateY** under Translate. In the multiplyDivide Inputs, select **InputZ** under Input1.

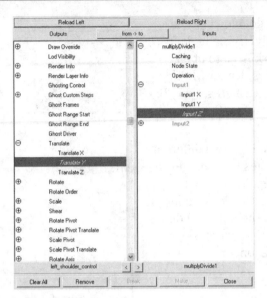

Figure 13-68

14. Now we need to switch things around. Select the **multiplyDivide** node and then select **Reload Left**. Select the **left_clav** and select **Reload Right**. Under multiplyDivide, scroll down and select **OutputZ** under Output. In the left_clav column, select **RotateZ** under Rotate.

Figure 13-69

15. Finally, double-click the **multiplyDivide** node in the Work Area to open its attributes. Under Multiply-Divide Attributes, type **20** in the last box to the right of Input2.

So there it is, two different approaches that will get the same results. I've heard a tech artist buddy of mine say that the only real difference is that expressions can take longer to compute than the node-based solution.

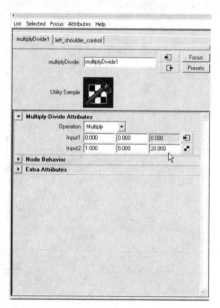

Figure 13-70

16. Now we will add a controller for the rotation of the forearm. With **left_arm_ control** selected, go to **Modify | Add Attribute ⬚**. When the dialog box opens, type **Forearm-Rotate** in the Attribute Name box. Under Numeric Attribute Properties, type **–45** for the Minimum value and **45** for the Maximum value. Click the **OK** button.

17. In the Connection Editor, load **left_arm_control** in the left side and **left_forearm** in the right side. Select **Forearm Rotate** in the left column and then **Rotate X** in the right.

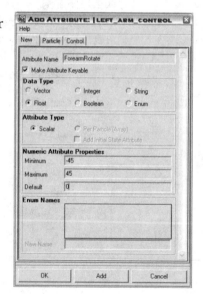

Figure 13-71

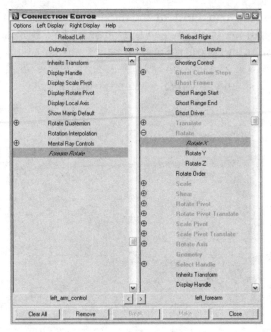

Figure 13-72

The last thing we will do with the arm is set up an automatic rotation of the clavicle as the arm is raised and lowered. Make sure the arm is back in its starting location.

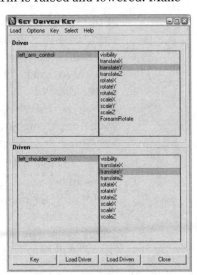

18. Open **Animate | Set Driven Key ▸ Set ☐**. When the dialog box opens, you should see a Driver area on the top and a Driven area on the bottom. Select **left_arm_control** and click **Load Driver.** Now select **left_shoulder_control** and click **Load Driven.** Select **translateY** from both the Driver and Driven lists, then click the **Key** button.

Figure 13-73

19. Select **left_arm_control** and move it up on the Y-axis by typing **10** for TranslateY in the Channel Box. Now select **left_shoulder_control** and move it up as far as it will go, then click **Key** at the bottom of the Set Driven Key window. The clavicle should now rotate when the arm is raised.

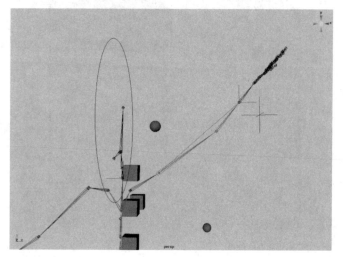

Figure 13-74

20. Now let's adjust for the clavicle relaxing when the arm is down at the side. Select the **left_shoulder_control** and move it as far down as it will go. Move the **left_arm_IK** down by typing **–10** for the TranslateY of the Channel Box. Click **Key** again. Now as you raise and lower the arm, the clavicle will raise and relax along with it. You can create a similar setup so that the clavicle reacts when the arm moves forward and backward as well. Try playing around with it on your own. You should now step through and repeat this process with the right arm.

Once you have both arms set up, you can work on the fingers. As I said before, there are two different setups that are commonly used for fingers. One is to set up attributes and then use the attributes to drive the rotation of the fingers using set driven keys. The second method is to set up the fingers with IK. We will begin by discussing the former.

Some animators prefer attributes to control the movement of the fingers. What we would normally do is add extra attributes to the left_arm_control. For example, we might add an attribute called fist that will curl the fingers into a fist position as we adjust the numeric value. And there can be as many attributes as you want. Usually there is one for every finger and then additional attributes that control all of the fingers at once. The aforementioned fist along with a relaxed hand or extended fingers would be good examples.

I will run though the setup for one finger here. This should give you enough information to set up additional attributes for whatever you want. The first thing we will do is add an additional attribute to the left_arm_control.

21. With **left_arm_control** selected, select **Modify | Add Attribute ☐**. When the dialog box opens, name the new attribute **indexCurl**. Leave Data Type set to **Float** and Attribute Type set to **Scalar**.

22. Under Numeric Attribute Properties, type **–2** for the Minimum, **10** for the Maximum, and **0** for the Default. Hit the **OK** button to finish. Now if you take a look at the Channel Box, beneath Visibility you should see your new attribute. Highlight **indexCurl** and middle-mouse-button drag back and forth in your viewport. The value should go from –2 to 10. Be sure to set the value back to **0** when you are finished.

23. So now we have our attribute and we need to connect it to something. Open **Animate | Set Driven Key ▸ Set ☐**. Select the **left_arm_control** and press **Load Driver**. You should see the list of attributes appear in the right column under Driver.

Figure 13-75

24. Now select **left_index_1**, **left_index_2**, and **left_index_3** and then press **Load Driven**. The three joints are displayed on the left side of the Driven column. When each one is highlighted, its attributes appear to the right.

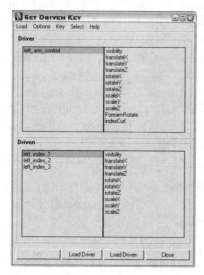

Figure 13-76

25. Highlight the **indexCurl** attribute under Driver and then highlight **rotateZ** under left_index_1. Press **Key**. Repeat the process with left_index_2 and left_index_3. Now select **left_arm_control** under Driver and, in the Channel Box, set the value of indexCurl to **10**. In the scene, select **left_index_1** and then Shift-select **left_index_2** and **left_index_3**. Rotate the joints so that they curl down into the palm.

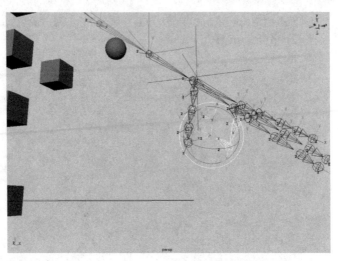

Figure 13-77

26. Press **Key** again for each of the joints. Now when you move the value on the indexCurl attribute, the finger should respond by curling and uncurling. Set indexCurl to **–2** and then select the joints in the same manner as before and rotate them slightly so that the finger appears hyperextended. Key each of the joints again. The rotation of the index finger joints is now controlled by the indexCurl attribute.

This should give you an idea of how attributes can be used to control the fingers. You may also in your infinite wisdom see a number of ways to use attributes for other purposes. Next, we will take a look at using IK to control the fingers.

27. Begin by selecting **Create | Polygon Primitives ▸ Cube ⬜**. When the dialog box opens, set the Width, Height, and Depth to **0.25**. Move the cube up so that it is positioned in front of the index finger. Name it **left_index_control**. Duplicate the cube for each of the fingers and the thumb. Name them **left_middle_control, left_ring_control, left_pinky_control**, and **left_thumb_control**.

28. Select each of the cubes and then select **Modify | Freeze Transformations.**

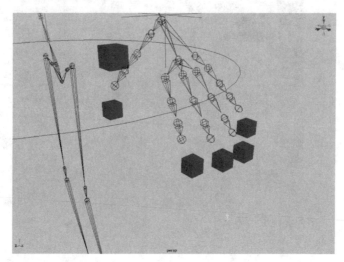

Figure 13-78

29. Select **Skeleton | IK Handle Tool** ⬜. When the dialog box opens, be sure Current Solver is set to **ikSCsolver**. Select **left_index_end** and then **left_index_1**. Repeat this same process for the remaining fingers as well as the thumb. Name the IK handles accordingly, using this convention: left_(finger name)_IK.

30. Select **left_index_IK** and then parent it to **left_index_control**. Do the same with each of the remaining fingers and the thumb. You should now be able to control the bending and finger position using the cubes. As a final step, parent the cube controls to **left_arm_control**. That's about it for the IK hand setup. If you have difficulties with the finger joints getting all wacky, try limiting the rotational axes.

So there you have it. Two completely different setups to control finger movement. As stated, you can use attributes to control just about anything. It really depends on how you would like to approach animating your character. Make sure you repeat the process on the right arm. When it comes to the hand, perform only the operation that you find most comfortable.

Creating Leg and Foot Controls

1. Select **Skeleton | IK Handle Tool** ☐, set Current Solver to **ikRPsolver,** and then select **left_ankle** and **left_thigh.** The IK handle for the left leg should be visible. Name the handle **left_leg_IK.**

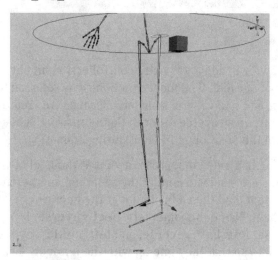

Figure 13-79

2. Create another IK link set to **ikSCsolver** from **left_ball** to **left_ankle,** and then one more from **left_toe** to **left_ball.** Name the IK handles **left_ball_IK** and **left_toe_IK,** respectively.

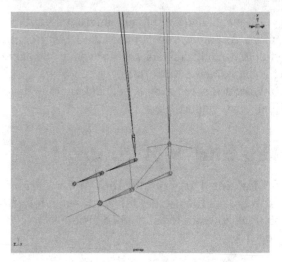

Figure 13-80

Next, we will add a few extra controllers to simplify the movement of our foot. The most common rig is referred to as a *reverse foot control*; it is so named because we create a joint structure in a reverse order to that of the foot. This will then control the position of the foot during animation.

3.   Starting in a side view, create a joint at the heel of your skeleton. Create a second joint at the toe, then another at the ball of the foot, and then a final joint at the heel where you started the chain. Name the joints **left_heel_reverse, left_toe_ reverse, left_ball_reverse**, and **left_ankle_reverse**. Move the joints so that they line up with the left foot. As a final step, select **left_heel_reverse** and then freeze its transformations.

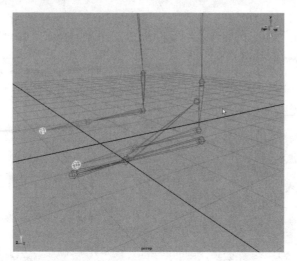

Figure 13-81

4. Select the **left_toe_IK** and parent it to **left_toe_reverse**. Parent **left_ball_IK** to **left_ball_reverse**, and finally parent **left_leg_IK** to **left_ankle_reverse**.

5. Create a cube and position it to the right of the foot. Select **Modify | Freeze Transformations** to zero the coordinates of the cube. Name the cube **left_foot_control**.

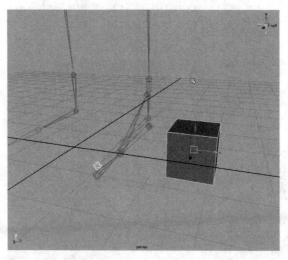

Figure 13-82

6. Select **left_heel_reverse** and parent it to **left_foot_control**. This box can now be used to position the foot. Move it around and check it out. You can at any point zero the Translate XYZ of the cube in the Channel Box to return the foot to its original position. In addition, rotating the joints of the reverse foot setup will rotate the foot as well.

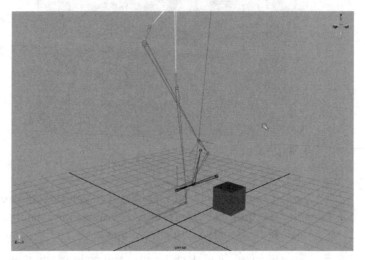

Figure 13-83

7. Select the **pelvis_control** and move the skeleton up and down. Notice that the foot will stay put when the pelvis is lowered or stand on its toes when the pelvis is raised.

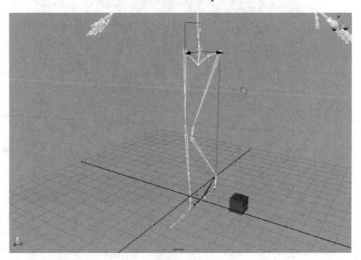

Figure 13-84

So let's add some attributes to the foot control that will allow us to control the reverse foot setup.

8. With **left_foot_control** selected, select **Modify | Add Attribute □**. When the dialog box opens, name the new attribute **ToeRoll**. Leave Data Type set to **Float** and Attribute Type set to **Scalar**.

9. Under Numeric Attribute Properties, type **0** for the Minimum, **10** for the Maximum, and **0** for the Default. Hit the **OK** button to finish. Now if you take a look at the Channel Box, you should see your new attribute ToeRoll. Highlight **ToeRoll** and middle-mouse-button drag back and forth in your viewport. The value should go from 0 to 10. Be sure to set the value back to **0** when you are finished.

10. Select **Animate | Set Driven Key ▸ Set □**. Select the **left_foot_control** and press **Load Driver.** You should see the list of attributes appear in the right column under Driver.

Figure 13-85

11. Select **left_toe_reverse** and press **Load Driven**. Select the **ToeRoll** attribute and then select **rotateZ** under left_toe_ reverse. Press **Key** at the bottom of the dialog box.

12. Select **left_foot_control** and type **10** next to ToeRoll in the Channel Box. Now select **left_toe_reverse** and rotate it up until the foot rises to a comfortable position, then hit **Key** at the bottom of the window. The foot should now rotate up when the ToeRoll attribute is at 10.

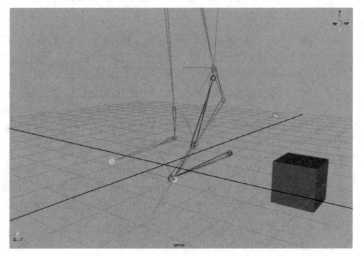

Figure 13-86

13. Let's add another attribute to our left_foot_control. With the **left_foot_control** selected, once again open **Modify | Add Attribute □**. Name the new attribute **ballRoll** and, under Numeric Attribute Properties, type **0** for the Minimum, **10** for the Maximum, and **0** for the Default.

14. In the Set Driven Key window, click on **left_foot_control**. The new attribute should appear in the window. Select **left_ball_reverse** and load it into the Driven window. As before, select the **ballRoll** attribute and then select **rotateZ** under left_ball_reverse. Select **left_foot_control** and type **10** next to ballRoll in the Channel Box. Select **left_ball_reverse** and rotate it so that the toes stay grounded and the heel rotates up, then hit **Key** at the bottom of the window. Now repeat this entire process of creating controls for the right foot and leg.

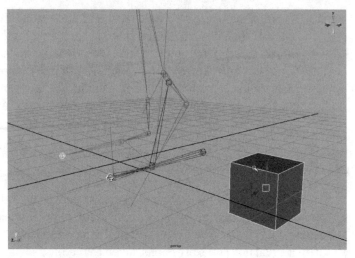

Figure 13-87

This is about as far as we will take our rig. You should now have a pretty good basic understanding of what is involved in the rigging process. Figure 13-88 shows a fully rigged skeleton with all the bells and whistles.

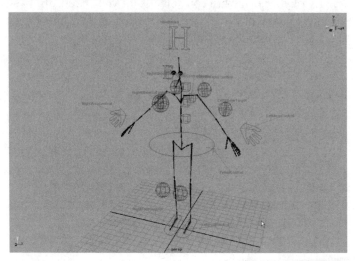

Figure 13-88

15. As a final step, create a new layer and name it **IK_L**. Select all of the IK handles and assign them to this layer. In the Layer Editor, select **T** to template the layer. Because all of the IK links are controlled by something else, there is no reason to have them selectable. Create one additional layer and name it **controls_L**. Add all of the controls to this layer. This will make it easier to turn the visibility off during renders.

Wrap-Up

We covered quite a bit in this chapter. Not only did we set up a skeleton for our model, but we also set up controls to more easily animate it. We learned how to set up attributes and set driven keys with a small dose of expressions added to the mix.

As you advance you may want to take the time to create controllers using Create | CV Curve Tool. This way you can draw out shapes such as arrows or even hands or feet. Obviously this is not necessary, but it looks pretty damn cool!

This should give you a good understanding of the rigging process and you should now have enough knowledge to create a basic rig of your own with controls to suit your needs. But as you can see, a great deal of work goes into setting up a rig, and in many ways we have just scratched the surface!

The Weighting Is the Hardest Part

The Process of Weighting Our Character

Refer to Chapter_14 on the companion CD.

Wow, isn't that a clever title for this chapter? Attaching the model to a skeletal rig is commonly referred to as weighting. In this process, the individual joints will influence each of the vertices on the model, thus making the character move. The art of proper weighting is a task that is very involved. You might even call it tedious at times.

In Maya, we call this process *skinning*. Luckily for us, Maya offers a pretty good tool set in order to make this process easier. Just like anything else, there are a number of different approaches to the skinning of a model. Some prefer to individually weight each of the vertices by using the Component Editor to give each joint a value that determines the amount of influence it has on each vertex.

Others prefer to paint the weights using the Artisan brush. We will cover a bit of both, but we will primarily use the Paint Skin Weights tool.

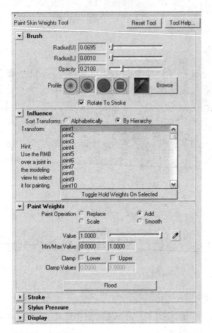

Figure 14-1

As stated, this can be a very time-consuming process, but the payoff is having a character that moves well. As we step through the process I won't go into great detail about how you should paint the weighting. Depending on the way you built your model, very detailed steps might not correspond to your particular model. Suffice it to say that this chapter should give you a good understanding of the process, and I have the utmost confidence you will be able to handle it!

ONE VERY IMPORTANT NOTE: Do Not Delete History as you work your way through the weighting process. Deleting history will also delete the skin cluster that attaches your model to the skeleton. This would not be a good thing. The alternative is to use Edit | Delete by Type ▸ Non-Deformer History. This will keep your weighting intact while deleting the history.

Normalized Weighting

Here is another buzzword to add to your word of the day calendar: *normalized*. Normalized weighting refers to the idea that no matter how many joints influence the movement of any vertex, their influence must always add up to 1.0.

So hypothetically we have a vertex that sits at the middle of the elbow. This vertex would be infuenced by both the upper arm joint as well as the elbow or lower arm joint. Since it resides right in the middle, the two joints would more than likely have equal influence: 0.5 for the upper arm joint and 0.5 for the lower arm joint. So if you do the math, and this is an easy one, $0.5 + 0.5 = 1.0$.

There is really no limit to the number of joints that can influence a particular vertex. I have found that on average three joints is usually the norm. This really depends on the type of joint you are dealing with. For example, the joints around the shoulder move considerably more than those on a joint that merely pivots, such as the knee joint, so more joints would be involved in weighting the shoulder area.

Like I mentioned in Chapter 13, it is very difficult to get real human motion on a character regardless of how good the modeling, rigging, and skinning may be. There are a few ways to compensate for problems in these areas, though. The method I prefer is using blend shapes to correct any unwanted deformations of the mesh. In this process you can use driven keys to drive the blend shape. This can really come in handy for problem areas such as the shoulders.

We also have the ability to mirror weighting. This speeds up the skinning process quite a bit. In a similar fashion to the modeling process, with mirror weighting you concentrate the majority of your efforts on one side of the model only.

Skinning Basics

So the first step in the weighting process is to attach the model to the skeleton. Select the mesh and then Shift-select the pelvis joint of your skeleton. Select Skin | Bind Skin ▶ Smooth Bind. We will be using the default setting for our purposes. Your mesh should now move whenever you rotate a joint on your character. Give it a try. At any point you can return your character to its default pose by selecting any joint and then Skin | Go to Bind Pose. This gives you the luxury of being able to move the joints all over and then easily return the character to the default pose.

Unfortunately, you may see some problems where Maya doesn't do such a hot job of assigning the weighting by default, as shown in Figure 14-2. This is to be expected. Many areas like the shoulder and hips will need a good deal of TLC before they will properly deform.

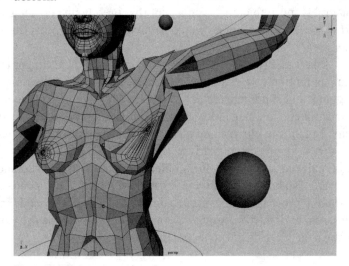

Figure 14-2

One important thing to mention is that you don't have to be in the base pose to adjust the weighting. This means you can apply animation to the skeleton and be able to adjust the weighting of the mesh as joints rotate into various positions. This will give you an accurate indication of how the mesh is deforming, making it considerably easier to adjust any problem areas.

It is also important to note that you are applying the weights to the cage mesh. As you make adjustments, you can apply a smooth node to the model to see how well it is deforming and then delete the node. You may instead want to create a Subdiv Proxy [v7: Smooth Proxy] to see the final mesh under the control mesh. Either way, you will need to use the control mesh to see any real-time deformation.

Painting the Weights

Let's start with the legs. First we'll set up a simple animation so that we can see the deformation of the knee as the pelvis moves up and down. We will use the controllers we created in the previous chapter (also available on the CD in Chapter 14\scenes).

1. At the bottom of the screen under the Time Slider you will see two boxes on the left and two boxes on the right, each containing numeric entries. The boxes on the left indicate the frame in which the animation begins. The boxes to the right indicate the number of frames in the animation. For our purposes, type **100** in the boxes on the right so that we will have a total of 100 animation frames to work with.

2. Select **pelvis_master_control**. Make sure the Time Slider at the bottom of the screen is all the way to the left. Set a key frame for the pelvis control by pressing the **S** key on your keyboard. You should see a vertical line on the Time Slider, indicating that a key frame has been set.

3. To the right of the Time Slider is a button that has a key symbol on it. Click the key. The key should turn red, indicating that auto keyframe is active. Now move the Time Slider to **20**. Using the pelvis_master_control, move the pelvis down so that the knees are bent.

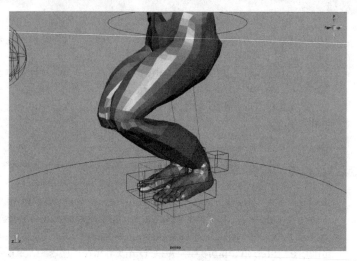

Figure 14-3

4. A new vertical line should appear in the Time Slider at frame
    20, indicating a new key has been set. Move the slider back
    and forth to see your character move up and down. Now you
    will be able to adjust the
    deformation of the leg at
    various stages of it bending.

5. So this is where we utilize
    the Paint Skin Weights tool.
    With the mesh selected,
    select **Skin | Edit Smooth
    Skin ▸ Paint Skin Weights
    Tool ⧠**. When the dialog
    box opens, you will notice a
    number of different settings
    that are very reminiscent of
    the Sculpt Geometry tool.

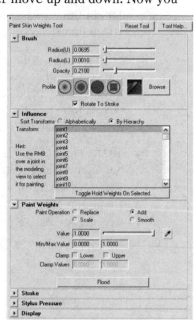

Figure 14-4

When painting the weights, the influence of each joint is by default more of a whiter shade. As the influence falls off, it will become increasingly more gray and then black where there is no influence (see Figure 14-5). As you paint, the color will change to indicate more or less influence depending on the brush settings you use. You can also use Multi-Color Feedback, which can be set under the Display tab of the Paint Skin Weights Tool window. Once again, we will concern ourselves with the left side (screen right) of the model.

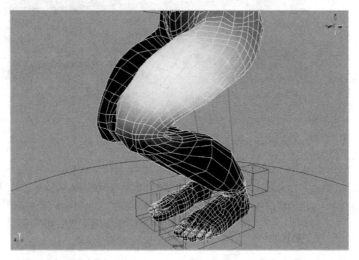

Figure 14-5

Chances are that as you move the slider you will notice that the leg loses some of its volume as it is bent.

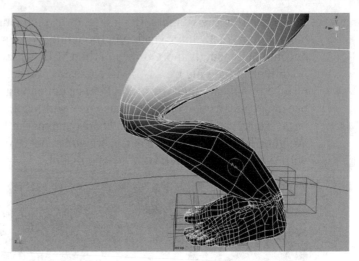

Figure 14-6

This is obviously something that we don't want.

6. Move the slider to around frame **15**. In the Influence section of the Paint Skin Weights Tool window, select the **left_thigh joint**. You may also select the joint by clicking on it in the scene with the middle mouse button and selecting **Paint Skin Weights**.

7. Under Paint Skin Weights, select **Add** for Paint Operation and then set Value to around **0.25**. This will give you a manageable value to begin the painting process.

8. Begin to paint the vertices on the back of the leg behind the knee. The idea is to close the gap between the back of the thigh and the calf. In order to get the weighting as close as possible, click on the **left_knee** with the middle mouse button and add a little influence by painting the verts. Utilize the Smooth operation as well as Add to get the best results. Switch back and forth between **left_thigh**, **left_knee**, and **left_calf**, adding and smoothing so that it looks similar to Figure 14-7. Remember to check the smoothed version of your model to see the end results.

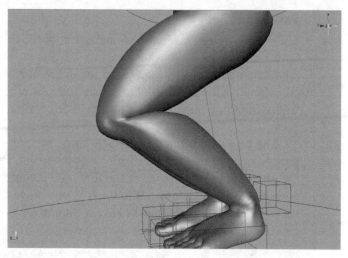

Figure 14-7

9. Continue this process to include the entire knee. One little trick is to add a bit of influence from the thigh a little farther down the calf and vice versa. This will give the appearance of the calf and thigh muscles compressing as they push against each other.

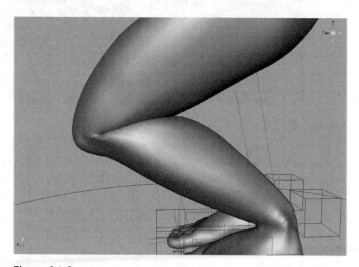

Figure 14-8

10. **Save your file!**

Let's move up and take care of one aspect of the thigh and butt. I say one aspect because we are only keying in on the forward rotation of the thigh when the figure moves into a crouching position. We will have to account for other instances where the thigh may rotate out to the side or when it rotates back.

The area where the thigh rotates up to meet the hip is probably one of the more difficult areas to weight. Proper placement of the thigh joint is the first step in getting good deformation. Take a look at the thigh as you move the slider back and forth. You will most likely see some problems at the aforementioned hip area as well as problems with the butt.

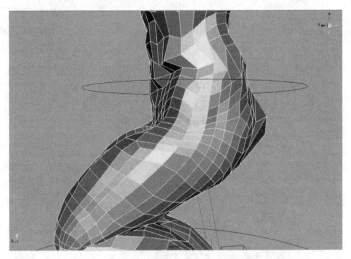

Figure 14-9

Let's start with the butt. The first thing we will do is try to even out the movement of the vertices as the thigh rotates. The idea is to evenly weight the area to the thigh and the pelvic bones. When the thigh rotates, we want to see nice even spacing between the edge loops as they are deformed.

11. In order to accomplish this we need to work back and forth between the thigh joint and the two pelvis joints. Use the Add and Smooth brushes until you get a nice rounded deformation when the thigh is rotated.

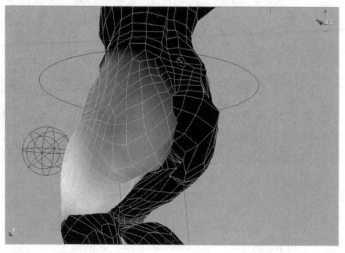

Figure 14-10

To really get a grasp on keeping the deformation spaced evenly, think of the shape of an accordion (or if you're not much into the polka scene, a paper fan) as an example. In both cases, as the folds move farther apart, they maintain a nice even spacing. This is what you should look for in the deformation of your mesh.

Moving on, the area in the crotch region should be more heavily weighted to the pelvis joints. The butt cheek should have a higher weighting concentration given to the thigh.

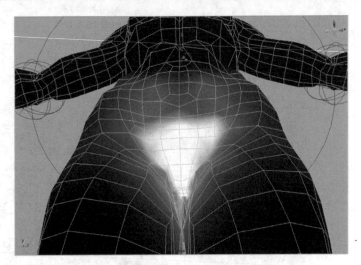

Figure 14-11

12. Let's focus in on the front of the thigh area near the hip. This is where you will really reap the benefits of maintaining a smoothness to the deformation. In this situation, begin by getting a pretty even weighting distribution between the thigh joint and the lower pelvis joint. Next, we want to close the gap between the thigh and the hip where they meet. This involves moving back and forth between the thigh and lower pelvis and adding influence. At the most extreme rotation, it is acceptable for the top of the thigh to intersect the geometry of the hip, and in some cases it might be unavoidable.

13. Check the thigh and compare it to Figure 14-12. Try to make the fold look as smooth and natural as possible.

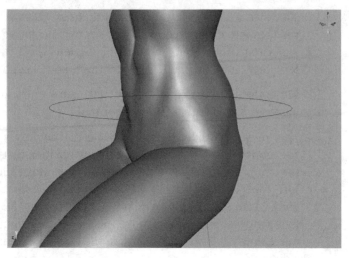

Figure 14-12

14. The interior of the thigh where it meets the pelvis can also cause some difficulties. Once again, try to get an even spacing of the edge loops to diminish the stretching that may occur (see Figure 14-13). You may find it necessary to move the right leg out of your way to better see your weighting. Just grab the right foot control and move it. When you are finished, return the foot control to its original position by typing **0** for the translation values.

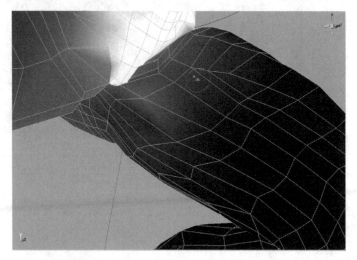

Figure 14-13

15. Next, we will add a few more keyframes so that we can move the legs into other positions to check our weighting. Move the slider to the first frame of the Time Slider. Select the **left_foot_control** and then press the **S** key to set a keyframe.

16. Move the slider to frame **20** and make sure a new keyframe has been set for the **left_foot_control**.

17. Now move the slider to frame **30**. Select the **pelvis_master_control** and move it to its starting position by typing **0** in the TranslateY setting in the Channel Box. Move the **left_foot_control** so that the leg extends from the side of the body. Make sure a new key has been created for the pelvis and foot controls. Now as you move the slider, your figure should move down and then up, and then the leg will extend to the side.

18. Note how the weighting that you have done for the thigh reacts to the new animation. One problem area might be some collapsing at the top of the hip.

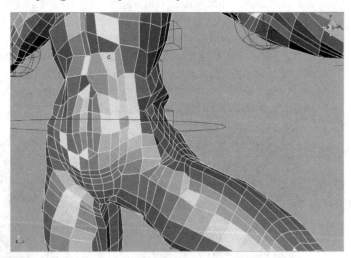

Figure 14-14

This is due to the fact that some of the vertices on the hip are being influenced by the thigh. It may look great when the leg is bent forward, but not so hot when it sticks out to the side. Quite the dilemma! We will have to create a nice balance between the different positions of the legs.

19. Begin by adding a bit more influence from the lower pelvis to the hip bone.

20. Move the slider back and forth and see how the crouch position is affected by the change in weighting. It may look fine or it may need some additional adjustments. Consider how the character is to be animated and what movements will occur more in the animation.

    The rule of thumb is to weight the character with emphasis on the weighting scheme that gives you the most bang for your buck. For example, if your character is going to sit or crouch more than it does the splits, you may want to give more emphasis to the weighting that suits that type of animation.

    If you have to have it all, you can always use blend shapes to fix the issue.

    Next, we will move down to the foot. This should be a walk in the park compared to weighting the thigh.

21. First, we will make a minor adjustment to our animation. Move the slider to frame **35** and select **left_foot_control**. Move the control by typing **0** in the TranslateX setting of the Channel Box. This should move the foot back to its original position.

22. Select the **pelvis_master_control** and press the **S** key on the keyboard with the mouse pointer hovering over the Time Slider to create a new key at its current position. Move the slider to frame **40** and then move **pelvis_master_control** up so that the character stands on its toes.

23. Select the mesh and then the Paint Skin Weights tool. Paint the foot and ankle joints until the foot deforms properly.

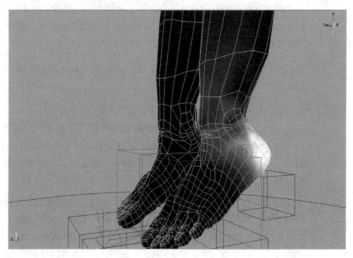

Figure 14-15

24. **Save your file!**

25. At this point we can mirror our weighting over to the right side of our figure. With the mesh selected, go to **Skin | Edit Smooth Skin ▶ Mirror Skin Weights ☐**. When the dialog box opens, select **YZ** for Mirror Across and make sure Direction Positive to Negative (+X to –X) is checked. Now as you scrub through the time line, the right leg of the model should have the same weighting as the left.

    The one minor issue that arises is any overlapping geometry will not get the correct weighting. If this should occur, and it more than likely will around the butt and crotch, you will need to go back in and fix the weighting. This is a task that should be done at the end of the weighting process when you are no longer mirroring the weights.

26. Now we will move up to the torso. With the Time Slider set to **40**, select **spine_master_control** and create a keyframe by pressing the **S** key. Move the slider to frame **45**. Move the **spine_master_control** forward on the Z-axis until the

character is bent over (see Figure 14-16). A new keyframe should appear for the spine_master_control in the timeline.

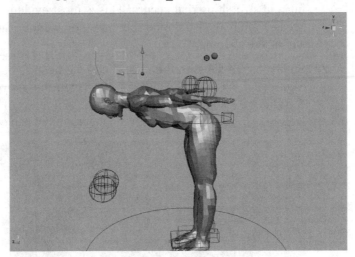

Figure 14-16

27. Move to frame **50** and move the **spine_master_control** back on the Z-axis so that the back is severely arched. A new keyframe should appear for the spine_master_control in the timeline. Adjust the individual spine controls so that the arch is a bit more realistic.

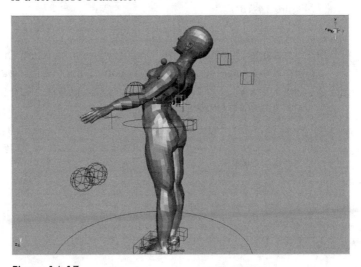

Figure 14-17

Now as we move the slider back and forth, the torso will bend forward and back. There tends to be some unnatural intersecting and stretching that occurs. This is most evident with the breast. You may also notice some problems under the arms and at the abdomen.

28. So just as we did with the lower body, we need to use the Paint Skin Weights tool to smooth out our weighting. As you move the slider back and forth, use the Paint tool to evenly blend the weighting over the torso until it appears to deform correctly.

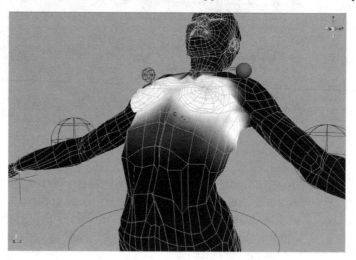

Figure 14-18

29. The stomach where it overlaps the hip area when the model bends over can be quite troublesome. This can be made to look considerably better if you use the pelvis tilt to adjust the position of the lower pelvis.

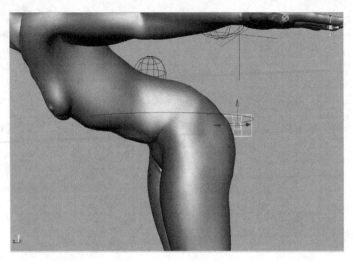

Figure 14-19

30. **Save your file!**

31. Once you have the torso in relatively good shape, we can move along to the arms. Move the slider to frame **55**. Select the **spine_master_control** and type **0** for the TranslateZ setting. This will return the control to its default position. Select **left_arm_control** and press the **S** key to give it a new keyframe.

32. Move the slider to frame **60** and move the **left_arm_control** up on the Y-axis so that the clavicle is raised as well (see Figure 14-20). Make sure a new key is created for the control.

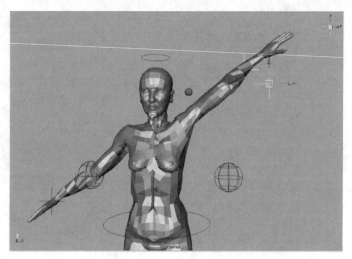

Figure 14-20

33. Move the slider to frame **65** and move the **left_arm_control** down on the Y-axis so that the clavicle is lowered. Check to make sure a new key has been created.

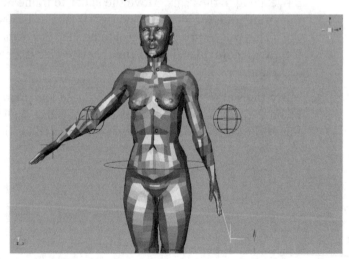

Figure 14-21

34. When the arm is raised, the palm of the hand generally faces forward. This rotation takes place mostly at the shoulder. Go back to frame **55** and create a keyframe for left_elbow_ control. Move to frame **60** and move the **left_elbow_control** on the Y-axis until the palm of your character is facing forward.

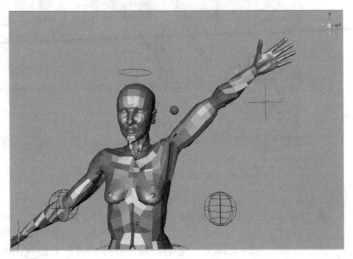

Figure 14-22

35. Move to frame **65** and return **left_elbow_control** to its default position, making sure a new keyframe has been created. As you scrub the slider back and forth, the arm should rotate as it is raised and lowered. This should give us a pretty good indication of what kind of work we need to do on the shoulder.

36. Like I have stated before, it's not easy to get perfect deformation of the shoulder. Work back and forth, moving between the **left_clav, left_shoulder**, and **spine_5** with the Paint Skin Weights tool. It will take a bit of effort to get a good deformation, so take your time. You should ultimately end up with something like Figure 14-23.

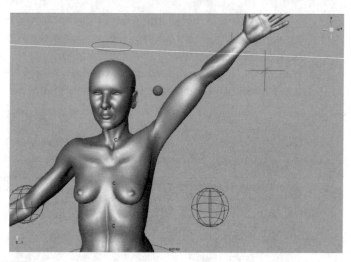

Figure 14-23

37. Move the Time Slider to frame **70** and move **left_arm_control** back to its starting position, making sure a keyframe is added. Move to frame **75** then move **left_arm_control** up on the Y-axis and then in toward the body on the X-axis until the arm is bent at the elbow. Make sure a new keyframe has been created.

38. In a similar fashion to the knee, use the Paint Skin Weights tool to get a clean deformation.

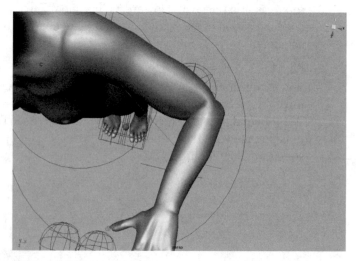

Figure 14-24

39. Now the cool thing here is that more than likely there are very minor adjustments to do on the hands. You may have a stray vertex here or there that move with the wrong joint, but aside from that it should only involve some minor tweaks. Most notably, as you curl the fingers, make sure they deform in a similar manner to the elbows and knees.

Figure 14-25

40. **Save your file!**

    The final step in the skinning process is to weight the head and neck.

41. Starting at **55** on the Time Slider, set an initial keyframe for the head and the neck. Rotate the head and the neck on subsequent frames just as we have done for the rest of the skeleton. Be sure to create keys where the head is rotated forward and backward and left and right at a minimum.

42. To start off the head we will take a slightly different approach than the one we have been using. In this case we will set the weighting using the Component Editor. Rotate to a side view and in Vertex mode, select all of the vertices for the head. Avoid selecting vertices of the neck.

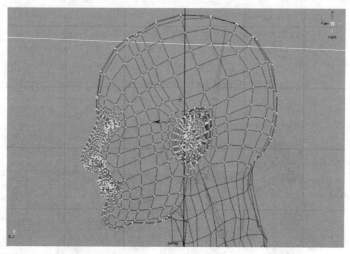

Figure 14-26

43. Select **Window | General Editors ▸ Component Editor.** If it is not already selected, move the top slider portion over and select **Smooth Skins** (see Figure 14-27). With Smooth Skins selected, you should see a list of all of the selected vertices down the left side of the dialog and then the list of bone names along the top.

	head	head_end	jaw	jaw_end	left_ank
Hold	off	off	off	off	off
Group2Shape					
vtx[0]	0.482	0.433	0.037	0.015	0.000
vtx[1]	0.477	0.425	0.043	0.018	0.000
vtx[2]	0.487	0.467	0.020	0.008	0.000
vtx[3]	0.487	0.471	0.018	0.007	0.000
vtx[4]	0.386	0.018	0.285	0.028	0.000
vtx[5]	0.398	0.020	0.275	0.027	0.000
vtx[6]	0.405	0.019	0.271	0.026	0.000
vtx[7]	0.407	0.019	0.273	0.026	0.000
vtx[8]	0.537	0.010	0.113	0.005	0.000
vtx[9]	0.558	0.010	0.107	0.005	0.000
vtx[10]	0.570	0.019	0.112	0.006	0.000
vtx[11]	0.548	0.019	0.120	0.007	0.000
vtx[12]	0.047	0.000	0.875	0.051	0.000
vtx[13]	0.068	0.000	0.835	0.059	0.000
vtx[14]	0.021	0.000	0.886	0.082	0.000
vtx[15]	0.012	0.000	0.920	0.062	0.000
vtx[16]	0.303	0.003	0.461	0.079	0.000
vtx[17]	0.354	0.004	0.370	0.040	0.000
vtx[18]	0.352	0.009	0.356	0.046	0.000
vtx[19]	0.339	0.007	0.397	0.067	0.000
vtx[20]	0.449	0.373	0.077	0.036	0.000
vtx[21]	0.455	0.276	0.073	0.024	0.000

0.4820	0.00		1.00

Load Components	Close

Figure 14-27

44. Alongside each vertex number the amount of weighted influence is displayed. Select the influence box for all of the vertices under head. Type **1** to add **100** percent influence to all the selected vertices.

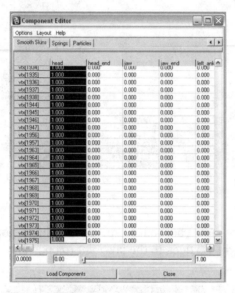

Figure 14-28

45. Move the slider to rotate the head. You will then need to use the Paint Skin Weights tool to balance the falloff of influence where the head meets the neck. Be sure to check the head at various positions to get the best weighting.

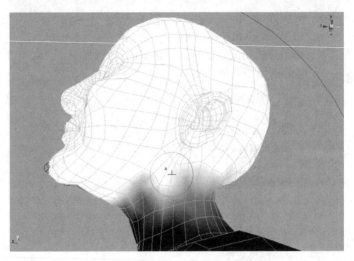

Figure 14-29

46. Depending on how you want to animate the head, you may want to weight vertices to the jaw joint to open and close the mouth.

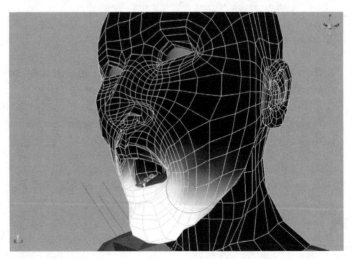

Figure 14-30

47. As you may remember, along with our character mesh we had a few additional geometries: the eyes, mouth, hair, and eyelashes. All of these objects should be simply parented to the

head joint with the exception of the lower teeth and tongue, which should be parented to the jaw.

A Bit about Blend Shapes

I mentioned blend shapes earlier in this chapter, so I feel you deserve a bit of explanation as to how they are used. For some of you, this might be obvious, but once again, let's not forget about the newbs!

Blend shapes are used most often to create facial animation. In this case, you create duplicate geometries and move the vertices on the duplicate to form a variety of facial expressions. When the blend shapes are applied to the original geometry, Maya takes into account the offset of the vertices in the blend shape object. If the vertices have moved from their original positions, the blend shape slider's movement causes the geometry to morph to its blend shape counterpart.

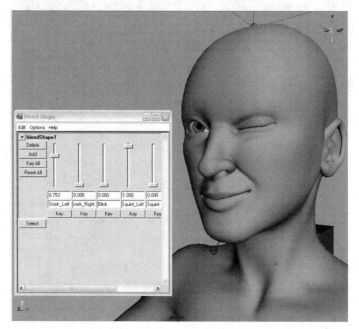

Figure 14-31

This is a very effective way to create quality facial animation. One important thing to remember when creating blend shapes for facial animation is to keep blend shapes for the lower part of the head separate from the upper part. For example, have one blend shape for the smile and then a separate blend shape for the squinting eyes.

Blend shapes are also, as I have stated, very useful in cleaning up deformation issues that may occur on your model during animation. You can have the rotation of the joint drive a particular blend shape to make the deformation appear more convincing, as shown in Figure 14-32.

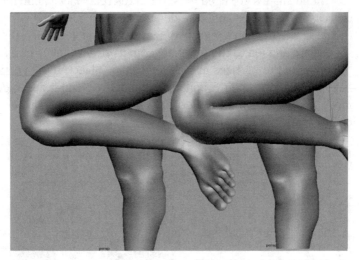

Figure 14-32

Wrap-Up

This chapter gave us but a glimpse into weighting a character. We learned to use the Paint Skin Weights tool to get a nice deformation on our character. As I stated way back at the beginning of the book, we won't be getting into the animation process. We did, however, learn to set keyframes so that our figure had a rudimentary "range of motion."

I want to emphasize that this chapter along with the previous one are meant to give you enough information to set your character up for animation and by no means cover the subject to the depths that it deserves. I encourage you to pursue this subject further even if you don't intend to focus on animation.

As far as animating the face is concerned, one of the best books written on the subject is *Stop Staring* by Jason Osipa. It really takes into account the nuances associated with believable facial animation.

Final Thoughts

A great deal of work has gone into the creation of this book. In teaching and working in the game industry, I have dedicated a vast amount of time into getting where I am now.

I stress the point of being passionate. Art is something that allows you to express who you are. I hope you got as much out of this book as I have put into it. Making it through is a testament of how dedicated you are to your craft. This is an industry that will keep growing and opening up new opportunities for anyone with the ambition and drive to take advantage of them.

Take what you have learned here as just a primer for the endless coats of paint you will add as you continue to build your skills and learn what this industry is all about — talented people who love what they do.

"Nothing in the world can take the place of persistence. Talent will not; nothing is more common than unsuccessful men with talent. Genius will not; unrewarded genius is almost a proverb. Education will not; the world is full of educated derelicts. Persistence and determination alone are omnipotent."

—Calvin Coolidge

Index

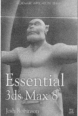

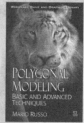

About the CD

The companion CD contains the images from the book, Maya image and scene files to help build the character, AVI movies that show the modeling process in real time, and Mel scripts for installing the Go Tools character modeling tool menu. The content is organized as follows:

▶ Chapters_Images—This directory contains all the images from the book and is organized by chapter.

▶ Scripts—This contains the goModTools.mel and mhClearDeadNodes.mel scripts that are discussed in the book. See the Read_Me file for information on how to use these to install the Go Tools.

▶ Videos—This folder contains self-extracting AVI files that step through the blocking and sculpting process and provide examples of Go Tools operations. AVI files will play in the Windows Media Player. Note that the AVI files are best viewed with a screen resolution of 1024 x 768 or better.

▶ Maya8_CharacterModeling.exe—This file contains scene and image files used to build the character. When extracted to the C: drive, Maya will find the associated images for each scene.

Please see the Read_Me file for more information.

 WARNING:
By opening the CD package, you accept the terms and conditions of the CD/Source Code Usage License Agreement. Additionally, opening the CD package makes this book nonreturnable.

CD/Source Code Usage License Agreement

Please read the following CD/Source Code usage license agreement before opening the CD and using the contents therein:

1. By opening the accompanying software package, you are indicating that you have read and agree to be bound by all terms and conditions of this CD/Source Code usage license agreement.

2. The compilation of code and utilities contained on the CD and in the book are copyrighted and protected by both U.S. copyright law and international copyright treaties, and is owned by Wordware Publishing, Inc. Individual source code, example programs, help files, freeware, shareware, utilities, and evaluation packages, including their copyrights, are owned by the respective authors.

3. No part of the enclosed CD or this book, including all source code, help files, shareware, freeware, utilities, example programs, or evaluation programs, may be made available on a public forum (such as a World Wide Web page, FTP site, bulletin board, or Internet news group) without the express written permission of Wordware Publishing, Inc. or the author of the respective source code, help files, shareware, freeware, utilities, example programs, or evaluation programs.

4. You may not decompile, reverse engineer, disassemble, create a derivative work, or otherwise use the enclosed programs, help files, freeware, shareware, utilities, or evaluation programs except as stated in this agreement.

5. The software, contained on the CD and/or as source code in this book, is sold without warranty of any kind. Wordware Publishing, Inc. and the authors specifically disclaim all other warranties, express or implied, including but not limited to implied warranties of merchantability and fitness for a particular purpose with respect to defects in the disk, the program, source code, sample files, help files, freeware, shareware, utilities, and evaluation programs contained therein, and/or the techniques described in the book and implemented in the example programs. In no event shall Wordware Publishing, Inc., its dealers, its distributors, or the authors be liable or held responsible for any loss of profit or any other alleged or actual private or commercial damage, including but not limited to special, incidental, consequential, or other damages.

6. One (1) copy of the CD or any source code therein may be created for backup purposes. The CD and all accompanying source code, sample files, help files, freeware, shareware, utilities, and evaluation programs may be copied to your hard drive. With the exception of freeware and shareware programs, at no time can any part of the contents of this CD reside on more than one computer at one time. The contents of the CD can be copied to another computer, as long as the contents of the CD contained on the original computer are deleted.

7. You may not include any part of the CD contents, including all source code, example programs, shareware, freeware, help files, utilities, or evaluation programs in any compilation of source code, utilities, help files, example programs, freeware, shareware, or evaluation programs on any media, including but not limited to CD, disk, or Internet distribution, without the express written permission of Wordware Publishing, Inc. or the owner of the individual source code, utilities, help files, example programs, freeware, shareware, or evaluation programs.

8. You may use the source code, techniques, and example programs in your own commercial or private applications unless otherwise noted by additional usage agreements as found on the CD.

 WARNING:

By opening the CD package, you accept the terms and conditions of the CD/Source Code Usage License Agreement. Additionally, opening the CD package makes this book nonreturnable.